Personal Computers and the Baha'i Community

Personal Computers and the Baha'i Community

V. Mitra Gopaul

Kalimat Press
Los Angeles, California

LIBRARY OF CONGRESS CATALOGING IN PUBLICATION DATA

Gopaul, V. Mitra
Personal computers and the Bahá'í community.

Bibliography: p.
1. Bahá'í Faith—Government—Data processing.
2. Microcomputers. I. Title.
BP377.G67 1988 004.16'0242979 88-13737
ISBN 0-933770-70-7

Kalimat Press, 1600 Sawtelle Boulevard, Suite 34, Los Angeles, CA 90025

Dedication

To my mother and father,
for their love and self-sacrifice.

To Gaye, my wife, for her love and friendship.

Acknowledgement

I am grateful to Lisa Blake, a pioneer on the island of St. Vincent, who first gave me the idea of writing a computer book for the Baha'i community.

Since I proposed the idea of this book to Anthony A. Lee at Kalimat Press, he has always been encouraging and helpful. Also a special thanks to the staff of Kalimat who have been involved in improving the quality of this book.

During the course of writing this book many people have contributed in different ways and I owe a debt of gratitude to them. My special thanks to Dr. William Deilh, Director of Louhelen Baha'i School, who has been helpful in improving the chapter on computer-aided learning and gave many ideas for computerizing management of Baha'i schools.

Finally, I am grateful to Gaye, my wife, and Laila, my daughter, for their love, understanding, patience, and support, especially while writing this book.

CONTENTS

INTRODUCTION

Baha'u'llah, expounding on the greatness of His Revelation, made reference to these words: "Knowledge is twenty and seven letters. All that the prophets have revealed are two thereof. No man thus far hath known more than these two letters. But when the Qa'im shall arise, He will cause the remaining twenty and five letters to be made manifest" Kitab-i Iqan p. 243 44). This generous, unprecedented source of understanding in the Baha'i Revelation is about spiritual realities, no doubt it also increases man's knowledge about the physical world to promote spiritual goals. Consequently, in the last century we have seen unimaginable growth and activities in many fields of science. In fact, there are too many list them all here. One obvious development is that scientific discoveries, eventually translating into technological innovations, are changing human life.

Among all the sciences and technologies, the ability to build faster, cheaper, and smaller computers has not only touched large populations, especially in the industrialized countries, but is also a key tool in the many scientific successes of the latter part of this century. Let's just take one historical event, such as landing on the moon: this was only possible because of computers aboard the spacecraft and in control centers around the earth. There are other events, not so dramatic as space travel, that show computers are used in both diverse fields and on an international scale. Some of these achievements are the establishment of global communications networks, microscopic scans of the human body, complex trade transactions at global levels, and the advent of international research centers working on a single project. Every time we do banking, use a telephone, or make airline reservations, there are thousands of computers working together to make these routine tasks happen.

Among many other things, computers are an essential tool in establishing the global village where information travels fast and people get a feeling of closeness in spite of long distances. This was demonstrated when a gathering was held to pray for peace in the world. Almost one billion people were joined together in this worldwide mission, shrinking the thousands of miles of distance between the participants and the TV set. Again, to make this global meeting a success, computer communication was essential.

In the Baha'i Faith, we have seen new technology used since the early 1920s; currently, computers are used at every level of the Baha'i Administration. As the Baha'i world grows in complexity and size, computers will play an increasingly important role in ensuring the prompt, accurate flow of information. This book is about using computers in carrying out the work of the Baha'i Administration.

In the last decade, there has been a sudden burst in the use of computers, mainly of the kind called personal or microcomputers. These are relatively inexpensive, and generally they are easy to use. Because of these two advantages, we find personal computers useful in the Baha'i Faith. In this book most of the applications are geared toward using programs for treasurers and secretaries, educators, administrators and researchers, and so on. Each subject is dealt with in such a way that an immediate, relevant use of software is shown at different administrative levels.

TO THE READER

Are you thinking how this book can be useful to you? If you are the least bit interested in a modern revolution--computer technology--and its application to the Baha'i Faith, then these pages have many things to offer. In this decade the marketing of computers has exploded, bringing down prices so that more people can afford them. At the same time, another expansion is taking place: it is the emergence of the Baha'i Faith from obscurity. We are attracting the attention of the general public. This new recognition will soon swell our membership to a great number. This means our need to handle information will greatly increase; there will also be a demand on the Administration to produce quick and decisive results. Since computers have the capacity to manage huge amounts of information at impressive speeds, it is logical to consider their uses within the Baha'i Faith.

The reader of this book must be familiar with computers in general and must have some working knowledge of software, such as the word processor and data base manager, but you are not required to be an expert in any of these areas. If you consider yourself a beginner, learning more about these programs and applying the ideas discussed in this book will definitely put your computer to use. Here, the focus is to discuss ways of using software in the Baha'i Faith. However, detailed instruction for running any program are not included. Operational steps are always covered in the manual accompanying the software package.

For experienced programmers, this book provides designs for various applications, such as finances, membership, the management of schools, and so on. The discussions are such that you may use any piece as you find it, or change it to suit your resources and situation. If you are a secretary, it gives ways of managing minutes of meetings, membership lists, and ideas for managing and protecting information in the computer age. There are ideas for teachers to create lessons, Baha'i librarians (or distribution representatives) to improve sale transactions, and computer hobbyists to start a computer bulletin board.

Not to mislead the reader, we want to make clear that this book is not about programming or using any particular program. It only presents several ideas--over a dozen--on how to put a personal computer to work in the Baha'i Administration. These suggestions are discussed in various degrees. Some go into detail concerning how to convert an idea into a working program, while in other cases they give only a general view of making commercial programs useful. In some examples you will be required to develop programs, but only using a language for nonprogrammers.

We hope that by making these ideas available we will encourage the use of computers for administrative work. Perhaps individuals or institutions will take initiative to design and develop programs to suit their own particular needs, as well as share their experiences with others. In time, some of these programs will mature to cover many situations and include many functions. When the user base becomes large enough, we hope that a network will evolve, one through which users and developers can exchange views and programs just like in any other computer user group. This will also eliminate duplication and possibly promote higher computer standards within the Baha'i community.

An important reason for not including programs here is that the world of microcomputers is changing fast. In the last decade, we have seen the rise of many computers that created numerous users, and then disappears within a few years (such as the Osborne computer and some Commodore and Radio Shack computers). Technological changes have forced some of them off the market. Similarly, programs such as word processor, data base managers, and spreadsheets have a lifetime of two to five years. Vendors are always bringing new and improved products to market. When the old ones become unavailable their support gradually disappears and the user base shrinks. The design ideas in this book, however, have particular relevance to the Baha'i Administration with no dependence on any computer. They are universal: with the right tools they will work in any size computer, although our emphasis has been mainly on personal computers such as the IBM-PC, IBM-PS/2, the Apple or the various clones. To write these programs, one's greatest difficulty would be to choose a computer with software tools that will not be obsolete in a few years.

ABOUT THE BOOK

The content of this book can be broadly classified into two categories. One category discusses the usage of several computer software--for instance, how to do secretarial work, develop instructions, text retrieval, and computer communication. When you buy any of these programs, the accompanying operation manuals describe only the steps of how to use them, with perhaps some examples of common situations. However, in this book we have shown how software can be directly applied to carry out work in many areas of the Baha'i Administration. Minutes of meetings are vital records, yet they are difficult to organize in such a way that you can pull out any decision quickly without sifting through piles of paper. A text retrieval program can easily organize all the minutes, providing speed and flexibility in searching for information.

The other category requires development work, converting application designs into working programs. It may sound like only experienced programmers should tackle this area. However, there are computer languages on the market, geared toward nonprogrammers, that are called fourth-generation languages. They are easy to learn, and allow beginners to complete useful programs within hours. One such program is DBASE III, popular among users of microcomputers.

The designs vary from simple tasks, such as managing membership in a community, to computer administration of a Baha'i School. In all cases, the topics are developed fully, including design specifications, screen layouts, and printout formats. Wherever relevant, we have also made suggestions on how to implement these designs. In software development, programming (coding) is one of the last stages of the process. By giving extra attention to a workable design, programming becomes easy. Therefore, the choice of the tools to do the programming and the implementation of the program are left up to you. In the areas where development is required, the tool suggested is data base management software available for all the popular computers, such as IBM-PC, IBM-PS/2, Apple, Atari, and Commodore.

Chapter 1 is for beginners who need an introduction to computers and associated equipment. In addition to describing different components, it discusses the basic functions of the word processor, data base, telecommunication, and spreadsheet.

The secretary, at any level of administration, has to deal with many different kinds of information: minutes, membership, correspondence, and so on. In Chapter 2, one section is devoted to organizing computer information and storage media, such as diskettes. In fact, this information applies to any computer user. We also show how computers can be used to organize minutes, correspondence, newsletters and membership lists.

Chapter 3 describes how a data base management system (DBMS) can be useful in finishing a simple but complete program. Our example is management of membership with emphasis on how to use software features.

Chapters 4 through 7 provide several design ideas on how DBMS are used in such fields of the Faith as teaching, fund raising, distribution services and schools.

Computers and communications make a powerful combination in establishing a flow of information. Chapter 8 shows how this technology can bring individuals, committees, and Assemblies around the world closer together. Perhaps its importance will be felt more as the network of Assemblies grows in size and capacity, requiring prompt communication. Electronic mail, computer conferencing, and the bulletin board are only some of the ways of achieving efficient communication systems.

Educators have been some of the first users of computers, and they have always pondered on how computers can benefit the learning process. Chapter 9 describes some of the current theories advanced by researchers in this field. Also, we have focused on characteristics of software used to prepare instructions, with particular emphasis on Baha'i education. Also, to promote discussions and standards, there are examples of forums using computers.

In this information age, text is the most popular form of communication. In the Baha'i Faith, the Holy Writings are our most valuable resource, and routinely we collect other documents as records and instructions. Chapter 10 describes a computer retrieval system that allows the user to locate words and phrases within context.

CHAPTER ONE

GETTING STARTED

This chapter is about the basics of computers. It introduces types of application software that will be discussed throughout this book. The software reviewed includes word processors, data base management systems, electronic spreadsheets, and data communications. The hardware discussion covers the screen, keyboard, CPU, printer, and disk. Anyone with computer experience may want to skip on to the next chapter. To a reader who has little or no exposure to computers, this introduction provides a start in understanding the basic points of computer hardware and software. The ideas are presented in simple terms and, whenever applicable, examples are given for further clarification. Of course, in one chapter it is impossible to explore in great detail areas such as computer hardware, word processing, data bases and so on. If interested, you can consult other sources on these subjects, and we have provided some suggestions of books and magazines in Appendix A.

1.1 BASIC COMPUTER

Probably the most significant technical advances in this century have been in the field of computers. The first one was built with vacuum tubes, switches, and miles of cable; all contained in several huge metal cabinets occupying the entire floor of a building and weighing thirty tons. It was mainly used for calculations, performing 1,000 times faster than the electromechanical machines of the day. Since then, the computer has been improved in complexity, speed, and flexibility, ranging in application from controlling spacecraft navigation to accounting for small businesses. Currently, size varies from a mainframe computer department occupying several floors of a skyscraper to personal computers small enough to be held on the lap. Today, the "knee-top" portable computer can calculate twenty times faster than the first all-purpose computer. Regardless of its size or application, every computer is a processing machine requiring the input of information and delivering to us the processed results in forms convenient for our use.

Our main interest here is small computers, generally known as micro- or personal computers. It was in the mid-1970s that this family of computers became commercially available in stores, thus creating a new era in computer marketing. Within a decade we have seen these personal computers in all different sizes, shapes, and price ranges. On one hand, there is the box that looks like a keyboard, that has enough computer power to do some word processing, some programming, and run games using the home television set. On the other hand, a microcomputer may have a detachable keyboard, monitor, and cabinet. Perhaps it is also connected to other devices such as a printer, or to telephone lines. Such high-end personal computers are used for business, and for scientific purposes, engineering, and other applications. Besides the price, there are many other aspects of high-end micros that set them apart from the rest. The different components, such as the cabinet, keyboard, CRT, and so on, are becoming lighter in weight and are more portable. Moreover, they can operate from the power line of a house or office building, and they do not require any special environment (such as air conditioning) which often is necessary for mini and mainframe computers. In its short history, there have been many personal computers from different companies--many old names and some new. The level of activity in this technology has increased in many ways, therefore competition is allowing only the tough companies to servive. Some common computer companies are Apple, Atari, Commodore, and IBM. Each has a variety of hardware and software with varying prices. By visiting some computer retail stores, you will be able to collect information about the different products.

Within the microcomputer category, there is the portable category, which means the machine is easy to transport from one place to another. Many are packaged to include a display unit, keyboard, and necessary connections--all in a cabinet small and light enough to carry like a handbag. In some units, the display is a small (5 inch) CRT while others have a flat screen with liquid crystal display (LCD). Both the number of lines and number of characters per line vary from one brand to the next. These computers are so small that they fit in a normal size brief case. Some run on batteries. One main advantage of the portable is that you can take it to meetings or use it at home, and continue working wherever you are.

For a first time computer buyer, it can be a confusing job deciding which hardware to buy. One must be sure that, when everything is put together, it will do exactly the job intended. Let's begin by understanding the functions of the different pieces of hardware and software. The following discussions will help with that.

The most essential part of any computer is the Central Processing Unit (CPU). It is a *ceramic chip*, usually half the size of a chocolate bar, packed with electronic circuitry that gives the computer its processing power. To achieve this power, the CPU follows step-by-step logical instructions from the *memory*, made of an array of electronic chips and usually residing very close to the CPU. These instructions, when grouped together, are called a *program*. All the processing activities inside the CPU are generally invisible to the user. But the entering of information and the display of the results are done through devices known as input and output (I/O), as shown in Figure 1.0.

```
                 ....................
                 :                  :
                 :       CPU        :
   INPUT >-----:                  :--------> OUTPUT
                 :      MEMORY      :
                 :                  :
                 :..................:
```

Figure 1.0

One output device is the screen, also called a monitor or Cathode Ray Tube (CRT). To feed into the computer, information such as text or commands, we use an input device called a keyboard--much like a typewriter keyboard. Both the keyboard and the screen link the user with the processing capability of the CPU. To store such information, correspondence, or files of names and addresses of Baha'is, there are mass storage devices such as floppy disk drives or hard disks. Since we can feed to and retrieve information from these disks, they are both an input and output device.

Besides these basic components of a computer, a serious user will need other equipment (such as a printer, communication equipment, a mouse, and so on) to make the system more versatile. All these different parts are called hardware. They are connected by cables to the CPU, which controls their functions.

```
............             ********************
:          :             *                  *      ...............
: PRINTER  :.......      *       CPU        *------>:     SCREEN   :
:..........:      :      *                  *<--:  :..............:
                         *                  *   :
                ________ *                  *   :
              :        : *                  *   :
              : INTERFACE:<>*               *<- :
              :________: *..................* : :  ................
...............   :      *      MEMORY      * : :  :              :
:             : :        *                  * : ----:   KEYBOARD   :
:COMMUNICATION :..:      *     PROGRAM      * :    :..............:
:             : :        *                  * :
:..............: :       *       DATA       *      ...............
                  :      *                  * :    :             :
...........       :      *                  * :>: MASS STORAGE :
:          :      :      *                  *      :             :
: MOUSE    :.......:     ********************      :.............:
:..........:
```

Figure 1.1 Basic Computer

Figure 1.1 is a block diagram showing the relationship *between* the CPU and the rest of the hardware. The screen, keyboard, and mass storage device are connected directly to the CPU, while the printer, communication, and mouse are linked via an interface. In this case, an interface is another piece of hardware to provide compatibility between the computer and the peripheral equipment to allow the data to flow in both directions. Each line also shows an arrow indicating the direction of data flow. For example, the screen only receives whereas the mass storage device receives and transmits information. Now let's look in more depth at the hardware and software, and at some applications.

HARDWARE

In a computer system, every piece of hardware consists of a cabinet, nuts, bolts, cable, printed circuit boards, and so on. But at the heart of it all are the electronic circuits--thousands of transistors sealed in small chips--that perform the functions of the equipment. Without delving into much detail, we will describe only the features or functions of some of the common hardware attached to a computer.

SCREEN

The screen is one of the most common hardware parts. It displays reports, information, text, and the like, and echos keystrokes. Its size ranges from 9" to 12" diagonally and is either monochrome (with green, white, or amber characters on a black background) or color. You may notice a rectangular block or a hyphen blinking on the screen that shows the position where the next character will be entered on the screen as you type. This is called a *cursor.* There are usually 80 columns across the screen and 24 lines from the top to the bottom, which is about one half of a typed page.

As mentioned previously, the screen is the window through which you can determine whether you have pressed the right key. If an unacceptable character is typed, as part of a command, a message is usually flashed on the screen to warn that the input information is incorrect. Another message may request you to try again. The screen is also a place to watch for messages describing unexpected situations or problems.

The source of the information to be displayed can be from the keyboard, disk, or program, but it always goes through the CPU, as shown in Figure 1.2. In many home computers, it is possible to use your TV set as a monitor. Remember, it is not possible to connect every computer to the TV, for this requires special electronic circuitry. Instead of showing only letters and numbers, some computers with graphic controller cards can create graphs, drawings, and charts.

```
                      ..........         ............
PROGRAM-------------->:        :         :          :
                      :   C    :         :  SCREEN  :
DISK----------------->:   P    :-------->:          :
                      :   U    :         :          :
KEYBOARD------------->:        :         :..........:
                      :........:
```

Figure 1.2 Basic Components of a Computer

KEYBOARD

To process anything, the computer requires information. Text, numbers, or program commands are fed to the CPU through its memory. One of the possible sources of the information is the keyboard. Its layout is similar to the typewriter keyboard, with the numeric and alphabetic keys arranged for touch-key typing. In addition, on the right side there is often a pad with numeric and arithmetic keys. Extra rows of keys on the top or left side, called function keys, are programmed in such a way that by pressing them the computer receives an entire command line. Depending on the computer, the user can customize the function keys, matching the key to a task frequently used. Let's say to process monthly fund contributions, you may have to type "FUND" and press "RETURN." A function key can be programmed so that by pressing it, the command "FUND" is automatically typed and the CPU starts the task. It should be mentioned that the arrangement of the numeric pad and the commands of the function keys differ from one computer brand to the next. For more details about programming the function keys, consult the operation manual of your computer.

A coiled cord often attaches the keyboard to the cabinet of the computer. This cord carries electronic pulses when a key is pressed. When you type a character, there is an immediate response: it appears on the monitor. This is the way you as a user are assured that the proper code has been sent from the keyboard to the CPU. If it is a letter or the minutes of a meeting, you would type it as you would on a typewriter and the document appears on the screen as it would on the typing paper.

Sending a command to the computer from the keyboard depends on how your computer is programmed. For example, to save typed minutes of an L.S.A. meeting, in one computer will simply require you to type "SAVE" and press the RETURN key. In another, you may have to press two keys, CTRL and one other key; and in another, you may have to press a function key. To find out which command corresponds to which key, the manual accompanying any program, such as a word processor or accounting package, will explain the control keys and their functions.

Place the keyboard in the most convenient and comfortable place, such as in front of the computer on a desk or on your lap, to type your commands or text. In Figure 1.3 the arrows show the character traveling from the keyboard to the computer and then echoed on the screen.

```
............      ...............      ............
:          :      :             :      :          :
: KEYBOARD :-------->:  COMPUTER  :--------->:  SCREEN  :
:..........:      :.............:      :..........:
```

Figure 1.3

PRINTER

With the advent of personal computers, and their capacity to store many millions of characters, our appetite to use printed paper to convey information has not diminished. At this stage in the development of the Baha'i Faith, it is necessary to have paper, such as letters and reports, as a means of communication or to keep paper copies in a manual file system. The printer is used to put text on paper.

The two most common, and perhaps the least expensive, printers these days are the formed character impact (often called letter-quality) and dot matrix printers. The former gives you print quality equal to that produced by a standard typewriter. Dot-matrix printers (letters formed with a series of dots), often appear less professional than the impact or daisy-wheel printers, because of the rough appearance of the dot-composed letters. The dot matrix printer is faster and cheaper and the output is quite acceptable for documents used mainly for filing rather than correspondence. Both use inked cloth or mylar ribbons and are connected to the computer by a cable. If the ink in the ribbon is used up, the old ribbon cartridge is easily removed and replaced by a new one. Laser printers are attracting a lot of attention now, especially in the desk-top publishing business. The main advantages of the laser printer over others are quality and variety of print functions. For a large quantity of print, it is sometimes an economical choice.

To print a character the computer sends (Figure 1.4) a character code to the printer. The incoming signal is decoded and it then activates the mechanical parts to print the appropriate character. Besides printing ordinary characters, some printers can also draw pictures.

```
                                   *****
                                   * I *
                                   * N *
...........        ..........      * T *     .............
:         :        :        :      * E *     :           :
: PROGRAM :------->:  CPU   :---->* R *---->:  PRINTER  :
:         :        :        :      * F *     :           :
:.........:        :........:      * A *     :...........:
                                   * C *
                                   * E *
                                   *****
```

Figure 1.4 Connecting CPU to Printer

DISK STORAGE

When using a computer for personal use, business, or Baha'i work, large amounts of data are processed; therefore, a place is required for permanent or for short-term storage. There are several inexpensive ways to store information; the most common medium is the floppy (flexible) diskette, used within a floppy disk drive. The diskette is a thin mylar ring covered with a layer of magnetic material, protected by an envelope. The magnetic material on the diskette records the data. The diskette is inserted into the disk drive and the door is closed. A motor spins the diskette, like an album record, and a head in the drive moves back and forth to fetch or write the data on the diskette (like the stylus and cartridge of a turntable).

The floppy disk drives and diskettes come in three sizes: 3 1/2, 5 1/4, and 8 inch widths. Currently, the most common in personal computers is the 5 1/4 inch, but this may change in the future as more compact devices are developed. Once the information is recorded on the diskette, it stays permanently. There is a notch on the 5 1/4 and 8 inch diskettes, that when covered on 5 1/4 and uncovered on 8 inch, disables the head of the drive from writing anything on the diskette and protects the data from being inadvertently erased or destroyed. In this state, it can `only` read information. Your important work can thus be protected, but you cannot store any more data on the disk, nor can you modify or update information already there.

The storage capacity of a diskette can range from 70,000 to 1,200,000 bytes, depending on the size, density, and whether recording is possible on both sides. With this kind of storage, one diskette with a capacity of 1,200,000 characters can hold up to 480 pages of text. Or, if there were a record of believers with name, street, city, state, and postal code, it will take 1,200 such records to fill this disk space. Further advances in the technology of mass storage are promising us smaller, cheaper disk drives, with increased capacity to hold data.

HARD DISK

As the Baha'i Faith grows, it may become necessary to gather huge amounts of information in one mass storage place: for example, various data on many thousands of new believers. In a situation such as this, many diskettes would be needed. In a matter of months you would be surrounded by many boxes of diskettes, making it inconvenient to keep track of new, used, and updated ones. Again, technology has provided us with the means to hold from 5 to 50 million (mega) characters in one storage space.

A hard disk, as the name suggests, is made of a nonflexible material that is coated with a magnetic surface like the floppy disk. In the same manner as the floppy disk, it holds characters and reads, writes, or erases with a head moving forward and backward searching the right position where the characters are to be found. Unlike the floppy disk, a hard disk is sealed in a metal case and turns at a very high speed.

Compared to the floppy disk, it is much faster to read from or write to a hard disk. If you have several million pieces of data stored, it can search the right record within a tenth of a second. It is available in different storage sizes for different popular personal computers. Imagine many diskettes stacked together: for instance, 10 million characters in a hard disk is equivalent to 20 diskettes, and there is no need to remove or insert any part.

So far, we have discussed the screen, printer, CPU, and the disk. All together, they form a very basic computer system. Sometimes, it is necessary to add more equipment to a computer. If you want to connect your computer to another to send and receive information, you will probably use a <u>`MODEM`</u>. This is another hardware device which provides an interface between the computer and the telephone line for communication. Special programs are also required to make use of the additional equipment. For more details on data communication refer to section 1.5.

SOFTWARE

So far we have seen how the different pieces of hardware are connected to the CPU, the central "nerve system" of the computer. The communication of data between the equipment, such as the screen, keyboard, or disk, and the CPU is a direct consequence of instructions executed by the CPU. Many instructions, put together in a logical fashion, are called a program. Programs can read the characters from the keyboard, show text on the screen, or read a believer's name and address from the floppy diskette. These programs, usually on disk, are called software. Software can be classified into two types: operating system programs and application programs.

DISK OPERATING SYSTEM (DOS)

Each computer has its own operating system (OS) and most vary from brand to brand. The Apple computer, for example, has different OS functions and methods from the IBM-PC. However, some computer companies choose "standard" disk operating systems (DOS) such as MS-DOS or CP/M, to interface between the programs and the OS. Such computers are said to be compatible, since the software and data are usually interchangeable. There are many computers advertised as IBM-PC compatible, meaning the functions of the software and hardware are similar to, or the same as, the IBM-PC.

Operating software is a collection of small programs, called routines, which do all the repetitive chores and internal tasks. These tasks are mainly receiving data from any of the input devices and sending it to other output equipment. Each piece of equipment has a code name in the system, for instance, "PRN" is for printer, "CON" for screen or console, and "A" for the disk drive. The typed command "COPY FROM A:MYFILE TO PRN:," first makes the computer copy a file called "MYFILE" from disk "A" to the printer "PRN." The operating system manual, which accompanies computer, explains in detail the use of these OS commands.

The DOS also accomplishes other important tasks: it interprets the commands you type, loads the appropriate program, and executes the task. This part of DOS, called the "command interpreter," is the only link between the user and the computer. Without it, the computer is of no use to us.

The commands of the DOS can be divided into two categories. First, there are system commands--the kind we saw earlier to copy from one file to another. The other type is the program that belongs to the application of the computer, such as word processing, accounting, or data base. In either case, the "command interpreter" first checks for the correctness of the command syntax (to see if it is legal), then it loads the program from the disk and executes it. However, if it is not correct, it will display an error message on the screen. At this point you have to type correctly. Sometimes, it is possible to give a command with correct syntax, but one that is not intended. In this case, the computer will go ahead and do the chore as requested. For example, if you type "COPY FROM A:MYFILE TO A:YOURFILE" it means replace the content of "YOURFILE" with "MYFILE," both files found in drive "A:." The computer interprets precisely the command typed on the keyboard. If it was meant only to add the second file you have nonetheless already lost the original content of "YOURFILE." As you can see, there is no room for ambiguity in the computer. In section 2.1, there are some ideas about avoiding mishaps in a computer environment.

APPLICATION SOFTWARE

How can the computer be used beneficially in service to the Cause or one's daily life? For any personal computer, there are thousands of programs available to do many useful tasks--such as accounting, word processing, data transfer, and so on. Generally, application software is designed to do a specific job directly related to our practical way of life. In this section, we will discuss some of the most common types of application software: word processing, data base management, electronic spreadsheet modeling, and data communication. Throughout this book we will see how these programs can be useful in the Baha'i Faith, and some common features of each software type will be described. For in-depth discussion and information, refer to the operating manual accompanying the software or to a book on your software.
Figure 1.4a gives the interconnection of the operating system, application software, and the different hardware devices. To use any equipment, such as the screen, printer, keyboard, or mass storage, the application software always has to present a request to the DOS, that will do all the chores of either receiving or sending data to any of these devices. The arrows in the interconnection indicate the direction of data flow.

```
................
:   WORD       :    .......    ..........
: PROCESSOR    :<--->:      :--->: SCREEN :
:..............:     :      :    :........:
                     :      :
...............      :      :    ..........
: DATA BASE   :<---->:      :--->:PRINTER :
: MANAGER     :      :  D   :    :........:
:.............:      :      :
                     :  O   :    ..........
...............      :      :<---:KEYBOARD:
:   DATA      :<---->:  S   :    :........:
:COMMUNICATION:      :      :
:.............:      :      :    ..........
                     :      :<-->: MASS   :
...............      :      :    :STORAGE :
:ELECTRONIC   :      :      :    :........:
:SPREAD-      :<---->:      :
:SHEET        :      :      :    ..........
:.............:      :      :<-->: MODEM  :
                     :......:    :........:
```

Figure 1.4a Connection Between Software and Hardware Through DOS

1.2 WORD PROCESSING

Not long ago, application software, such as a word processor, was confined to business offices; its expense kept it out of the reach of most users. Now, with the proliferation of personal computers, and word processors priced from $100 to $1,000, have made them very approachable. Word processing has numerous advantages over typewriters; as we will see later, the most outstanding features are the ability to view the text while editing, save it on disk for future use, and print it in formats of your choice. Although a computer is definitely more expensive than a typewriter, the cost may be justified by time savings, ability to handle large volumes of text, ease of use, flexibility, and options that are impossible on a typewriter.

When you purchase a word processor package, you will receive one or more diskettes containing the software, and an instruction manual explaining how to use the program. There are numerous books published to supplement the manuals for most popular word processing programs. They are written in easy-to-understand language and contain practical examples. Such books discuss ways to use the software that are not found in the instruction manual and make you aware of common pitfalls to avoid.

Let's look at some of the basic features of the word processor: the typed characters are immediately stored in memory, which gives us the possibility to edit, insert a character between two letters, delete a character, move a line, or move a block of text from one point to another. To accomplish these functions, the operator gives specific and unambiguous instructions. These commands are explained in the program manual, and explanations are often available from the computer on a "help menu," that can be called up while you are in the middle of a word processing task.

The screen shows only 24 lines, with each line having 80 columns. But the computer can process one single document as large as a book. The screen is only a window. To view any part of the text you can scroll up or down. You can move the text by line or by page, which makes viewing the text very easy.

During word processing, you follow the "cursor," a special character on the screen that looks like a rectangle or hyphen (sometimes blinking). You can usually do on-screen formatting: this allows you to set the right and left margins, and also indent any section. You may be able to center words just by the stroke of a key. To enhance the look of your work, it is possible to underscore, create bold characters, and break the page at any point.

Somewhere at the top or bottom of the screen you will see the line number and column position of the cursor and also the page number of the text you are currently displaying. Once the margins are set, you can just type without paying any attention to the carriage returns; the word processor will automatically place the words onto the next line. This feature is called the "word-wrap." Unlike typing on a typewriter, nothing is fixed. It is easy to change the margins and move or correct the text until you are perfectly satisfied.

With the word processor you can save a document under any appropriate name; for instance, the minutes of the Local Assembly meeting of April 15, 1985 can be called "LSAM0415.85." This is a file that can be recalled at a later time for possible viewing, further changes, or printing on paper.

It will be a long time before the world eliminates paper as a means of communication. It is certainly important in the Baha'i community. In a computer system, the most common way to get "hard copy" is through a printer. Printers are becoming versatile: the mode can be changed from letter quality (slow but pretty) to draft (fast but harder to read). They can be adapted to print different pitch letters and graphics.

Word processing does not end with editing and printing. There are many other tools. One is the capability of merging lists of names and addresses with documents. Say you want to send the same letter to several believers. This is easily done by first producing a file of names and addresses, and then another of the letter. After giving one command, each letter will be printed with the appropriate name, title, and address. Furthermore, a whole book or reports can be indexed and/or a table of contents generated. There are programs that check spelling and grammar, and give the number of times a word has occurred in the text. In Appendix B we have listed popular software with descriptions of the functions.

1.3 DATA BASE

A data base is an organized collection of information. For example, quotations from the Baha'i Writings filed by topics in a box, can be called a data base. If you want to know what the Baha'i Writings say about a particular subject, you refer to that section and pull out the right quotation. New quotes or new subject area files are easily added. A computerized data base is an electronic file cabinet with a built-in clerk. This electronic secretary can produce all sorts of useful reports from your files, ranging from financial statements to statistics on believers or seekers.

There are programs especially made to manage the data, called data file managers. They establish a data base, do file operations that create, delete, erase, and rename files, and store, update, delete or retrieve data from files. There is also another kind of software called Data-Base Management System (DBMS). A DBMS has all the basic capabilities of the file manager, but allows greater flexibility in handling files, and more capabilities in using the data base for applications such as maintaining membership and accounting records or reporting. In various parts of the book we will focus on DBMS as a tool to do specific tasks in the Baha'i Faith.

A computerized data base provides some definite advantages over paper and pencil. It is a more efficient way of storing information, which allows quick changes when necessary. It provides the ability to retrieve relevant information scattered in several places, and it can produce reports for making decisions. It can summarize and print out information in various formats ranging from lists to statistical reports and financial statements. Managing a huge volume of information is easy with this tool, even with many thousands of names, fund transactions, or inventory items of books, pictures, and pamphlets.

Now let's consider the method of organization used in a data base. The data base consists of one or more files, each a collection of similar information. For example, the names and addresses of believers in a locality can be placed in a file called "INFOFILE." INFOFILE is divided into portions, each called a record. The record might contain information about each member's name, address, age, and so on. In a file, there are many such records, each for a different person. It is like a card file. Within the file are cards (records) for each believer containing the same lines of information (fields). Of course, different names, addresses, and so on are in each record, and this systematically captures the same type of information on all believers.

In Figure 1.5 each record consists of a name, address, city, and state. Many records can be stored; here, only two are chosen.

```
Fields ------> :     Name         Address          City        State
               :
  :            :
 \ /           :
record 1       :    Jack Smith   123 Palm St.    Kalamazoo MI.
record 2       :    Ali Tabrizi  100 Ulm Rd.     Little Town ONT.
record 3       :    Prem Kapoor  2 Main St.      Boston MA.
  .
  .
```

Figure 1.5 File, Record and Field

The most common way of entering information to the data base is through the keyboard. Usually, the users design the screen input format to resemble the paper forms that they are accustomed to using in their manual system. Each field of the record has a place on the screen where data are either entered to the data base or displayed from existing records.

```
          Personal Data Entry

Name     :--------------
Address  : --------------
City     : ------------
Province : --------------
Age      : ---      Profession  : ----------------
Sex      : --
```

Figure 1.6a Data Entry Screen

For instance, in Figure 1.6a the screen, called "Personal Data Entry," is used to manage a record containing seven fields. The input format as designed here gives you a prompt (e.g., "Name") to enter a specific type of information, and the area with dashes shows how long this information can be. For example, "age" is 3 spaces so if you're ever 999 years old, there will be no space for your age on the list. This screen can be used to enter records as shown in Figure 1.6b. When you type the data onto the line where prompted, the information is put into the right fields in a data base record.

```
          Personal Data Entry

Name     : Sureway, Jennifer
Address  : 25 Haven Way---
City     : Sunnyville---
Province: Nova Scotia
Age      : 21       Profession  : Astronaut-------
Sex      : F
```

Figure 1.6b Input Screen with Data

A record such as this one can be entered, updated, or deleted from the data base. Similarly, information can be entered for numerous believers into the computer. If necessary, any one item can be changed and deleted later. If we now create another file called "CONTRIBUTION," the data entry screen may look like Figure 1.7.

```
          Monthly Contributions

Name          : ----------------------
Month         : ----------    Prov. (State) : ----------------

|<--- CONTRIBUTIONS      --->|

Total Amount  : $ ----------
Local fund    : $ ----------
National fund : $ ----------
Continental   : $ ----------
International : $ ----------
Other         : $ ----------
```

Figure 1.7 Monthly Contribution Screen

Given these two files, INFOFILE and CONTRIBUTION, one containing personal information and the other contributions, we can generate a few interesting reports. In these files you have data from believers from different states or provinces. For instance, in Figure 1.8 there is a list of all believers selected between the range of 15 and 21 in the age field.

Report - Believers between 15 and 21

Name	Address	City	Province	Age
Njoyi, Jane	155 Maple Grove Ave	Sunnyville	N.S.	15
Rungloll, Ravi	24 Rue du Saut	Sunnyville	N.S	15
Sureway, Jennifer	25 Haven Way	Sunnyville	N.S.	19
Tehrani, Kamran	5A Apple Ct.	Sunnyville	N.S.	20
Lavoie, Claude	16 Belle View Rd.	Sunnyville	N.S.	20

Page 1

Figure 1.8 Youth Listing

Contributions by state for month of Jamal 143

State	Total	L.S.A.	N.S.A	Inter.	Cont.	Other
GA	16000	5000	8000	1000	1000	1000
NH	25000	10000	10000	2000	2000	1000
NY	11000	6000	5000	----	----	----
SC	12000	8000	1000	1000	1000	1000

Page 1

Figure 1.9 Contribution Report

Figure 1.9 shows the contributions made in four states for different funds (these are only imaginary numbers) during the month of Jamal. Thus from the same data base, reports in different formats and containing different information are printed. With a DBMS, it is possible to combine information selectively from two or more files and then sort it by alphabet or number before printing. In Figure 1.8 the listing is sorted numerically by age, and in Figure 1.9 it is sorted alphabetically by state. Also, any range of any field can be selected, for instance, we chose between ages 15 and 24.

In addition to providing a flexible way of accessing and storing data, a DBMS is also equipped with a report writer. As we have seen, reports, youth listings and contributions, are easily produced by this tool. This part of the DBMS selects any field, sorts the entries if required, and produces printed copies. Also, it allows formatting of the report so that footer, header, and page number are inserted on every page automatically. The above two report forms can be set up in less than an hour with a report writer. Subsequently, reports will take but a few seconds to generate.

To use the DBMS, either to manage files or write reports, some degree of programming is required. The ease of use varies from one product to another, and some are made especially for nonprogrammers. The programming commands of some DBMSs resemble the English language; therefore learning how to use them fully can take only a couple of weeks.

1.4 TELECOMMUNICATION

Over a century ago, on May 24, 1844, was the birth of telecommunication, when Samuel Morse sent over the telegraph wire the message, "What hath God wrought ?" Since then, this new technology has evolved and passed through different stages, from telegraph to modern telephone, satellite, and fiber optic communication. At present, the latter medium has touched our lives in many different ways. It is used to transmit voice, computer (digital) data, and facsimile (TV picture). Lately, with the introduction of microcomputers, communication of data using the telephone has taken an upturn. In this section, we will discuss some current developments in the areas of personal computer and data communication, and in later chapters we will see how they can be used within the Baha'i Faith.

TELECOMMUNICATION INGREDIENTS

Let's start with describing the basic principle that allows the exchange of computer data in a telephone line. The telephone lines, as they exist now, are appropriate only to carry voice or analog signals (analog signals consist of electrical waves with varying voltages). However, computers work with a different signal, called digital. In terms of electronics, this signal has only two states "ON" or "OFF," "ONE" or "ZERO." Each state can be assigned a value and a unit. For instance, "ON" can be 5 volts while "OFF" is 0 volt. This is called the binary (two state) system. The working of the computer is based on a combination of many of these "ON" and "OFF" signals or pulses. Figure 1.10 shows digital pulses with two voltages while analog signals are shown as a continuous line with varying voltage levels.

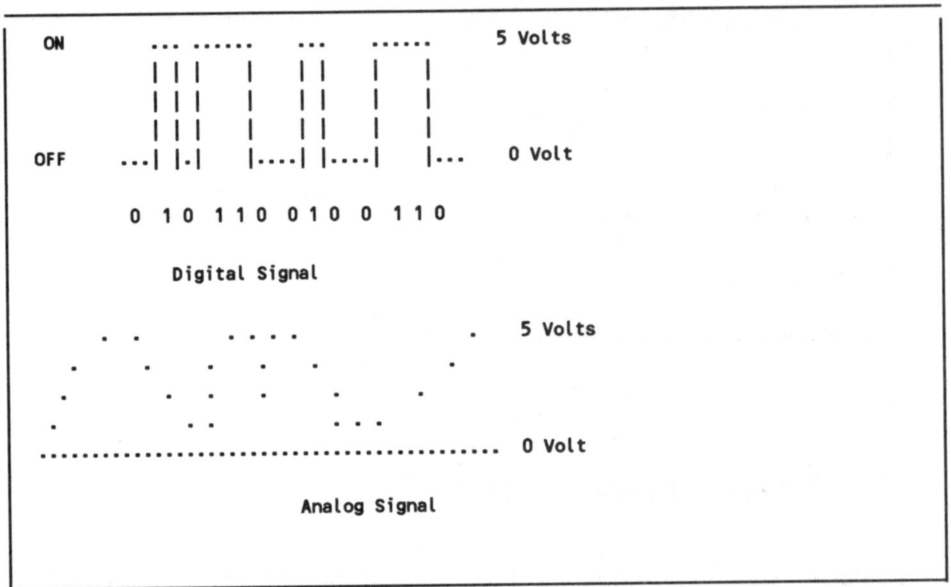

Figure 1.10 Digital/Analog Signals

Now to send a digital signal over the telephone, it has to be converted from digital to (analog) voice. To receive, the analog signal has to be changed back to digital. The equipment that does this is called a modem, a combination of two words: MOdulator and DEModulator. The modem can be in a separate box, or it may be part of the hardware built into the computer. All modem transmission speed is measured in "baud." A 300 baud modem receives or transmits at 300 bits per second, translated to roughly 30 characters. To communicate between two computers, a modem at both ends is required and their baud rates must be the same. If the modem is a separate unit, then it is connected to the computer through a wire cable and a serial port. (This serial port uses a convention called RS-232, an electronic standard for digital communications). If the modem is part of the computer then it connects directly to the telephone jack.

Besides the hardware, communication programs are required for sending or receiving digital data. Though all popular computers have such software available, functions differ from one program to the other.

```
                   Digital signal
                         |
                        \ /
....    ........... 00101001          00101001      ............
:             :   ..........         ..........   :            :
: SENDING     :   :        :         :        :   : RECEIVING:
: COMPUTER    :--->: MODEM  :         : MODEM  :-->: COMPUTER :
:             :   :........:         :........:   :            :
:.............:     :                    :        :...........:
                    : i                  : i
  Analog signal --> ====i====.......... ====i====
                        i                    i
                        |                    |
                        i  TELEPHONE LINE    i
```

Figure 1.11 Computer Data Communication

In Figure 1.11 the sending and receiving computers are far apart and between them are modems and telephone lines. First, the sending computer transmits bits to the modem, which translates them into analog signals. Then at the receiving end, the reverse process occurs, changing voice to digital signals that are passed to the computer as "ones" and "zeroes."

ELECTRONIC MAIL

When combining the power of computer and communication, we get an unusual but powerful system to transfer information called electronic mail. The electronic mail system (EMS) employs computers, telephone lines, satelites, and other communications equipment as a means of transferring information. Its flashing speed, reliability, and sophistication have caused a growing interest in the business community and to some extent in the public sector, as an alternative to traditional mail. Imagine sending a letter, report, or urgently required membership list that reaches its destination--across a building, city, continent, or world--within seconds or minutes.

First, you would compose the words in any format using a word processor. Then, using the modem and communication software, you make the telephone connection and send them. Yes, it is so simple that a person with little or no experience with computers can use it.

To use E-mail (electronic mail), a network has to be established for many subscribers though all the activities are controlled by one or several central computers. Such networks vary in size and complexity. For example, a company may have a network within a building for its employees: without physically moving anything, messages, memos, and other documents are passed from one place to another. Another network may be across a city, country, or continent. Figure 1.11a shows networks in three different sizes: within a building (also called local area network), across a continent (North America) and a global network that covers many countries. There are already many commercial electronic mail services available. Here is a list of a few.

1. CompuServe
2. Source
3. E-Com (the U.S Postal E-Mail service)
4. Inet (Bell Canada)
5. Delphi
6. QLS Systems (Kington, Ont)

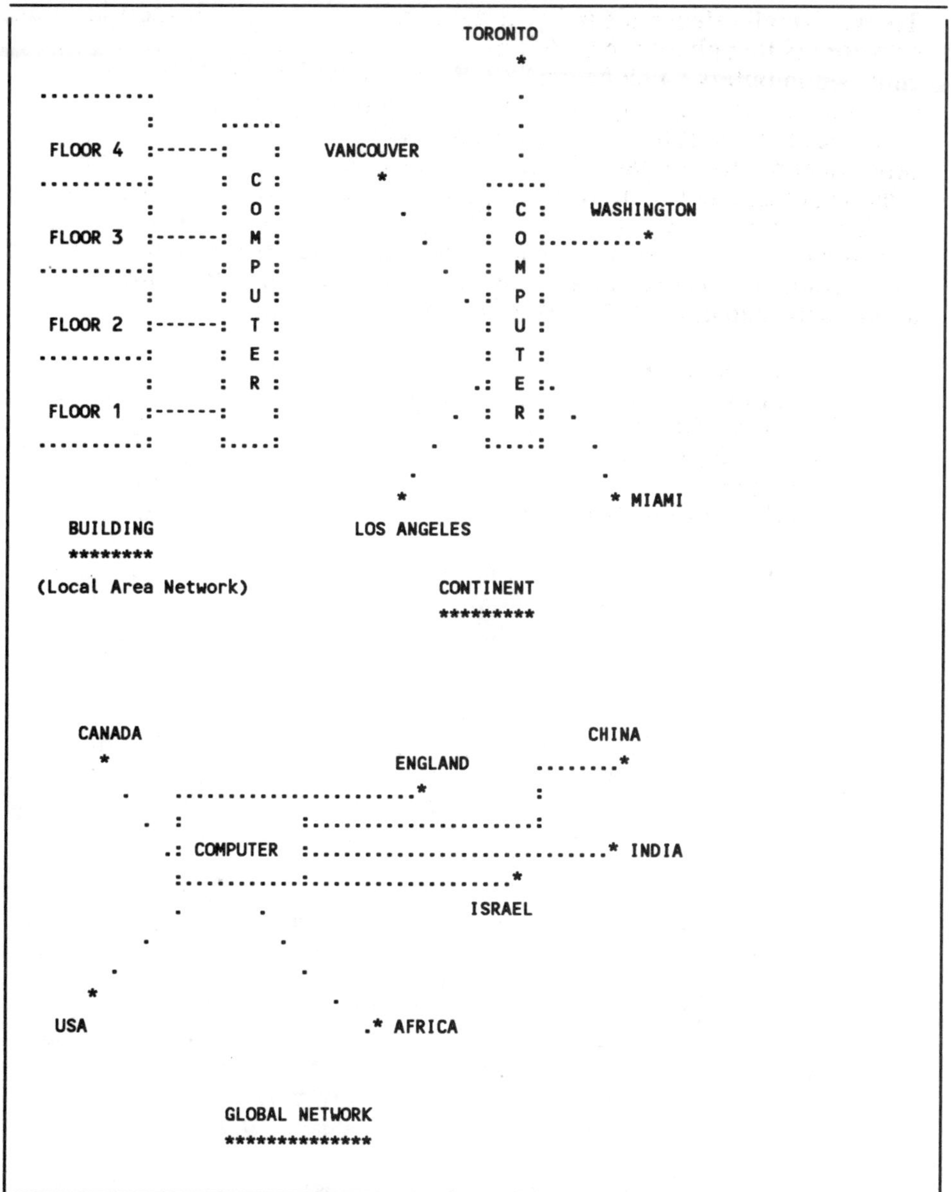

Figure 1.11a Electronic Mail Networks

These companies provide services for microcomputer users (IBM-PC/XT/AT, IBM-PS/2, Apple, Macintosh, Atari and Commodore). Depending on the service, you can send mail electronically anywhere. Not only words, but pictures, graphics, and other images can be transmitted. Because such information is difficult to convert in a digital signal, a special facsimile (fax) machine is required to separate the dark, light, and shaded areas of a picture.

To use any commercial EMS, such as the traditional mail, one requires a mail box. It can be acquired by applying to any of the commercial information services and paying a subscription fee. All your incoming mail is placed in your box; so anytime you look into the directory and request a report, it shows the senders, subjects, and time of receipt. At this point, you have several options: a hard copy through your printer, a copy onto a file on your microcomputer disk, or no copy. Mail can be sent to any subscriber of the host computer or broadcasted to one or many boxes at one time. All the mail reaches its destination in an instant, regardless of the place--locally, nationally, or internationally.

There are some information services that offer "gateways" to other services, giving you a window to a very wide world. In this way continents are connected, just like with the telephone system. Since there is a network of Baha'i communities throughout the world, this service can be beneficial in exchanging information in a timely and reliable manner.

So far we have looked at transferred messages accomplished by EMS and how one message can be sent to more than one recipient. This can be expanded to support on-line communication among a particular group with common interests. This is called "computer conferencing."

How does electronic mail service compare to traditional mail? First, electronic mail is much faster--almost instantaneous. It is also possible to insure the receipt of a message almost immediately after it has been delivered. The reporting mechanism in the EMS is built-in and it can be as precise as the minute. Except for certified mail, the postal system has no good method of reporting the arrival of correspondence.

However, the postal system does provide some security, preventing vital and confidential information from falling into the hands of the wrong person. In this area, EMS requires improvement, so that only authorized personnel have access to "key" information. You can protect the transmitted data through an enscription software, available for most micros at a reasonable price. With a known address, mail can be sent to any destination in the world; but the EMS is limited in its flexibility and its ability to deliver messages universally. However, because of a great demand for this service, subscribers are increasing, making it possible to reach a wider range of people.

A PARALLEL

It seems that a parallel can be drawn between the growth of the Baha'i Faith and that of tele-communications. The first wired message was sent the day after the Bab declared His Mission and initiated a New Era. Later, 'Abdu'l-Baha often used the telegraph to convey important messages across the world. During the ministry of the Guardian, Shoghi Effendi used telegrams extensively to communicate with the believers in many parts of the world. Currently, the Universal House of Justice uses Telex and electronic mail systems to broadcast messages, news, and urgent requests to all corners of the globe.

BULLETIN BOARD

Commercial EMS provides a reliable, instant service, but the major drawback in some cases is the cost. A bulletin board system (BBS) provides an alternative. It evolved through the interaction of the computer hobbyists in their search for a way to communicate using the microcomputer. There are already thousands of bulletin board systems established throughout Canada and the United States. Most of them do not require any fee other than the telephone charges to connect. It is also a place where computer buffs and other interest groups may exchange ideas and share their work with other users in areas of software news and design. Their software is generally available without cost. Such programs are called public domain software and can be used without violating copyright laws. One micro acting as a host can be established as an inexpensive electronic mail system. In a later chapter, we will look in detail at how EMS and BBS can be used to facilitate mailing and communication in the Baha'i Faith.

1.5 ELECTRONIC SPREADSHEET

Imagine a chart with each column representing one Baha'i month and each row assigned to the different Baha'i Funds as shown in Figure 1.12.

```
Month -->        1 2 3 4 5 6 7 8 ..          ...17 18 19  Totals

      Funds
        :
       \:/
      Total
  contribution : - - - - - - - -                   --

      Local    : - - - - - - - -                   --

    National   : - - - - - - - -                   --

  International: - - - - - - -                     --

  Continental  : - - - - - - -                     --

        Other : - - - - - - - -                    --
```

Figure 1.12 Spreadsheet

Imagine also that the Local Spiritual Assembly decides that the monthly contribution to the Local Fund should be divided into small portions and given to other Baha'i Funds. However, all the portions are not the same, but rather are divided as follows:

```
1. Local          50 %
2. National       30 %
3. International  10 %
4. Continental    10 %
```

Each cell on this chart is the intersection of a vertical column and a horizontal row, holding an amount. Each cell in the contribution row is the amount donated each month. However, columns of other rows represent a percentage of that monthly contribution. We might add another column that shows the total of the amounts in each row. This arrangement is called a spreadsheet.

This chart can easily be constructed with electronic spreadsheet software. Compared to pencil, paper, and calculator, this method of producing a spreadsheet is much faster, more flexible, and less prone to errors. Each cell can be a formula representing the relationship between values in specified cells.

```
For example:

Local Fund = 50 % of the monthly contribution.
Total = sum of all amounts in a row.
```

To use the spreadsheet, first, create an entry form on the screen to enter the data. Give each cell a name, a value, and a formula. The data are represented in a tabular form, making it an ideal tool to create a model for analysis and evaluation of alternatives. When a new value is entered, the changes ripple throughout the whole chart as the values of the cells change based on the changes of information in the other cells.

Depending on the program and computer memory, a spreadsheet can have up to 2,048 rows and 256 columns. The screen, having only 80 columns and 24 rows, provides only a window to the whole sheet. Each cell is stored in the memory while the work is in progress, requiring the computer system to have enough memory to support all the activity of the spreadsheet. With one cell of the electronic sheet and the format of the screen layout, many operations are performed. Some common features are as follows:

copy - move value from cell to cell.
delete - remove a column or row.
format - designate a cell to be text; decimal or control how cells, rows, and columns are shown on the screen.
insert - add columns and rows.
save - save a spreadsheet into a file.
load - read a file and display on the screen.
print - produce printed copy of part or all of the spreadsheet.

The main function of an electronic spreadsheet program is number crunching, that is, doing scores of calculations in seconds. However, it should not be substituted for data base software, although both have overlapping features to store and retrieve information. Each has functions to accomplish specific objectives, and to get the best results each should be used accordingly.

1.6 INTEGRATED SOFTWARE

So far we have discussed various application programs such as word processors, data bases, telecommunications, and spreadsheets--each as a complete program and functioning entirely on its own. In a computer system with many activities, there are situations when transfer of information is necessary from the file of one application to another. For example, it is possible to build a mailing list file, used by the word processor, from a DBMS file. Until recently, this transfer was difficult or impossible, especially if the products were not from the same vendor. Each application stores data in a file in a special way, and there is no industry standard to follow. To copy the data, one has to understand the file structure, which usually only the designers and developers of the program know. But, there is a new trend in the industry toward *integrated software*, which integrates word processing, data base, communications and electronic spreadsheets into one package. Each section is a small module of the whole, able to run and operate on its own. The interesting and important aspect of such integration is that each module is capable of transferring data to the other. For instance, the data base can supply the word processor with names and addresses to produce letters to many believers. Integrated software may even allow data communication and use electronic mail systems. Furthermore, information can be gathered from all these parts to be fed into the spreadsheet program to do analysis and forecasting.

CHAPTER TWO

SECRETARIAL HELP

The secretary of any institution of the Baha'i Faith has the great responsibility of managing and organizing a great deal of information. In the case of an Assembly, there are minutes, correspondence, reports, and other miscellaneous data brought to its attention. The secretary has to prepare the minutes of each meeting, outline an agenda, and maintain incoming and outgoing correspondence. Furthermore, in many cases, this person has to keep the list of names and addresses of all believers with most up-to-date personal information. It should be mentioned that it is not necessary for the secretary to do all these tasks. The institution can delegate any number of them to other officers or to anyone else who is capable. But, as we know, the secretary does most of them.

Given the workload of the office of the secretariat, we will devote this chapter to exploring the many ways the computer can be used to do the minutes, correspondence, membership lists, newsletters, and so on. These ideas to ease the work of the secretary can be implemented by most word processors on almost any equipment. We will also touch on another kind of program, not popular, but useful in locating text patterns, called text retrieval software.

If you have any fear of computers, let us help you banish it forever. To many, the thought of using a computer can, at first, be a frightening and intimidating experience. It is easy to understand such fears. In science fiction movies and on TV, the computer is portrayed as a powerful, intelligent machine, capable of doing complex, extraordinary tasks. Certainly, some of this is true; computers are indispensable for space voyages, modern banking transactions, modern telephone systems, and so on. But the bizarre performances of computers seen in movies and on TV are only products of some scriptwriter's imagination. It is important to remember that computers are only machines capable of doing routine chores at incredibly fast speed. A computer can be programmed to perform calculations or sort data but it is essentially just a big programmable calculator, and can never emulate or surpass other human qualities.

Personal computers, which are the focus of our attention, are small compared to mini- and mainframe computers. The software that accompanies these products may sometimes do complicated tasks, but it is not difficult to understand how to use it. The inexperienced user may find new computer vocabulary, strange codes of operation, commands, and other aspects of computer operation overwhelming at first. Sometimes, this also happens to experienced computer users. But, with time and patience, it is possible to understand and appreciate the many capabilities of software.

We should also remember that a little organization and precaution can always make the experience more pleasant and less frustrating. In the following section, we will discuss choosing files and diskette names, cataloging your work, labeling diskettes, and other matters of organization.

2.1 GETTING ORGANIZED

Proper organization always has many benefits. This is especially true with computers. Our main concern is the organization of two levels of information: 1) the structure used by the computer to store data on a diskette and 2) the method used by the user to classify the different types of information.

Common computer applications include word processing, data base management, data communication, and the electronic spreadsheet. Any one of these software applications requires the collection of data that is stored as files in a storage unit like the floppy disk. Handling this information, as with a manual system, requires certain organizational skills. The types of files stored on a particular diskette and the file names are up to you to decide. A well thought out plan can sometimes save time and prevent problems. In the rest of this section, we will discuss ways to avoid some of the pitfalls of computer operation, arrangement of your diskettes, protection of files, and the use of such features of the operating system for secretarial work in the Baha'i Faith.

DISK DIRECTORY

Every diskette has a directory--a small space designated to store all the names of the files. The data is placed in the rest of the disk, scattered in different spots. There is a linking mechanism, embedded in the DOS (Disk Operating System) to join every directory name with its associated data for reading and writing files. The number of directory names allowed on a disk depends on storage size, density, and whether both sides can be used. For example, double-sided, double-density diskettes for an IBM-PC can hold up to 128 directory names. Each directory entry contains file name, file size, time and date, and other information useful to DOS.

By typing a command, you can view the directory on the screen. It also provides many options, such as selection by a single or group of names, sorting by the names or dates in a descending or ascending fashion. With so many names in the directory, the access time is very fast. Finding a file with any option is almost instantaneous. As part of the DOS, there are several other commands that are useful for "housekeeping" in everyday use of the files. Some of these are:

1. copy files
2. rename a file
3. delete or remove files
4. print a file
5. make directory
6. remove directory

In a directory with about 100 files, with many names closely resembling one another, it is easy to write over a file accidentally, thus destroying your work. In DOS, there is a way to avoid such mishaps. Each file has two statuses: READ/WRITE to allow both reading and writing data on the file, and READ ONLY by which DOS prevents any data to be written on it. Thus if you do not want a file to be changed in any way, set the status to READ ONLY.

COPYING AND BACKUPS

In computer operation, one of the most common occurrences is loss of files. One day, to your surprise, you may find that you cannot use the valuable minutes, correspondence, and so on, because the file or directory is corrupted. It is a very frustrating and depressing experience, and it happens equally to experienced programmers and novice users. Such a failure can be attributed to either hardware or software.

Such a disastrous situation can be avoided if regular backup of your work is done. This involves making a second copy of each file on another diskette. In some cases, this may require just duplicating a whole diskette. If you attach a great importance to some of your work, you may want to have two copies.

When is the best time to make a backup? One method is to back up files after a session or at the end of a day. Let's call it the daily backup. On another diskette, every half or full week you may copy all the working files. This way, you reduce the chances of completely destroying a file.

Copying files is very straightforward. For example, a DOS command,

```
> COPY A:MINUTES1 TO B:MINUTES1
```

will duplicate a file in drive 'A:' called MINUTES1 in drive 'B:'. But, if you want to copy numerous files, the command is:

> COPY A:MINUTES* TO 'B:'.

Here, the asterisk (*) is called the *wild card*. It simply means to select from diskette directory and copy all names with the first seven characters as "MINUTES" and the rest can be any character. This wild card is useful and frequently used. If it is necessary to backup a whole diskette, then there is a program (BACKUP for IBM-DOS), with which you can duplicate one diskette onto another without having to select any directory name.

WHAT'S IN A NAME

Before using the computer for any application, some thought must be given to the nature of the data. For secretarial work, you may find that you will be doing minutes, correspondence, and newsletters. In addition, you may also keep a record containing personal information about each believer in your Baha'i community. With a community of, say 100 members, you will be handling a considerable amount of data.

One useful file management technique is to use an efficient naming system for quick identification of files. The length of a file name is limited--most computers allow only 8 to 11 characters for each name. In many personal computers, a file name is made of two parts. There is the name with a maximum of 8 characters and an extension of 3 characters, each part separated by a period(.). For example, MINUTES.001 has MINUTES as the name and 001 as the extender. As part of a directory name, the extender can be omitted, for instance, LETTER. It is very important to make the best use of this range of characters by choosing a method to identify the type of file easily and possibly the information associated with it.

On the keyboard, there are symbols such as $ (dollar), () (parentheses), and % (percent). These symbols, along with letters and numbers, can be used to name a file; in this way a group of files can be easily identified and perhaps other information gathered, such as month and version of the copy. This method will also allow one disk to keep files of various types, and we can easily group them by giving the right directory command option.

Here is a list of symbols with designations of the types of files and examples to show their uses.

1. "&" and a file name for minutes of meeting, e.g. &APR1285 is the minute for meeting held in April 12, 1985

2. "@" and a file name for correspondence, e.g. @NSA0229.82 is a correspondence to NSA on Feb. 29, 1982 @SMITH.Z is a correspondence to Z. Smith

3. "&" and a file name for information of a believer in the community, e.g. &SMITH.R is an information file of Smith R.
&BAGDADI.F is an information file of Bagdadi F.
&LAFLEUR.G is an information file of Lafleur G.

4. "$" and a file name is for newsletters,
e.g. $JAMAL is newsletter for the month of Jamal
$BEAUTY is a newsletter for the month of Beauty

5. "#" and a file name for calendars,
e.g #JAMAL is a calendar for the month of Jamal
#BEAUTY is a calendar for the month of Beauty
#AUGUST is a calender for the month of August

After organizing our filing system according to the different categories with symbols to identify each one, we can display part of the directory by group selection. Let's see all the minutes on the disk for the year 1985.

Let's give a command, using the wild card option, like this: "DIR &*.85". It will show all the minutes of the year 1985, as in Figure 2.1.

```
&JAN05.85
&JAN17.85
&FEB05.85
&FEB20.85
&MAR05.85
&MAR15.85
&APR19.85
```

Figure 2.1 Minutes for Year 1985.

Similarly, "DIR NSA*.*" will display all correspondence to the N.S.A., as in Figure 2.2.

```
@NSA0229.82
@NSA0301.85
```

Figure 2.2 All Correspondence to the N.S.A.

From our examples, we can see how easy and flexible it is to name and access files on a disk.

EXTENDED DIRECTORY

The method of file names just described gives only an abbreviated label, with file type and possibly the date. Sometimes, you may want to know more about file content. To know what is in each file you would have to go through all of them. This can be a time-consuming and boring task if you have to search through hundreds of files to find the information you want.

> @NSA0229.82 - Feb 29, 1982, asking National Spiritual Assembly if it is timely to hold a peace conference.
>
> @NSA0301.85 - Mar 01, 1985, accepting the request from the National Spiritual Assembly to increase the mass teaching activities.

Figure 2.2a

We can extend the directory of the disk by creating a file where each disk directory entry will have a description of the file. To make it a standard of your file organization, call it "CONTENT" and keep one on each disk. Use the word processor to create it. To take advantage of this extended directory, its content must be kept updated. After each session, the content file can be routinely changed to reflect the status of the directory. Figure 2.2a is such an example.

LABELING DISKS

After working with the computer for a while, the number of disks in use will increase. Generally, these disks can be classified into three categories: first, there are the original disks you received when you purchased the software, whether DOS or application program such as a word processor. These diskettes must be kept in a safe place and used only to make a working copy. To further protect these valuable programs on the diskette, a silver tag is placed on the notch for a 5 1/4 inch diskette to prevent the head of the disk drive from writing on it while in use. Second, you will have working diskettes containing all your regular work such as minutes, letters, newsletters, and so on. Finally, there are the backup disks, copies of all your working and software distribution diskettes. The backups are added protection for your valuable work from unexpected failure of the computer hardware. As part of your routine, you should backup your work after each session.

To avoid confusion, the disks need organization for quick identification. Accompanying the box of diskettes, there are labels that should be placed on each. Always use a soft, felt-tipped pen on the label to avoid damage to the magnetic surface of the disk. If you use a pencil or pen on the label while affixed to the diskette, you could lose some of the written data or permanently render the diskette useless.

The diskettes can be divided and labeled separately in three different categories : program, working, and backup disks. For further identification, color coding can be used to subdivide each category, making the organization system more efficient. For example, minutes can be marked as blue, correspondence as red, newsletters as green, and so on. The small surface of the label can be economically used to write information that will identify the material on each disk.

CATALOG

After a period, your collected disks will include all three categories, each containing its own different file types. Out of many scores of disks, it is difficult to pick one and remember its content. Of course, you can display on the screen the content of each directory when looking for a file name, but this is time consuming. For disks not used very often, or ones that are part of archives, you can make a printed copy of the directory and the file "CONTENT" and insert it along with the disk in the paper envelope. By reading this list, you can find out at any time the contents of the files of a disk, a vital step to proper organization of your information. This method works best if the list is updated whenever changes are made. If this method is too awkward for you, there are many commercial programs with features that do all the cataloging.

2.2 MINUTES

One of the main responsibilities of the secretary is to prepare the minutes of the meetings of Baha'i institutions. Because of the need for preciseness in recording the exact views and decisions of the institution, and the need to record other transactions, this can be a time-consuming job. The secretary has not only to produce the minutes, but also to file them in such a way that any of the subjects discussed can be called up in as little time as possible. There are two aspects of managing the minutes of the Assembly that can significantly improve the quality of work. One is the organization of the minutes with the proper classification of the diverse items, and the other is a fast way of grouping and retrieving items from the minutes. When we look at the capabilities of a personal computer with a word processor, it can definitely be used in both these areas, making the work of a secretary of an institution more efficient and less time consuming.

Besides having all the correct information, it is important that the contents of the minutes be well organized. They should be easy to read, and at a glance the different sections should be distinct. For example, the layout should separate the main body from the rest, with each item standing out as an individual entity. They should clearly show the item number, reference to previous minutes if necessary, and a heading describing the subject.

Let's consider for a moment the number of items the local Assembly has to deal with in its meetings during the course of a year. The frequency of meetings among institutions varies from once a week to once a month. With weekly meetings averaging 10 items per set of minutes, there will be 520 actions in a year. These decisions are vital and indicate the direction in which the institution desires to proceed on any matter with which it is concerned. Also, each decision is a policy binding the community over whom the Local Spiritual Assembly has jurisdiction. But, with the number of decisions made over a year, it is difficult to remember every single one. If the secretary is requested to locate a set of minutes with certain decisions on any given subject, he or she can spend many hours searching through piles of minutes accumulated over many years. To do a summary manually of each set of minutes, through the use of an index, also seems excessively time consuming and even impractical.

COMPUTER SOLUTION

If a computer is used to record the minutes, it gives the secretary the opportunity to print meaningful reports in any organized fashion and quickly locate any item in past minutes. We have seen the flexibility that a word processor provides, making it an appropriate tool for typing the minutes and storing them in files easily identified by an appropriate name. After having all the minutes in the computer, there are many ways to use them. One step would be to print out related data or display it on the screen; another would be to locate a common heading as part of an item from a set of minutes. This type of searching is easily accomplished with a computer. Whenever a heading is found, the whole item of the minutes, or a part of it, can be placed in a new file.

Among the desirable features in managing the minutes, one would be to locate data in the fastest possible way. To achieve this speed in the software, the computer can search for keywords. In our application, we define these keywords and embed them in each set of minutes, associating them with a description of one of the categories of items noted earlier.

Here are the definitions of the keywords:

> Minute Identification - It is a group of numbers identifying the minutes, consisting of the Baha'i year followed by a hyphen and the minutes' number.
>
> xxx-xx

```
      : :...
      :   :
    year  minutes
```

e.g. 144-12 means Baha'i year 144 and
12th meeting of the year.

Item ID - A group of numbers and letters showing the category, year, and the minutes it belongs to.

```
          xx-xxx-xx
       ....:  :  :...
       :      :     :
     category year  minute
```

e.g. RC-144-15 means report from committee
in year 144 of the 15th set of minutes.

Categories - letters, the first denoting the main category and the next is a subcategory.

```
            xx
       ......:.......
       :            :
    Category     Subcategory
```

e.g. RC means main category is 'Report'.
subcategory is 'Committee'.

The selection of main and subcategories in Figure 2.3 is only general; bear in mind that it can be expanded as required by the scope of the institution with which you are associated. One important thing to note is that it is necessary that the letter chosen as a code for each category be a unique character, and the same applies to each subcategory. However, the codes for both main and subcategories overlaps.

Code	Main Category
R	Reports
C	Correspondence
I	Institutions
G	Current goals
T	Teaching
P	Proclamation
S	Consolidation
F	Feast/Holidays
E	Education
X	Restricted: personal matters

Code	Sub Category
C	Committee
T	Treasurer
I	In
O	Out

Figure 2.3 List of Codes for Categories

Each item of the minutes should start with this item identification, followed by a reference number, which can be an item ID of previous minutes. The reference number is optional, required only if necessary. To identify a reference number as a keyword, it is necessary to enclose it in parentheses--for two reasons. First, it provides a distinction, while reading, between an item ID of the minutes and a reference number to items found in other minutes. Second, while searching, the software has to make the same distinction. Following it, enter the subtitle (a short phrase showing the items' subject matter), and then the text of the minutes as you would ordinarily enter. Figure 2.4 shows an example of minutes with keywords.

Note that the format is flexible, except that every keyword has to be associated with some part of the minutes. In Figure 2.4, the minutes' identification is 143-3 (as the third minutes of the Baha'i year 143). This identification is unique for each set of minutes and the number to the right of the hyphen denotes the number of the meeting for the year. It should be placed on the first line in the left corner of each page of the minutes. Also, it would be convenient to call the file by the minutes' ID, namely, 143-3.

Next is the item ID. For instance, P-143-3 means the item belongs to proclamation main category as well as to minutes 143-3. Following it, the preamble and decisions are entered. Similarly, there are several such item IDs. Notice that there are two that include both main and subcategories. For example, if we look at Figure 2.3, we find RT-141-3 means this item belongs to main category of REPORTS and subcategory of TREASURER.

```
141-3
 /:\
  :               Minutes of the Meeting of the
  :            Spiritual Assembly of the Baha'is of
minute                        Unityville
Identification
                                     March 24, 1985

Present : Gail Beautiful, Ron Beautiful, Ali Kind, Lim Hoisum,
          Leela Yogi, Janet Frugal, Louiggi Joyeux.

Absent  : Jim Close, Henry Happy.

Meeting opened with prayers at 8:00 PM.


P-141-3   Proclamation
/:\
 :         Preamble : The town of Unityville will
           hold the annual
 :         parade on July 10, 1985.
 :
Item ID
          Decided: 1) To purchase balloons with the following
                      messages one on each side.

                   - Let's come together,
                       Let all people of the world unite
                   - Baha'i Faith
                       Unityville

                   2) Make an attractive display showing all the
                      principles of the Baha'i Faith.
                   3) Rent a helium tank.
                   4) During the parade, give the inflated
                      balloons to children and set up the
                      display.
       reference   5) A committee will be appointed to carry
           :          out the above.
          \:/
S-141-3   (S-141-2)     Family Unity Month (May)

          Preamble :  Participation in Family Unity month
initiated by the Municipal Government.

          Decided   :   Samson Smith to invite an assistant to the
 :-->Main category      Auxiliary Board to a meeting of the
 ::---->Subcategory     community to discuss the many ways we can
 ::                     participate.
\::/
```

```
 RT-141-3  Book purchase for public library

          The cost of books to be donated to the local public
          library will be $ 30.21.

F-141-3   Feast of Glory

          Feast of Glory to be held on April 9, at the Smith's,
          starting at 8.00 PM.

CI-141-3  Correspondence in

          Letter dated March 15, 1985 received from National
          Spiritual Assembly re: Peace Movement.


The next meeting to be held at 8.00 on March 31.


Minutes Approved.




--------------------                  --------------------
   Chairman                             Secretary
```

Figure 2.4 Minutes

REPORTS

We have seen one example of minutes with embedded keywords. Over a period of time, say one year, many minutes will be accumulated that record numerous decisions made by the institution. As mentioned earlier, it is not easy to track one project through different minutes. Let's take the example of a Summer Proclamation/Teaching Project in a community. Usually, preparation for such a demanding activity will start months before the event. Some of the decisions of the Assembly may be to appoint a committee, define the committee's work, set a budget, and so forth. During the life of this project, the Assembly will also have to deal with other matters. As you can see, the diversity of the items in the minutes over a period of time can be very difficult to keep track of. There is another important aspect to managing minutes. Long after an event, you may want to go back and put together all the decisions made for reference or classification purposes just for curiosity. But such a task is difficult. Our minute managing system will be to produce reports (either in printed form or on screen display) from the different categories of items in the minutes scattered all over the disk. Let's look, first, at some of the desirable features of this system:

A. It can select one category of item identification (ID), from many files of a diskette.

In Figure 2.5, the report shows all the entries, decisions, or reports concerning consolidation during the year 141. Note, each item ID has a prefix "S" for consolidation, and the last item has a reference number that happens to occur in the previous minutes. As in this example, similar reports can be printed for any other category, such as treasury, proclamation, or any other area of concern to the Institution. The great benefit of such a report is that related decisions over a time period are grouped together for reference.

B. Sometimes it is useful to print all items from different minutes of one particular subject (heading). Figure 2.6 is an example: the subject is Family Unity Month (May).

On this report, all the items from different minutes are printed. Note, each item includes the item identification, heading, preamble, and decision. The uses of such a report are many, but one important one is to place all decisions, reports, and suggestions of one kind together in printed form.

Report to Show All Items of the
Category "Consolidation" for the Year 141

S-141-1 Regular Deepening

Decided: To ask the Consolidation Committee to continue the excellent work of consolidation and ask the secretary to write a letter to the Committee conveying to it the Assembly's appreciation and support.

S-141-2 Family Unity Month (May)

Preamble: It was announced by one of the members that the government has designated the month of May as Family Unity Month.

Decided: The secretary to find out more information from civic officials about Family Unity Month.

S-141-3 (S-141-2) Family Unity Month (May)

Preamble: Participation in Family Unity Month initiated by the municipal government.

Decided: Samson Smith to invite an assistant to the Auxiliary Board to a meeting of the community to discuss ways we can participate.

Figure 2.5 Minutes Report, Selection by Category

Report - Family Unity Month

S-141-2 Family Unity Month (May)

Preamble: It was announced by one of the friends that the government has designated the month of May as Family Unity Month.

Decided: The secretary to find out more information from civic officials about the Family Unity Month.

S-141-3 (S-141-2) Family Unity Month (May)

Preamble: Participation in Family Unity Month initiated by the Municipal Government.

Decided: Samson Smith to invite an assistant to the Auxiliary Board to a meeting of the community to discuss ways we can participate.

Figure 2.6 Report by Heading

C. While going through minutes of past meetings, have you ever come across some unfinished and forgotten business? This is likely to happen if adequate followups are not done. With a computer system, such outstanding items are easy to locate. Figure 2.7 is an example of such a report. All three items require attention of the Assembly at future meetings. Such a report shows any item that may have been overlooked. For instance, under the heading "Family Unity Month (May)", looking at Figure 2.6 we see that Samson Smith has been given the responsibility of inviting an assistant to the Auxiliary Board, and this has to come up again on the agenda of a future meeting, to ensure that this duty is carried out.

Report - Active Items

P-141-1 Proclamation
S-141-1 Regular Deepening
S-141-2 Family Unity Month (May)

Fig 2.7 Report to Show All Active Items

D. At the end of each Baha'i year, reports for each main category can put together all the decisions of the institution for future reference. In the example of Figure 2.3, there are nine such categories. Depending on the activities and needs of an Assembly, you can produce some or all of the reports. If this is done yearly, for any given subject you will be able to access the exact item you want among hundreds of decisions. To make this system more efficient, you can produce an index of the whole year's decisions using the word processor, if it has such an option.

E. Finally, the system should give the user the option either to display the information on the screen or print it on paper. The printed version is for a permanent or working copy, while the display on screen gives the operator the flexibility to check an item quickly.

IMPLEMENTATION

To implement the design to print reports of minutes requires a program to search for any of the keywords in the minutes file. After finding any keyword, it should either print it or place the heading of the whole item into a collection file to be printed later. Further, the program should select a number of files of the same group as the ones for the whole year. Then, it must go into each file and pick any item, category, or heading that you have specially requested or are searching for.

There are different ways to implement this job of managing the minutes. A word processor can be used as a tool to implement this idea. Again, keywords play a useful role. Some word processors accept commands from a file, rather than a user having to type them on the keyboard. In other words, a file can contain a series of commands--as if you were entering them through the keyboard--and the word processor will execute them one at a time sequentially. For instance, let's search for "Proclamation" in all the minutes of the year 141. Make sure all the files are on one diskette. The sequence of events will be as follows:

A. Find a minutes file with 141 as part of its ID.

B. For each file found, search for "P-141" (P is for Proclamation) as part of the item ID. For each item, write the whole line into a file called "PROCLAIM."

C. Look for another file, and if no more file with 141 as part of its ID is found, then terminate.

These three steps have to be translated into commands acceptable to the word processor you are using. (In Appendix B, there is a list of word processors that accept commands from a file.) Once set up, all the reports related to the minutes are done automatically by invoking the word processor with the command file.

But, any word processor without the command file facility can be used to implement part or most of the minutes management scheme. But this method takes time and is repetitious. Consider making a summary of the minutes instead, and later creating key information will be easy. After completing the minutes, search for each item ID. Write the ID and the heading in a summary file called "SUMMARY". This file will contain a summary of all the past minutes of the current year. To find related items many minutes, you can produce another file containing summaries of any subject found in the minutes, or you can print portions of the files to produce the report necessary to your specific requirements.

To further enhance your minutes management system, some word processors also provide such special features as creating a table of contents and index. In our case, we can merge all the minutes into one huge file, then create a table of contents and index for it, giving you the flexibility to reference any transaction from a collection of months or years of minutes.

Last, software to build a text retrieval system is available for microcomputers. Generally, it is used in offices or libraries where huge amounts of text are handled and searched. It is not a word processor, but it works with text already prepared by a word processor. One of the main functions of text retrieval software is to locate instances of words or phrases within context. This feature can be used in minute management and is described in more detail in Chapter 10.

2.3 CORRESPONDENCE MANAGER

Any institution of the Baha'i Faith can be overburdened with correspondence. Along with this task, regular maintenance of names and mailing addresses of institution representatives, civil officials, and individual believers *is* required. It requires further organization to follow-up after correspondence is sent. On the computer market, there is correspondence management software for sale. In this section, we will look at some of the facilities it provides.

The CM (correspondence manager) works with a word processor, and maintains the list of names and addresses for which it produces individual or multiple correspondence. Other features include follow-up to track phone calls and further letters at specified dates. At any time you can print your history of correspondence with any individual or institution.

In a CM program, information is organized into three categories: names and addresses of persons and institutions, status of correspondence and phone calls, and code of the originator. In each case, data are entered through a screen. In the name and address category, significant data on a person (such as, birthday and follow-up date) are kept. Some built-in features of the software include: adding of records, deletions, update, and inquiry about the records and status of any name. The status file stores references, with short descriptions of correspondence already sent or of phone calls. The originator consists of a code and the name of the person who is responsible for sending the correspondence (useful if there is more than one person working with the same computer.) CM can also generate lists of information related to any name. After the correspondence is entered through the word processor, the CM can be used to send it to one or multiple addresses. For instance, letters to all members of a local community informing them of the election of the Assembly can be printed with individual names and addresses.

CM also facilitates follow-up of any further correspondence or phone calls--a very desirable feature if you are dealing with many letters on a daily basis. Let's say that you have made a request to the mayor of your town to visit with the representative of the local Assembly. After a month, you have received no reply, and during this time you have dealt with many other letters and phone calls. It is conceivable that the letter to the mayor's office may escape your attention. But with CM it would not happen: you can enter the follow-up date with each status of the correspondence. On a regular basis you can print the correspondence according to follow-up date. CM also provides the capability to sort correspondence by name, address, and postal code. The names and the status are shown one at a time on the screen.

Every time a record or piece of correspondence is brought up on the screen for changes, the program gives you the option to record the transaction. Therefore, at any one time you can have a complete history of any person or institution. On the screen, or on hard copy, you can obtain the name and a list of all the dates, actions, and the originator's name.

2.4 MEMBERSHIP

It is always a tremendous task for any Baha'i institution to keep an up-to-date accurate list of the names and addresses of believers and other institutions, because people are moving frequently in and out of the community or Assemblies and committees are acquiring new addresses. The importance of a correct list is always realized too late at such critical times as Regional (or District) Conventions and Assembly elections. A record with proper information is also very essential for the Treasurer and other officers of the institution to carry out their duties efficiently.

Let us look at how computers can be beneficial in providing quick and accurate information. There are software packages called *data base managers* which enter numerous pieces of information into the data base, maintain it through addition, deletions, and changes, and make lists in many different formats. We will discuss these in detail in a later chapter. Here, we will look at how names and addresses can be processed by a word processor, the program that is most common among the users of personal computers. This is not a complete system for maintaining membership records because it is limited in its flexibility and capability compared to a data base manager. But it may be sufficient to keep a small number of records, use the names and addresses in mailing and make some hard copy lists.

INFOFILE

It is better to have one disk solely for keeping all the names in one place, avoiding confusion when locating a file, and also to prevent mixing files of different categories. For example, files of minutes and membership information should be kept on different diskettes.

With the word processor, let's create a file called "INFOFILE," a form that consists of all the names of different fields of a record. On the right side of each field put some dash characters (-) to show where the information related to each field will be typed. You can design the screen form any way you like, and the length can be longer than one full screen. The file "INFOFILE" is only one example and it may look like Figure 2.8.

```
                              UNITYVILLE

              Profile of ---------------------


Name : --------------------------            Address :


                                      -------------------------
Phone (H) : ---------------           -------------------------
Phone (B) : ---------------           -------------------------
              Ext - -----             -------------------------
                                      ---------



Profession : ------------------        Present services

Special talents :                     1) ----------------------
                                      2) ----------------------
1) --------------------------         3) ----------------------
2) --------------------------         4) ----------------------
3) -------------------------


Marital Status : ---------         Spouse : -----------------

                   Children :

              1) ----------------------
              2) ----------------------
              3) ----------------------
              4) ----------------------
```

Figure 2.8 Data Entry Screen

Having "INFOFILE," now let's create an information file for a believer, called Tom Savoir.

1. Create a file called "SAVOIR.T," and copy 'INFOFILE' TO 'SAVOIR.T'.

2. Load the word processor program and the file "SAVOIR.T."

3. Insert appropriate information in the fields.

4. Save the file "SAVOIR.T."

The instructions to do the above four steps can be found in the word processor manual. Now you have a file for Tom Savoir in the diskette for membership and it looks like Figure 2.9.

```
                              UNITYVILLE

                Profile of Tom Savoir-----------


Name : Tom Troy Savoir------------            Address :

                                        364 Sunny View Drive------
Phone (H) : 416 776 8956----            Apt 1256-----------------
Phone (B) : 416 567 9876----            Unityville, Ontario-------
              Ext - 4456-               Canada--------------------
                                        B9A 917--


Profession : Carpenter---------          Present services

Special talents :                        1) Serving on L S A-------
                                         2) Member of ABS----------
1) Plays violin---------------           3) Member of Teaching-----
2) Very good public speaker----          4) ----------Committee----
3) --------------------------


Marital Status : Married---          Spouse : Michelle----------

                     Children :

                1) Jason-----------------
                2) Andre-----------------
                3) Caroline--------------
                4) ----------------------
```

Figure 2.9 Input Screen with Information

Similarly, create profile files for all members in a community or all regional and national committees. Notice the name of the file in our example is made from the family name and initial separated by ".". In some cases, the family name and initial may exceed the 8 or 11 character limit of a file name. In such situations, you will have to abbreviate to suit the limit and still allow for the name to be easily recognized and differentiated from other files. You can also choose a different method in naming files, combining alphabets and numbers. Similarly, profiles can be created for committees.

For a quick check, the profile is easily displayed on the screen or printed on paper. To change any information, load the file on the word processor and do the editing as you would on a normal document.

Sometimes it is necessary to list a short form of each profile, with just name and address, leaving out other details of the file. With the word processor, however, there is no direct way of doing this as one would do with a DBMS report writer. With the word processor it is only possible with an extra step.

First, create a file called "SHORT." With the help of the word processor, copy to this file from each information file the lines of information you are interested in, such as names, addresses, and other data. After copying all the names and other information into the file called "SHORT," you can print its contents and it will look like Figure 2.10.

This file has another benefit; if it is always kept updated, it can be used to create a list file for the word processor to merge letters with names to print multiple correspondence. This is accomplished using instructions given in the *mail merge* section of the word processor manual (if this feature is provided).

```
                    MEMBERSHIP LIST

Name : ---------------------------          Address :

                                      -------------------------
Phone (H) : ---------------           -------------------------
Phone (B) : ---------------           -------------------------
              Ext - -----             -------------------------
                                      ---------

Name : ---------------------------          Address :

                                      -------------------------
Phone (H) : ---------------           -------------------------
Phone (B) : ---------------           -------------------------
              Ext - -----             -------------------------
                                      ---------

Name : ---------------------------          Address :

                                      -------------------------
Phone (H) : ---------------           -------------------------
Phone (B) : ---------------           -------------------------
              Ext - -----             -------------------------
                                      ---------
```

Figure 2.10 Membership List

Imagine you are asked to verify information about a name in your data base created by the word processor. Within seconds, the record can be brought to the computer screen and changes can be made. Also the large storage capacity of the computer allows us to handle more information than a manual system. As the Baha'i community grows, the advantages of this flexibility and speed become more obvious.

2.5 MAILING LIST

In the Baha'i Faith, at the present time, one of the most common means of communication between people and institutions is through print. It may be just one letter to one person or the same letter addressed to many. If you are sending newsletters to hundreds of believers, this requires that many names and addresses be typed. Obviously, this is time consuming and prone to errors. In word processing there are options called *mail merge and label printing;* both useful in mass mailing.

MAIL MERGE

Mail merge enables one to take a document, such as a letter, combine it with other information stored in a data base, and print out personalized copies. The data base consists of names, addresses, and other pertinent information, created by a word processor (or Data Base Management System) with data pulled from other files created by a DBMS or profile files and "SHORT" files discussed earlier. It is a mailing list; formatted according to the instructions provided in the operation manual. The letter is also created by the word processor.

Now, let's look at the ways to use the Mail Merge option and apply it to some relevant uses in the Baha'i Community. The details of implementation are different from one word processor to the next. But, there are three basic steps common to all Mail Merge systems. They are:

1. Create a document (such as a letter).
2. Compile a mailing list consisting of names, addresses, titles, and so on.
3. Print numerous copies of personalized letters, reports, memos, etc.

Figure 2.11 is a sample Mail Merge letter with *fill-in* spaces. The letter shown is similar to any other letter, except that it has spaces where the Mail Merge program will insert selected information from the mailing list.

```
..File: MAILING3
.PO
.DF DATABASE.DAT
.RV N,firstname,name,address,city,province,postal.


LOCAL ASSEMBLY OF THE BAHA'IS OF
UNITYVILLE


<firstname> <name>                                April 1, 1985
                 :
<address>        :--> Fill in places
<city>           :
<state>          :
<postal>.......:


Dear <firstname> :

This is to let you know that Ridvan is approaching. This is a festive time for
Baha'is throughout the world. Also, it is when we elect the members of our local
Assembly. The election will be held on the evening of April 20, at 8.00 PM at the
home of the Moore family. Your election call is enclosed along with a current list
of the adult believers who reside in Unityville.

<firstname>, if you will be unable to attend the annual meeting, please fill in the
enclosed ballot and forward it to me before April 20.

The Assembly hopes you will be able to attend the meeting. We look forward to seeing
you and send you our best wishes for a happy Ridvan.

Best Baha'i greetings,



Mary Humble

secretary

/mh

encl.
```

Figure 2.11 Sample of Mail Merge Letter.

The second step is to create the mailing list (data base file) as shown in Figure 2.11a. The mailing list is made of many records; each is a collection of information that will be inserted in various places in the letter created in Figure 2.11. In this list, there is a number for each record, followed by first name, family name, address, city, state and postal code. The entries can be as numerous as allowed by your word processor.

```
1,John,Vital,364 Mingle Rd.,Unityville,Ontario,M4C-1Z2
2,Mila,Radiant,99 Flight St.,Unityville,Ontario,M4C-5T5
3,Habib,Humble,2 Clearwater St.,Unityville,Ontario,M4C-6Y6
4,Vida,Audacious,4 Heaven Way,Unityville,Ontario,M4C-5Y7
5,Ritesh, Rungloll,24 Rue de Saut,Unityville,Ontario,M4C-7Z6
6,Vikram, Rungloll,24 Rue de Saut,Unityville,Ontario,M4C-7Z6
```

Figure 2.11a Mailing List

The field contains such information as first name, family name, address, and the like. To print each letter, just give the command as required by the software. Both letter and mail list file are merged, creating for each mailing list a copy of the letter with the information in the fields placed as indicated by the fill-in places. The first letter will look like Figure 2.11b

LABELS

After making multiple letters using Mail Merge, you will need the names and addresses printed on the envelopes. Printing mailing labels for envelopes is easy and straightforward once a data base is established. The file 'SHORT' (with names and addresses) can be printed on one column labels. Be sure to adjust the lines between records so that each name is printed on a new label. This is a cumbersome way of printing labels, however. Some word processors have built-in programs to print labels in several columns, with the option to print a test pattern to ensure that the paper is properly adjusted on the printer. Figure 2.11c is an example of two column labels.

LOCAL ASSEMBLY OF THE BAHA'IS OF UNITYVILLE

John Vital April 1, 1985
364 Mingle Rd.,
Unityville
Ontario
M4C-1Z2

Dear John:

This is to let you know that Ridvan is approaching. This is a festive time for Baha'is throughout the world. Also, it is when we elect the members of our local Assembly. The election will be held on the evening of April 20, at 8.00 PM at the home of the Moore family. Your election call is enclosed along with a current list of the adult believers who reside in Unityville.

John, if you will be unable to attend the annual meeting, please fill in the enclosed ballot and forward it to me before April 20.

The Assembly hopes you will be able to attend the meeting. We look forward to seeing you and send you our best wishes for a happy Ridvan.

Best Baha'i greetings,

Mary Humble

secretary

/mh

encl.

Figure 2.11b Sample of Mail Merged Letter

John Vital 364 Mingle Rd. Unityville Ontario M4C-1Z2	Habib Humble 2 Clearwater St. Unityville Ontario M4C-6Y6
Mila Radiant 99 Flight St. Unityville Ontario M4C-5T5	Vida Audacious 4 Haven Way Unityville Ontario M4C-5Y7
Ritest Rungloll 24 Rue de Saut Unityville Ontario M4C-7Z6	Vikram Rungloll 24 Rue de Saut Unityville Ontario M4C-7Z6

Figure 2.11c Mailing Labels

2.6 NEWSLETTER

In the Baha'i community the local or regional newsletter is an important organ for transmitting information to the believers. A regular newsletter is especially vital in a large Baha'i community where all members have to be informed about Feasts, Assembly reports, and community events by mail.

In preparing a newsletter from start to finish, the many stages are as follows :

1. Gathering news,
2. Writing and editorial,
3. Artwork and printing format,
4. Printing and duplicating.

In all of the above areas we will look at where a computer can be applied to relieve people of routine tasks and allow time for creativity and originality.

News gathering can be the most interesting aspect of any newsletter. You can collect news from within and/or outside the region. The most up-to-date events and stories will keep readers well informed while making the reading interesting. The format and the content are decided by the needs of the community. However, we all agree that a variety of topics will add more life and diversity to this organ. Here is a list of suggestions about where news can be found:

1. Assembly or committee minutes, statements, and reports,

2. Community announcements of upcoming events, teaching stories, and pioneering stories,

3. Regional news and events, with a touch of international reporting for those stories that are not covered in the national newsletter. (For example, news of friends from the local community who are pioneers overseas),

4. Summary of guidelines and directives from the National Spiritual Assembly,

5. Book reviews and commentaries,

6. Quotations from the Writings.

In a computer system, a file can be opened for each category mentioned above and the incoming news can be entered in draft form with the word processor. In a way, each file is like a shoe box where the respective pieces of news are thrown in. Unlike the shoe box system, you can make changes with great ease and the printed form is in one continuous place rather than in bits and pieces on scraps of paper.

After the news has been collected, the fun part of the newsletter starts--writing the articles. With the help of the word processor you take the raw ideas of the draft file and expand them into clear and logical prose. With your knowledge of word processor function you can write and edit as much as you desire.

The newsletter can be divided into several sections:

1. Assembly informations,
2. Calendar of events,
3. Uplifting stories,
4. Regional/International events,
5. Recent directives and guide lines of the National Assembly,
6. etc.

The sections can be chosen in such a way as to reflect the character and needs of your community.

After the composition is done, you must decide on the layout and the printing format of the entire newsletter. It can be one or many pages, printed on one or both sides. The elegance of the print depends on the combined capability of your word processor and your printer. One kind of word processor can only do margin justifications, pagination, and perhaps print bold and underscored characters, while at the other extreme with a versatile word processor you can do multiple column formats, graphics, proportional spacing, and use different fonts of characters. Remember to make room for any photographs you want to insert.

The next step is to print the newsletter. The method of printing definitely depends on the number of copies required, and the budget with which you are working. Perhaps it is economical to use the dot matrix or daisy-wheel printer for as few as twenty one-sided copies, without pictures. For anything more, it may be preferable to go to a photocopying or printing company. For these last two choices, you should have good print quality from the computer-generated original, preferably from a daisy-wheel or letter quality printer. After this step, make mailing labels using the printing option of the word processor.

CHAPTER THREE

DATA BASE: MANAGING MEMBERSHIP

In Chapter 1, the idea of using a computerized data base was introduced. We discussed a few basic principles such as maintaining information of community members in disk files. That chapter showed how data from several files can be combined to produce reports. Later, the word processor was put to work to manage membership lists; as you will recall, that is limited in its flexibility and capability to accomplish complex management of information. The word processor is mainly for managing words. Obviously it places some severe restrictions on information management; but it is useful in the absence of data base management software.

In this chapter, we will further describe a computer data base system, and explore in detail its powerful capabilities: creating files in a data base, manipulating the records, and retrieving the data for reports and charts. Our tool is a popular software program called Data Base Management System (DBMS), now available for almost every brand of personal computer. A few popular software systems for micros are DBASEIII, RBASE:5000, and Oracle. Our example is the management of membership information in the Baha'i community.

Before going any further, let's refresh our memory about the nature of a data base system. As mentioned earlier, it is a collection of data, organized in a manner to simplify retrieval and changes of any information. For example, a data base can simply be a collection of bills, which is indexed, labeled, and placed in a shoe box, or it can be a complex filing system found in a computer disk.

DBMS, as computer software, can be used to manage Baha'i membership lists, from the local community to the regional and national level. It is popular because it is easy to learn, and it handles huge amounts of data with flexibility, speed, and accuracy. For individuals having a personal computer and interested in using it for the Faith, building this application for a community or committee can be an interesting and rewarding experience.

The project we are undertaking is, for some of you, a major computer task, and to ensure its success we should proceed carefully. Recent experiences show us that many computer projects have failed, at a cost of many thousands of dollars, leaving participants with a bitter taste in their mouths because they failed to provide the solutions they promised. The biggest culprit behind such failure is lack of proper planning. Let us acquaint ourselves with some rules that may lead to a happy ending. Here are some steps to follow:

DETERMINE YOUR REQUIREMENTS: This step defines the needs; and in our case, it describes different tasks that you would want the membership management system to accomplish. On paper, you develop the ideas related to the project, with clear descriptions of the limits of its capabilities. Emphasis is not placed on how this is to be accomplished.

OUTLINE THE COMPUTER SOLUTION: After carefully studying the requirements, you must decide if a computer can satisfy your needs. If it does, you should first provide an overview of the solution, then show how different parts--as small tasks--contribute to the solution. In computer terms, you must show the input information, processing steps, and the results (output).

LOGIC: Remember the CPU operation is based on the logic steps of a program. It is necessary that the tasks in the outline of the solution be specified in a logical manner. The logic of this step should be sound for the computer solution to work properly. To explain further, let's take a common example such as buying bread from the grocery store:

a) get the money,
b) drive or walk to the "XYZ" store,
c) buy the bread,
d) return home.

These four steps seem reasonable, and they have a logical order, but if any two steps were interchanged the whole process will not make sense. For example, it would be illogical to switch items "a" and "d."

CODING: Now that we have defined our requirements, formulated the solution, and analyzed the logic, we are ready to translate the steps of each task into a program. In other words, this is the step when programming takes place. A program, written in a computer language, describes all the steps, big and small, for the computer to accomplish the task.

DEBUGGING: After coding (programming), the job is not yet finished. Even after meticulous planning and careful programming, it is possible to leave out some steps, rendering the work incomplete or nonfunctional. This phase of finding the "bug" in the program can be time consuming and agonizing, but it's necessary it the program is to work properly.

TESTING & VALIDATION: This step proves that the solutions you have outlined really satisfy the requirements. Here, you enter the test data into the program and determine if the intended results are in fact produced.

USES: After you are satisfied with the validation and testing, install the software by entering all the read data required for the data base. Next, prepare a procedure manual, showing the routine steps to be performed during a period of time, say one week or month, to accomplish a smooth running of the system.

It is important to note that any of these steps can be modified at any time during the life of the program. Thus the process has an organic character which allows you to derive the greatest benefit overtime. No one step can be accomplished fully before moving on to the next step. For example, during debugging and testing you might not notice a few bugs but find them later during the operation phase. Obviously, you have to fix the bugs. Similarly, while outlining the computer solution, you may later find it advantageous to add a few more features to the requirements of the system.

This method is popular in the computer industry and every software project goes through these different phases. But, throughout this book, we have concentrated only on a few steps. They are:

1. definition of requirements,

2. design suggestions (computer solution),

3. implementation,

4. how to use them.

Here, the programming area--coding, debugging and testing--have been omitted. They depend entirely on the computer language or data base system of your computer. There are many commercial DBMS, and each one is different from the next. Therefore we cannot show the details of how each can be coded. As part of implementation, we have given general ideas to guide you through these three parts. In this book, we have concentrated on DBMS as a tool to develop data base application, but it should be mentioned that the designs suggested here can be implemented using any computer language or DBMS.

3.1 SOME FEATURES OF DBMS

Before we jump into the requirements of a membership management system, let us first look at the power of the data base software. Earlier, we mentioned the DBMS comes with numerous ways of managing information. In this section we will discuss some of the commands that will be used later in implementing the membership management system. In most DBMS, the information is changed using the structured query language (SQL). The major problem is that this is cumbersome to use, requiring the typing of long command lines. Many DBMS provide software modules, called application builders, to simplify the use of the software. We will be discussing these functions along with screen interface to show a whole record at a time, thus providing you with a complete view of data.

SELECT: The select function is also called RETRIEVE, LOCATE, or FIND, depending on your DBMS. Once information has been packed as records in a data base, it has to be brought out to the screen of the computer for changes or inspections. The SELECT command searches the data base and brings out the record you are interested in. To retrieve a field, such as the name or phone number of a member, it is used to identify which record to pick from the file (table). This command is so flexible that it can select a group of records according to the range of a field (for example, number 0 to 99), also sort in ascending or descending order.

UPDATE: This is an important command, allowing us to make changes to the data base. For example, if a community member changes address, first we call the whole record on the screen using the retrieve command, make the changes, and enter the changed record back into the data base using the UPDATE function.

NEXT: When retrieving a group of records, you may want to browse through one at a time. The NEXT function lets you look at each record within the selected group.

PREVIOUS: The NEXT function allows us to go forward in searching for a record, but the "PREVIOUS" function lets us go in the opposite direction. These two functions, NEXT and PREVIOUS, allow the user to browse through records in both forward and backward directions.

DELETE: Believers are always moving from one community to another, making it necessary to change the data base. Here, the record can be removed by using the DELETE function. Before using this function, the user must be extremely careful! After its execution, there is no trace of that record left. In other words, if inadvertently you press the DELETE key, the record is erased from the system completely.

INSERT: Every data base system should have a means of entering information to the files. The INSERT function takes a record, with the fields properly filled, and places it into the file.

SORT: In a data base, the records are stored in the order they are entered, not necessarily having any other kind of order. Sometimes, it is desired to bring out the data in a certain order, for example, alphabetically or numerically. The sort option in the SELECT command is useful to retrieve the records in an ascending or descending order.

DATA TYPE: The fields in a record can be considered as "holes" where pieces of information related to a record are placed. Each field contains different types of data: number, name, address, date, and so on. The following describes the most common data types in a data base software.

NUMBER: As data, the number type is divided into two categories: integer and real. An integer number contains only whole numbers (for example, 123) while the real number consists of two parts, the whole number and a fraction. For example, 123.02 is a real number made of an integer part (123) and a fraction (.02). In a computer system these two types of numbers have to be distinguished because each is stored in a different way.

CHARACTER: The letters, numbers, and other characters on the keyboard that are printable on the screen are considered characters. In this data type, first you decide the maximum length of the characters to be stored in a field. For example, a field to store names with length 30, allows up to 30 characters as maximum. When using a field of data type, you cannot exceed the maximum length defined. Of course, this length can be changed, if necessary.

DOLLAR AMOUNT: This is similar to a real number with integer but only 2 decimal numbers for cents are allowed.

DATE: The date is made of day, month and year. Some DBMS provide options in selecting the date format. Here are some examples:

12 Jan 85,
Jan, 12 1985,
12 January 1985.

CALCULATION: It is very likely that in certain applications calculations are required. Most DBMS provide basic arithmetic functions, which are:

addition
subtraction

division
multiplication
average
summation

To use them, it should be noted that the data types should be integer, real, or dollar. Here are two examples.

1. 12 + 34.67 - $ 2.50
2. John + 3.5

In example 1, an integer is added to a real number, then a dollar value is subtracted, which makes sense. However, in the second example, a character is added to a real number, which is illegal.

WINDOWING: To explain the computer concept of windowing, let's consider a situation. You are building a table in the workshop and the phone rings. Immediately, you leave the tools and run to answer the phone. After finishing the phone conversation, you continue the work on the table from where you left off. But in many personal computer programs, it is not possible to stop one task suddenly, without completing it, and move to another.

For example, you are inserting contributions to the Baha'i Fund into a transaction file of a computer, and you notice that the address of a believer in the membership file is incorrect. Without windowing, it is not possible to leave the program about the Fund, go to the membership program, make the changes, and return to the Fund transaction without disturbing it. Windowing allows multiple tasks within a program to be executed simultaneously. Remember, this feature is not provided by all DBMS. And from our example, it is obvious that windowing is a desirable facility. In fact it makes it possible to work concurrently on many tasks.

APPLICATION GENERATOR: Some DBMS on the market are so powerful that they can build an application, such as managing membership, within minutes. The user has only to define the data base file with record size and fields, and after a few key strokes of commands the data base software constructs an application program, consisting of a screen interface and basic functions for information maintenance, with function keys programmed for you to use. But if you want to design your own screen layout, build programs according to your own plans, and use the function keys to the best advantage, the application generator will do all these and more at truly impressive speed. A data base system with application building capability is certainly one of the most desirable tools to produce fast results in program development. Not every DBMS has a complete system but the latest ones have some form of application generator.

REPORT WRITER: The information we save in the data base files is invisible to the user. If we look at a diskette, we will see a magnetic disk with concentric circles instead of hundreds of names and addresses. One of the ways of seeing the data is to pull up part or all of it and print it on paper. In fact, all DBMS provide a facility, with commands to produce elegant reports and listings, called report writer. For each page of a report, you can define the header, body, and footer. Within any of these sections you can print information at any column of any line. This aspect of choosing lines and columns is called formatting. To use the report writer of a DBMS, the programming language is generally easy to understand, allowing the user to produce formatted reports in a short time. For details of how to use the report writer, refer to the manual of the DBMS you are using.

SHOPPING FOR DBMS

If you are seriously looking into a DBMS, the main question is what to buy. In this section, we will discuss some of the most important issues in searching for the best software for your needs. By no means can this be an exhaustive or thorough study of the different commercial data base management software and their features, but it provides an entry point. You can gather more information through magazines and books to decide on a suitable software for you.

While looking to purchase a DBMS or any other software, do not be nervous or fearful. If the right steps are taken, this can be a pleasant and satisfying experience. But before buying, it is important to become an informed consumer. Knowledge of software without delving into theories of how it works, will give you enough information for your shopping. In this section, we will touch on some DBMS features, as well as a few other aspects such as ease of use, correctness of the manual, and support in times of difficulties.

SHOPPING LIST

There are hundreds of DBMS in different kinds, prices, and sizes, all emphasizing their strengths but ignoring their weaknesses. When investigating a software, you have to understand all aspects; it is your responsibility to decide whether a software will manage properly and efficiently the data of your application, namely a membership management system. Here is a list of functions required for our purposes.

1. Data base commands: some of the data base commands discussed earlier are SELECT, NEXT, PREVIOUS, DELETE, INSERT, and UPDATE.

2. Report writer: in some DBMS it comes as part of the whole DBMS package, while in others it is sold separately. In any case, it is a necessary tool if you want to print reports or listings.

3. Arithmetic operation: addition, subtraction, multiplication, division, and calculation of average.

4. Data type: integer, real, character, dollar, date, and text.

5. Access: multiple key (field) access of the record of a file. This will give you more flexibility in the way you can retrieve or sort data records.
6. Relation: the program should be able to extract, combine, and compare related data from multiple files.

In addition to these basic features, some DBMS will have additional functions as part of the package which can be accomplished with extra software modules. It is up to you to weigh the advantages of the extras and decide whether they will help the software development. Some DBMS are loaded with advanced features, and of course these are more expensive. For example, one of the added features in a DBMS may be windowing. It may only cost you a few hundred dollars more, but it enhances the quality of the product by giving it flexibility to handle more than one task at a time. Another popular feature is an application builder (generator) with a DBMS. It saves time as it automatically produces application programs. But keep in mind that it is the ease of use of the software that will really save you time; therefore, it is important to see how the editor DBMS, application builder, or screen generator work as an integral package.

As you can see, only these two features, windowing and application builder, can be of great benefit. Some other ones are: interface to word processor and electronic spreadsheet, and import and export of files from other data bases. As the data base technology further develops, there will be more facilities that emerge.

USER FRIENDLY

As you know, computers are penetrating into all aspects of our daily lives, forcing many of us (who a while ago had little or no interest in getting involved) to become knowledgeable about this new technology. There is tremendous pressure on the developers of this industry to demystify the uses of the DBMS. So, the present emphasis is to make the product "user friendly."

How do you judge if a DBMS is "user friendly?" This may mean different things to different people, depending on previous working experience on computers. One place to start is the manual. Look for clarity and simplicity of the DBMS commands, as well as step-by-step instructions in the form of a tutorial for you to learn. After investigating several products, you can finally judge which is the most "user friendly" for you. One trend is to equip software with "help menus", tutorials, or facts about how to use the commands of the data base correctly. For beginners, this saves the time of searching through the manuals.

ERROR HANDLING

If anything goes wrong, through your own mistake or because of system failure, what happens? The way the errors are handled should be one of your concerns while shopping for DBMS. A well-designed system should always let you know the source of the problem, not in coded form, but in plain easy to understand language. Also, it should not crash or return to the operating system--as both processes require bringing the system up from start, possibly losing valuable work. Rather, it should graciously recover from fatal errors, and in case of operation mistakes by the user, another chance should be given to make corrections. It is important to find out exactly what happens to the data base when the power fails. Such facts are not likely found in the operation manual nor will the sales person give you a precise answer. If you are not satisfied, ask for an expert on the product.

SUPPORT

In buying any expensive product, we are always concerned with maintenance and support after the sale. The concern is important, especially for a beginner, so question the dealer as to what exactly is provided as customer support. It may range, from toll-free telephone lines, with experts giving immediate answers to your questions, to absolutely no support.

Some other sources of help are from magazines, newsletters, and users groups. These depend on the popularity and age of the product. Again, it is worthwhile to find out any users group in your neighborhood. But keep in mind that the best service is always from the manufacturer.

TEST DRIVE

Last, you will want to trade places with the sales person and try the software. Before this stage, make adequate preparations, and list the features you desire. While testing the features, pay careful attention to the documentation. Here are some questions to ask.

1. Is the style of the language clear?

2. Does it provide tutorials for beginners?
3. Does it have an advanced section?
4. Is it well organized?
5. Are there plenty of explanations?
6. Is the manual indexed?
7. Is the manual complete and error free ?
8. Is there any discrepancy between the manual and the software?

3.2 REQUIREMENTS OF DATA BASE

One of the most important steps in using a DBMS is to understand the application clearly. In our case, it is the membership of a community. In this section, we will decide upon some basic functions of the management of data bases that will be essential, then suggest a few reports, and define the data base in terms of each record of a member.

Computerizing membership is a major undertaking for a person or Assembly, and one must first ask what size of community makes such a project worthwhile. A simple test is to check time and effort required to maintain accurately and regularly all the names and addresses of community members. In a small community, say with 50 members or less, only a few changes and additions may be required during a month. But, with over 300 members in a large city made up of transient people, keeping track of all the changes, such as insertions and deletions of names, may require a lot of time and effort.

In a community with a large membership, considering a computer system is a good idea. With the growth in the Baha'i Faith, it will be common to have communities with several thousands of members. In these circumstances, recording names and addresses on paper would be a staggering job.

In the example, our imaginary community, Unityville, will have a population of over 300 Baha'is: adults, youth, and children. The Spiritual Assembly of Unityville just decided to convert the manual filing of membership records to a computerized data base system, and you have been chosen to design, implement, and install the system.

The first logical step is to outline the requirements of this system. Here are the main aspects:

1. The data base is made up of a computer file with records, consisting of information of one member. Each will have the following kinds of data:

   ID number of member
   Name of the member
   Address
   Telephone
   Arrival date in the community
   Marital status
   Name of spouse
   Name of first child
   Name of second child
   Name of third child
   Name of fourth child
   Current profession
   Administrative position presently serving
   Date of birth
   Any special talents, languages spoken

2. With a screen interface, the operator manages the membership list, one record at a time, by using these functions implemented in the program that we are about to design.

   a) Insert a record with name, address, age, and so on to the data base.

   b) Delete a record from the data base.

   c) Update information of an existing record.

   d) Access (Select) a group of records, while showing one record at a time, move to the next record by pressing a function key of the keyboard called <NEXT>.

   e) Unlike <NEXT>, press another function key called <PREVIOUS> to go back one record at a time.

   f) Retrieve information either by ID number or name of the record.

3. Also, we will make lists of believers according to these categories:

   a) Short list with only number, name, address, and age.

   b) Long list with all the information.

   c) List of all youth, age between 15 and 25.

   d) List of all children, under 15 years.

e) List of only adults, over 21 years.

d) List of only Persian speaking Baha'is.

3.3 DEFINING & CREATING DATA BASE

In this step, we decide upon the size of the record for the membership file, called "MEMBER." Remember, the record is divided into fields, corresponding to name, address, telephone, and so on, of each member. Figure 3.1 shows a list of all the fields of the record with the name of each field, description, data type, and length (for character data type only).

File name: MEMBER

Name of field	description	data type	length
number	ID number of member	integer	
name	name of the member	character	25
apartment	apartment #	character	25
street	street number	character	25
city	city or town	character	25
province	province/state	character	10
postal	postal or zip code	character	7
h-telephone	home telephone	character	10
b-telephone	business telephone	character	10
a-date	arrival date in the community	date	
marital-status	1-married, 2-single	character	1
spouse	name of spouse	character	20
child-1	name of first child	character	20
child-2	name of second child	character	20
child-3	name of third child	character	20
child-4	name of fourth child	character	20
profession	name of current profession	character	20
admin-1	Baha'i administrative	character	25
admin-2	position presently serving	character	25
admin-3	or previously served	character	25
date-of-birth	date of birth	date	
talent	any special talent	character	25
persian	Persian speaking?	Character	1

Figure 3.1 Record Definition for "MEMBER" File.

Note, the information per record is more than you would normally care to have in a paper filing system. Here, we are taking advantage of the computer's capacity to handle data speedily. Depending on the needs of your own community, you can change the size of the record. Also note, some types have been broken down into more than one field. For example, street has two parts, one for apartment number and the other for street name. There are places for up to four names of children to be included as well as three places to show the different administrative positions a member is currently holding. There are two fields for telephone (home and business).

After having defined the data base file, we are ready to move to the next stage, the creation of the data base in your computer. To do this, we have to be aware of the facilities of the data base management software that allows us to maintain the data base, which is different than that maintaining the records of files. These facilities are part of the software package called utilities.

There are many such utilities, but there is one that is most essential: the function to create a data base. It sets up all the necessary building blocks to provide a foundation upon which many files can be built. The user's manual of your DBMS provides the exact commands for how to create a data base. Go ahead and create one and call it "DBMEMBER."

Next, we create a file for the membership, called "MEMBER." In this process, we establish the size of the record by defining each field as shown in Figure 3.1. Before we go any further, a few words have to be said about names in a data base system. Each DBMS has its own restrictions on how files (tables) or fields (attributes) are named. Therefore, it is important for you to check the number of characters allowed or which characters are legal as part of a name. For example, "date-of-birth" may be fine, while a name with spaces, such as "Date of Birth" is not acceptable. Or, names with spaces but enclosed with quotes may be legal, such as "Date of Birth." Therefore, care is needed in choosing field names, to ensure that they are acceptable to the software, as well as meaningful if abbreviated. In Figure 3.1, we have chosen to omit any space as part of the field name and in some cases we use abbreviations. The description with each name is to give information and to eliminate any misinterpretation.

To create the file "MEMBER", we will give an example to show the different steps that are necessary. These commands do not belong to any DBMS. They may or may not correspond to your software, but the process gives a general idea of creating a file in a data base. Let's establish a couple of rules: to distinguish between the software prompt and the response of the user, we have enclosed all the input to be typed by you with brackets [], while a carriage return is <cr>. In some software, it may be necessary to initialize the data base, and perhaps give it a name (like DBMEMBER).

Creation of the file "MEMBER" is done in the following steps:

```
[ create MEMBER ; <cr> ]

Field    #1  : [number <cr>]
type         : [integer <cr>]

Field    #2  : [name <cr>]
type         : [character <cr>]
length       : [30 <cr>]

Field    #3  : [apartment <cr>]
type         : [character <cr>]
length       : [20 <cr>]

      .
      .
      .

Field    #21: [birth-of-date <cr>]
type        : [date <cr>]

Field    #22: [talent <cr>]
type        : [character <cr>]
length      : [30 <cr>]

Field    #23: [persian<cr>]
type        : [character <cr>]
length      : [1 <cr>]

Field    #24: [.e <cr>]
```

Note after giving the command to create file "MEMBER," there was no prompt, indicating the process was successful. From that point, an interaction between the user and the software started to define one field at a time. In this case, there are 23 attributes, and each requires you to enter the field name, data type, and length if data type is a character. Also note, entering ".e" in the field # 24 ends the entry. Also, notice both upper- and lower-case characters as well as numerics are used as part of attribute names. To verify this entry, let's display all the fields by giving this command:

```
[display MEMBER ;<cr>]

The following is shown on the screen:

name                type      length

number             integer
```

name	character	25
apartment	character	25
street	character	25
city	character	25
province	character	10
postal	character	7
h-telephone	character	10
b-telephone	character	10
a-date	date	
marital-status	character	1
spouse	character	20
child-1	character	20
child-2	character	20
child-3	character	20
child-4	character	20
profession	character	20
admin-1	character	25
admin-2	character	25
admin-3	character	25
date-of-birth	date	
talent	character	25
persian	character	1

The display shows the information related to the fields is correct. If you discover any mistake, there are utilities to alter any of these parts of the fields. Some of these commands are for deleting fields, renaming fields, and changing data types or length. Also, you can delete or rename files. This concludes the creation of the data base and the file "MEMBER." Our next step is to use the fields by adding information.

3.4 SCREEN LAYOUTS

To manage the information in the data base, we require a screen interface, a program that converts the screen into a window to the data base. Through this interface, we can see only one of many records. In designing a screen layout, there are a few characteristics to keep in mind. First, the operator will be looking at it often. Therefore, a pleasant layout will be less strenuous on the eyes. In creating a layout, one starting point is to use the screen carefully. To strike a good balance, avoid crowding the screen with information only at one spot, rather, spread out the headings, fields, and descriptions to cover most of the screen. Another way to enhance the layout is to divide the screen according to the types of information. Always have a title or heading and describe the function keys, if they are used.

SCREEN 3.1 is an example with the title "Membership Maintenance." Note there are three main subheadings: address, family and administrative experience. Each dotted area corresponds to the field in the file we created earlier. In this area you type the information such as name, address, and so on. Associated with these, there are labels on the left hand side to identify the fields.

Functions such as SELECT, NEXT, PREVIOUS, and so on are listed at the bottom of the screen. Each corresponds to a key of the keyboard function (PF) keys. Some DBMS allow you to program these keys so that by pressing them, an operation is performed. To enter a record into the membership file, fill in the fields on the screen with information, then press function key F4. To bring a record from the data base, type the name or number and press F1. To update or delete use F5 and F6, respectively. You can improve the screen by using graphic capabilities, if provided in the DBMS. Boxes separate categories or highlighted areas can give emphasis.

```
                         Membership Maintenance

                                  UNITYVILLE

Name: .........................                 Number : ..........


ADDRESS                                  FAMILY
-------                                  ------

apartment:......................  status :.. [ M - married,
street    :......................               S - single]
city      :......................  spouse: .....................
state/prov: .........              child1: .....................
postal    :.......                 child2: .....................
Phone (H):..._..._....             child3: .....................
      (B):..._..._....             child4: .....................

ADMINISTRATIVE EXPERIENCE:
-------------------------
1 .......................      2 .......................
3 .......................

TALENT          : ............................
Profession      : ............................
Date of arrival : ................
Date of birth   : ................
Persian         : .. [ P - Persian speaking,
                       N - Non-Persian speaking ]

         <-----  FUNCTION KEY DESCRIPTION  ----->
F1-SELECT  F2-NEXT F3-PREVIOUS F4-INSERT F5-UPDATE F6-DELETE
F7-EXIT TO MAIN MENU
```

SCREEN 3.1 User Interface (Membership Data Base)

To create the layout, use the utility of the DBMS, such as an editor. Furthermore, you have to link this interface screen to the data base. Here the implementation varies from one DBMS to the next. Refer to the manual for more detailed instructions.

Before starting the reports of the membership system, we have to design a screen layout to give us the selection between the membership maintenance and reports. An example is shown in SCREEN 3.2.

```
                    UNITYVILLE
           MEMBERSHIP MANAGEMENT SYSTEM

                    MAIN MENU

    1 - Membership Maintenance

    2 - Reports

    3 - Exit to DOS


         SELECTION ( 1-3 ) : ..
```

SCREEN 3.2 Main Menu of Membership Management System

This screen does not concern the data base, rather it is used to select one of the three tasks. When the membership management system software is invoked, the user will be presented with this "Main Menu." Note, selection gives control back to DOS. The other two selections are Membership Maintenance and the Report Menu.

3.5 REPORTS

In a computer system, information from the disk files is produced on paper at fast speed. From the outline of our membership management system, there are five different reports to be done, and let's design the format of each.

REPORT 3.1 is a listing with all the information about each member.

```
                    UNITYVILLE


          Long Membership Listing       Date : ..............


Number: ..........  Name : .........................
                  Spouse : .........................
                Children : ...................
                           ...................
                           ...................
                           ...................

Marital status : ..  ( M - married,  S - single )


ADDRESS :                       ADMINISTRATION :

 ....................           .......................
 ....................           .......................
 ..............                 .......................
 ...........
 ......                         Phone (H): ... ... ....
                                      (B): ... ... ....
 TALENT : ....................................
 PROFESSION      : ............................
 DATE OF BIRTH   : ..............
 DATE OF ARRIVAL : ..............
 PERSIAN         : ..

                               Page 1
```

REPORT 3.1 - Long Membership Listing

Note, the formatting starts with the name of the community as the header, the type of report, and the date when the report was run. In the body, you will notice there are two types of information. One is directly printed from the file, each piece corresponding to the field of the previously described record, indicated by the dotted lines. The other is a label associated with the data. For example, all the fields related to the address are grouped under the heading "ADDRESS," similarly administration experiences under "ADMINISTRATION." However, other fields have their own label, such as "Number," "Name," "Spouse," and so on. At the bottom, there is a page number.

Next, REPORT 3.2 is a membership listing with less information. The heading and footer are similar to REPORT 3.1, except the listing title. But, in the main body only member, name, address, and age are printed. Note, as part of address, only the apartment number, street, and postal code are printed because we know the city (community) and the state (province). This listing is useful for quick reference of the community membership.

```
                    UNITYVILLE

         Short Membership listing          Date : ...........

Number      Name                Address                   Age
---------------------------------------------------------------
 ....    ................   ........................   ...
 ....    ................   ........................   ...
 ....    ................   ........................   ...
 ....    ................   ........................   ...
 ....    ................   ........................   ...
 ....    ................   ........................   ...
 ....    ................   ........................   ...
 ....    ................   ........................   ...
 ....    ................   ........................   ...
 ....    ................   ........................   ...

              page 1
```

REPORT 3.2 Short Membership Listing

The next three reports are similar except each lists members according to age. For instance, REPORT 3.3 is for adults of age over 21, which is especially useful when a list of eligible voters is required for election of the Assembly.

```
                              UNITYVILLE

Adult Membership Listing  ( OVER 21 )      Date : ............

Number       Name                    Address                      Age
-------------------------------------------------------------------------
  .....    .................    ...........................     ...
  .....    .................    ...........................     ...
  .....    .................    ...........................     ...
  .....    .................    ...........................     ...
  .....    .................    ...........................     ...
  .....    .................    ...........................     ...
  .....    .................    ...........................     ...
  .....    .................    ...........................     ...
  .....    .................    ...........................     ...

                 page 1
```

REPORT 3.3 Adult Membership Listing

In a large community, you want to find out all the youth between the age of 15 and 21, as in REPORT 3.4

```
                              UNITYVILLE

Youth Membership List (15 TO 21)        Date : ............

Number       Name                    Address                      Age
-------------------------------------------------------------------------
  .....    .................    ...........................     ...
  .....    .................    ...........................     ...
  .....    .................    ...........................     ...
  .....    .................    ...........................     ...
  .....    .................    ...........................     ...
  .....    .................    ...........................     ...
  .....    .................    ...........................     ...
  .....    .................    ...........................     ...
  .....    .................    ...........................     ...
  .....    .................    ...........................     ...

                 Page 1
```

REPORT 3.4 Youth Membership List

Last, there is a list of children under the age of 15, as shown in REPORT 3.5. This concludes the design of all the reports required for the Membership Management System.

```
                              UNITYVILLE

Children Membership List (0 TO 15)        Date : ............

Number       Name                   Address                      Age
------------------------------------------------------------------


 .....    .................    .........................    ...
 .....    .................    .........................    ...
 .....    .................    .........................    ...
 .....    .................    .........................    ...
 .....    .................    .........................    ...
 .....    .................    .........................    ...
 .....    .................    .........................    ...
 .....    .................    .........................    ...
 .....    .................    .........................    ...
 .....    .................    .........................    ...

                              Page 1
```

REPORT 3.5 Children Membership List

To transform these design ideas for the reports into a working computer software, we write a set of programs according to the instructions of the report writer. Each program should do mainly two things: format and extract data from files. These sample reports provide you with all the necessary formatting. To write the report program, consult the manual of the report writer. If you are not familiar with it and not quite sure how to start, use any examples, if provided in the manual. If there are several, choose the one that resembles our examples.

With a choice of five reports, a menu is needed to select any one of them, as on SCREEN 3.3. As with the Main Menu, use the utilities to build the Report Menu. When a selection is made from the Report Menu, it invokes the appropriate report program, and after the printing is over, the control goes back to this Report Menu screen for the next report or to exit to the Main Menu.

```
                    UNITYVILLE

           Membership Management System

                   Report Menu


  1.   Long Membership Listing

  2.   Short Membership  Listing

  3.   Adults ( age => 21 )

  4.   Youth  ( age 15 to 20 )

  5.   Children ( age 0 to 15 )

  6.   Persian

  7.   Exit to Main Menu

        SELECTION  : ( 1 to 7 ): ..
```

SCREEN 3.3 Report Selection Menu

3.6 CONVERSION AND USES

After having implemented the membership management system into an integrated software package, the next step is to transfer all the information from the manual files into this computer system. In this section, we will discuss all the different stages needed to load all the data, then verify it through making lists, and suggest the different ways the secretary and the treasurer can use this new system.

Before loading the information, some preparation is required. First, you have to gather all the information for each believer, also assign a number to each record. The number can be either the one used by the Baha'i National Center or your own. If the choice is to have your own numbering system, then you have to decide on the maximum number of digits, say four digits ranging from 0000 to 9999. One method is to assign a number to each alphabetical symbol. For example, the first two digits can be assigned to the letters:

```
A -- 01
B -- 02
C -- 03
  .
```

.
.

Z -- 26

The next two digits of the number will denote names within an alphabet category. The number for each believer is unique, appearing only once in the system. For example,

0101 for Adam, Aros
0601 for Fracichi, Alfred
0602 for Fracichi, Mildred

Where 01 is for letter "A" and 06 for "F."

As part of the preparation do the following:

1. Prepare a list of all the names of the members of the community, along with other information such as addresses, ages, telephone numbers, and so on.

2. Assign a number, whether your own or the national one, to each name on the list.

3. The record for each member, as defined earlier, has many more pieces of information than are normally used by a secretary of a community. The information that is not available can be left out. At a later date you can add it.

4. Enter all records, one at time, into your computer system. Screen 3.3 shows entry of one example.

```
                    Membership Maintenance

                          UNITYVILLE

Name: Audacious, Mary              Number : 0125


ADDRESS                            FAMILY
------                             ------

apartment: Apt # 29           .  status : M [M-married,
street    : 361 Orange Grove Ave.           S-single]
city      : Unityville            spouse: Henry
state/prov: Vancouver             child1: Jeffry
postal    : L7G 1T8               child2: Jason
Phone (H):613 751 3113            child3: Cindy
      (B):..._..._....            child4:....................

ADMINISTRATIVE EXPERIENCE:

1 ..........................    2 .............................
3 ..........................


TALENT : Guitar player
Profession      : Teacher
Date of arrival : June 15, 65
Date of birth   : Sept 05, 45
Persian         : N

    <-----  FUNCTION KEY DESCRIPTION  ----->
F1-SELECT  F2-NEXT F3-PREVIOUS F4-INSERT F5-UPDATE F6-DELETE
F7- EXIT TO MAIN MENU
```

SCREEN 3.3 A Membership Record

Type the membership information, then press the "INSERT" (F1) key to store the record into the file "MEMBER." Note, the administrative experience has been left out, for it was not available. At a later date, it can be added.

5. After every believer's record is in the system, verify the data. Make a long listing (as shown in Report 3.6) for all the believers and, after checking the information, correct any mistakes. To recall a record on the screen, use the "SELECT" function key (F1), make the changes, and update it with "UPDATE" function key (F5). Use other function keys to do addition, deletion, or look at next or previous records.

```
                          UNITYVILLE

      Long Membership Listing      Date : Jan 15, 1987


Number: 0125      .  Name : Audacious, Mary
                   Spouse : Henry
                 Children : Jeffry
                            Jason
                            Cindy
                            ....................

Marital status : M   ( M - married,  S - single )


ADDRESS :                       ADMINISTRATION :

 Apt # 29                         ........................
 361 Orange Grove Ave.            ........................
 Unityville                       ........................
 Vancouver
 L7G 1T8                          Phone (H): 613 751 3113
                                        (B): ... ... ....
 TALENT :  Guitar player
 PROFESSION      : Teacher
 DATE OF BIRTH   : Sept 05, 45
 DATE OF ARRIVAL : June 15, 65   .
 PERSIAN         : N

                           Page 1
```

REPORT 3.6 Long Membership Listing

6. Make short listings including adults, youth, and children. Report 3.7 shows a community membership listing.

UNITYVILLE

Short Membership listing Date : ....

Number	Name	Address	Age
0125	Audacious, Mary	Apt 29, 361 Orange Grove Ave.	42
0101	Adam, Aros	445 Maple Grove Ave.	35
0601	Francichi, Alfred	22 Green Rd.	65
0602	Francichi, Mildred	22 Green Rd.	60
0304	Chow, Bill	5111 Yonge St.	21
1307	Mehra, Prem	123 Queen St.	32
1901	Shirazi, Susan	011 Main Rd.	19
1925	Serra, Sue	112 Eglinton St.	45
1926	Serra, Joe	112 Eglinton St.	04
1266	Lim, Steven	22 Woodbine St.	12
.....	....	....	...
.....	....	....	...
.....	....	....	...

page 1

REPORT 3.7 Short Membership Listing

As you have already seen, it takes a lot of time and a significant amount of money to set up a computer application. To benefit the most from such a facility, it is important to realize all the possible advantages and uses. One of the great advantages of the computer is the speed at which it works. Just typing an ID number and pressing the "SELECT" key, you have a screen full of information almost instantaneously. This allows you to check information easily.

At the same speed, deletions and insertions are done. Also, the software prints reports much faster than manual typing. Any of these advantages are possible only if the information is routinely updated and the reports are used. Here are a few suggestions of how this system can be used:

1. A listing of all members for treasury work.

2. Committees may require any one or more of the four listings.

3. Just before annual election or by-election an up-to-date list of all adults helps the voting process.

4. Make mailing labels using the data base information.

5. Use the data base and word processor to print multiple letters.

For the sake of our design and implementation, we have focused on the community called "UNITYVILLE." But, most of the aspects discussed can apply to any region or committee that has to maintain information.

3.7 CONFERENCE AND CONVENTION APPLICATION

Now, let's see if a data base loaded with information on believers in a region can be useful at conferences. At such events, sometimes for security reasons, the Baha'i ID card has to be verified, after which a label with person's name and community is issued. This registration process takes a long time, often resulting in long lines and delays. This delay can adversely affect the whole program if the registration period lasts longer than expected.

To avoid delays at conferences and the disruptions caused by them, a computer can verify and print name tags. As participants of the conference arrive, the number associated with each ID card can be entered into the computer program, which will locate the record in its data file. If it exists, the registration is completed by producing a tag with participant's name and community on the printer, as shown in REPORT 3.8. If the person has no record in the system, either a record is created immediately, or other measures are taken to accommodate the believer.

```
SUNRISE REGIONAL CONFERENCE


    John Audacious

    UNITYVILLE        Nov/85
```

REPORT 3.8 Name Tag

It is important to understand how a computer can save time as well as ease the registration process in this situation. First, we know it is fast. Out of thousands of records it can select a single one within seconds. Also, it can print much faster and more accurately than anybody can write a name tag. Furthermore, old records can be easily updated and new ones added.

The computerized method can be used to verify names at conventions. With it you can print name tags, but the most important benefit is that a complete list, with corrections and changes, can be printed just before the casting of ballots. It can print names in alphabetical order or group them by community. It can print the names of only those who are eligible voters and delegates by checking the age and selecting only those over 21 years old on the convention day. If done manually, this is a tedious and time-consuming job, requiring that someone searches through the list, finds all the birth dates, and checks the exact age. As you can imagine, if the list is long, the manual process can take days. But, the computer can sort these two categories within seconds, and produce a complete list within minutes.

CHAPTER FOUR

TEACHING DATA BASE

The Baha'i Faith, as it emerges from obscurity, is undergoing a steady expansion. According to the promises recorded in its Writings, in the near future vast numbers will join as its adherents. At this stage, informing the general public of the spiritual and social principles and the laws of the Faith is the major thrust that will broaden the awareness of people and attract them to become part of it. Although it is the responsibility of each individual Baha'i to teach the Cause, the institutions participate in the teaching and expansion by encouraging the Baha'is, coordinating teaching and pioneering activities, and providing efficient and effective ways to promote the Faith of God.

No doubt, this future expansion will involve handling greater amounts of information: maintaining names and addresses of all the communities under one jurisdiction, managing all the teaching activities in each location, analyzing the different teaching methods applied in different places, and making sure new Assemblies are formed at a steady rate. When the numbers of both assemblies and Baha'is grow, managing information can become complex, rendering a manual system ineffective. The computer promises a solution. This solution has three main parts: regional information, regional pioneering, and quick access to information through telecommunication.

In Chapter 3, we discussed a computer data base to manage information for a community and print listings for the secretary, treasurer, or committees to use. The teaching data base is similar to the membership one in the ways that both use files to store data, and interface screens to maintain the data base. But, in this case, the application is more complex, for the data is grouped in different categories for each locality in the whole district. First, information such as name, address, status, and so on has to be kept. Also for each place, a history of all the teaching activities has to be managed. Along with the history, the reports should show the relationship between these activities and the results in terms of new believers.

On the pioneering side, this system should help the process of homefront pioneering by providing such information as availability of houses and apartments, possibility of employment, and so on. Many times the right kind of data is crucial if a person is to decide whether to pioneer or not. One of the ways of encouraging homefront pioneering is to provide information quickly through data communication.

Remote access of data is becoming more appealing to many people. The personal computer is becoming increasingly affordable; possibly it will become as common as radios and televisions are. With proper software and hardware, one can get important information just by connecting to a pioneering data base system over the telephone line. There is another benefit: the system does not necessarily require the attention of another person, an important factor if personnel is limited.

In this chapter, after defining in detail some of the desirable ways of using a DBMS for teaching and pioneering, and discussing their implementation, we will also show how to print statistical reports and histories of the teaching activities, and show how a computer network can be used in a district or region.

4.1 DESIRABLE FEATURES

The data base for teaching and pioneering is organized according to each locality, whether it is a group or Assembly. Each place in the region will have a record containing information such as name, address, status, and so on. With an application program, we load the system with data that directly relate to teaching and pioneering. After collecting information over a period of time, it can be used to produce statistical and analytical reports, which are used to understand some of the characteristics of propagating the Faith to the general public. In outlining the desirable features of this teaching and pioneering data base, we have to keep in mind the limited personnel resources in the Baha'i Faith, and how best results can be produced with a computer system.

The following lists all the capabilities we will be likely to want in this data base system:

1. LOCALITY: a single record of a computer file will contain data such as:

   name of the community
   community ID number
   address of the community
   status: Assembly, group, or other
   number of adults in the community
   number of youth
   name of the secretary
   name of the chairman
   date established as a group or Assembly

number of new Baha'is during current year

1. TEACHING: The system should also provide the means of collecting data related to each teaching or proclamation activity in a community as part of the history. The record of the history should contain the following :

   a) It should describe the different teaching methods used such as:

      musical event
      door-to-door approach
      advertising campaign in media
      delivery of literature through mail
      talks on Baha'i Faith
      etc.

   b) It should indicate which institution initiated the event, whether the Assembly or group or some other institution.

   c) It should also show the participants who helped the event happen, either the local members or, if help from outside the community was needed or recommended, the helpers.

   d) It should establish the aims of the teaching/proclamation project. Some in this category are proclamation to the general public, reaching the civic officials and political leaders, invitations to the public to participate in talks and discussions, individuals approached on one-to-one basis to inform them about the Baha'i Faith, and so forth.

   e) Other information such as date and duration of each project.

3. This system must have ways to maintain information that helps pioneering to localities:

   a) housing/apartment available
   b) job openings in the community or surrounding area
   c) number of pioneers required to establish an Assembly
   d) any offers to pioneer
   c) etc.

4. The system should provide all the facilities of maintaining a data base, such as:

   a) insert records
   b) delete records
   c) update records
   d) view records #

5. The reports are of the following types:

    a) a list of all the teaching activities during any period of time in a region
    b) number of declarations during the current year
    c) list of pioneers
    d) list of places where pioneers are needed
    e) list of all the youth in a region
    f) list of all communities with membership under 15

6. The system should also provide the facility to inquire about teaching activities and information related to pioneering from a remote home computer, using data communication equipment and the telephone line. Effectively, this aspect should in a way work similar to a computer bulletin board.

7. Finally, the system must have the capability to transfer information from the data base to the bulletin board.

4.2 CREATING A DATA BASE

The description of the teaching data base provides only the overview of its different functions. Now, we have to translate all these requirements in a workable computer system. To start, we have to establish a data base where all the information is going to reside, and a means of manipulating the data base through the help of keyboard and screen.

In the previous chapter, we created only one file ("MEMBER") as part of the data base; but in this case we have to decide if a single file will be practical. For each locality we have to maintain two types of information. One is the kind that contains data related only to the community. This kind occupies only one record of a file for each locality, such as name, address, secretary's name, and so on. In this category we can also include fields for pioneering. Another type of information is about teaching. For each teaching activity there will be one record, and possibly there may be more than one activity per community. In both these categories the type of information is different from the other: one for locality information and the other for teaching history data. From these considerations, we see that it is necessary to have two files: one for locality called "LOCALITY" and the other called "TEACHING."

As we have seen earlier, a file can be looked at as rows and columns. Each row represents a record while the columns of each row correspond to fields. Each is a piece of information about the community related to teaching. In creating the file, the fields (columns) have to be defined and they stay fixed. But the number of rows keeps changing as the records are added or deleted.

Our next step is to determine the number of fields for each file and the data type. In Table 4.1, we provide the description, name of the fields, and the data type for file "LOCALITY."

file name: LOCALITY

Description	Field name	Data type	length
Name of community	name	character	30
Community ID number	number	integer	
Status(Assembly,Group or Other)	status	character	1
Number of adults	adults	integer	
Number of youth	youth	integer	
Number of children	children	integer	
Name of secretary	secretary	character	30
Name of chairman	chairman	character	30
Date established (as Assembly or group)	date-est	date	
Number of declarants during current year	declarants	integer	
Housing/apartment available	residence	character	30
Job opening in the area	job	character	30
Pioneers required	pioneers-needed	integer	
Offers of pioneers	offers	integer	
Street	street	character	30
City	city	character	30
Province(state)	province	character	30
Postal code	code	character	7
Telephone	phone	character	12

TABLE 4.1 Record for "LOCALITY" file

Similarly, Table 4.2 defines the file called "TEACHING."

file name: TEACHING

Description	Field name	Data type	Length
Name of community	name	character	30
Community ID number	number	integer	
Method of teaching	method	character	30
Initiated by which Institution	initiated-by	character	30
Participation (any from outside)	participation	character	30
Activity	activity	character	30
Date project started	date	date	
Duration of project	duration	character	20
Coordinator	coordinator	character	30

TABLE 4.2 Record for "TEACHING" File

Many such records will be kept in the "TEACHING" file, each belonging to a different community. To connect each record to a community, note we have included two fields called "name" and "number." In other words, all the teaching records for one locality will have the same name and number. At this point, you can add more fields in either file, if necessary.

The details of how to create these two files, depend on the DBMS you are using; therefore refer to the appropriate manual. In Chapter 3 we have given a tutorial-like example of how to create data base and files of an imaginary DBMS. At the end of this phase, you should have two files "LOCALITY" and "TEACHING," with necessary fields established and ready to be loaded.

4.3 SCREEN LAYOUTS

To use the data base effectively, we must have a convenient way for the user to interact with it. The most common method is through a screen layout, showing one record at a time. The keyboard enters data and commands.

SCREEN 4.1 is an example of interface for the locality information called "Community Information Maintenance."

```
                    HEAVENLY REGION

                         Community Information Maintenance


Number : ..........        Name : ............................

ADDRESS                                Secretary :
                                        ......................
Street     : .........................
City       : .........................  Chairman  :
Prov/state : .........................   ......................
Postal     : .......                   Phone : ...-...-....

Status     : . [ Assembly, Group or Other ]

Adults     :  ....   Youth : ....       Children : ....

Date established : .............    New declarants : ...

  |<-----   Pioneer Information -------->|

Residence : ...........................
      Job : ...........................

Pioneers Req"d : ....  Volunteer pioneers : ....

    <-------  FUNCTION KEYS  ------->
F1 - SELECT  F2 - NEXT   F3 - PREVIOUS  F4 - INSERT
F5 - UPDATE  F6 - DELETE F7 - EXIT TO MAIN MENU
```

SCREEN 4.1 - User Interface

This screen consists of the title at the top, the body, and the function key descriptions. Each dotted line corresponds to a field defined in the Table 4.1. By using this screen interface and the function keys of the keyboard, the data base is manipulated in various ways as listed at the bottom of the screen.

Similarly, the interface screen layout of the "TEACHING" file is as shown in the SCREEN 4.2. The function key descriptions are the same. The title of the screen is "Teaching Information Maintenance" and the dotted lines of the body correspond to the fields of the Table 4.2.

```
                         HEAVENWAY REGION

            Teaching Information Maintenance


Number : ..........     Name : .............................



Method of teaching : ......................................
Initiated by (institution) : ..............................
     Participation : ......................................
         Activity  : ......................................
              Date : ............   Duration : ......

Coordinator :.......................

    <-------  FUNCTION KEYS  ------->
F1 - SELECT  F2 - NEXT    F3 - PREVIOUS  F4 - INSERT
F5 - UPDATE  F6 - DELETE  F7 - EXIT TO MAIN MENU
```

SCREEN 4.2 A Teaching Record

Note, the fields corresponding to method, initiations, participation, and aims are for description. Here you should allow the maximum length required, in most cases.

4.4 REPORTS

At regional levels of Baha'i Faith Administration reliable statistical reports of information can be extremely important in assessing current and past teaching activities, in planning future expansion, and in analyzing ways of fulfilling pioneering goals. As seen previously, it is easy to produce reports and lists from a data base using a DBMS. In this section, we will make suggestions for how to produce reports that can be used by regional or district committees.

Here is a list of the reports we will discuss:

1. Reports of teaching activities,
2. Number of new Baha'is in each community,
3. Lists of volunteer pioneers,
4. Lists of communities with less than 15,
5. Numbers of youth in each community,
6. Lists of all communities with less than 15 members,

7. Lists of communities in the region.

```
            HEAVENWAY REGION
                                   Report  Date : .........

Teaching Activities   from .......    to  ..........


  Number     Community Name    Activities
---------------------------------------------------------------

  .......    ...............   ..............................
  .......    ...............   ..............................
  .......    ...............   ..............................
  .......    ...............   ..............................
  .......    ...............   ..............................
  .......    ...............   ..............................
  .......    ...............   ..............................

                          Page 1
```

REPORT 4.1 Teaching Activity

REPORT 4.1 summarizes all the teaching projects of every community in a district. It is a very simple report, but can be very vital. At a glance it shows the degree to which each locality as an institution is participating in teaching. From this, one might initiate investigation as to why a certain community is lacking in teaching activities as well as find out the reasons for success in other places.

Note, this report selects activities within a period of time, say a month or a year. In addition to the activities, we have shown the community name and ID number. You can add more information if you wish.

```
            HEAVENWAY REGION

                         Report Date : .........

          List of New Believers

                                       Number of
Number     Community Name             New Believers
-----------------------------------------------------


.......    ................              ....
.......    ................              ....
.......    ................              ....
.......    ................              ....
.......    ................              ....
.......    ................              ....
.......    ................              ....
.......    ................              ....
.......    ................              ....


                 TOTAL ------------>     ....


                 Page 1
```

REPORT 4.2 List of New Baha'is

REPORT 4.2 is similar to the previous one, except that it gives the total number of new declarants in a community. For every effort we make we expect certain results; and in spreading the teachings of the Baha'i Faith the result is more believers. From a regional perspective, the progress of each community is established by analyzing the relationship between effort and result. Comparing the activities and the new believers of these reports can show how effectively the teaching activities are in attracting the general public to the Baha'i Faith.

The next two reports are about pioneering in a region. REPORT 4.3 lists all the communities that have volunteers who are willing to go homefront pioneering. REPORT 4.4 shows all the communities in a district that have fifteen members or less, and where pioneers are needed in any locality.

```
          HEAVENWAY REGION
                    Report   Date : .........

List of volunteer pioneers


Number      Community Name            Pioneers
-------------------------------------------------


 .......    ................             ....
 .......    ................             ....
 .......    ................             ....
 .......    ................             ....
 .......    ................             ....
 .......    ................             ....
 .......    ................             ....
 .......    ................             ....
 .......    ................             ....


                TOTAL ------------>  ....


                 Page 1
```

REPORT 4.3 List of Pioneers

```
             HEAVENWAY REGION

                       Report  Date : .........

          List of communities with less than FIFTEEN

Number      Community Name            Pioneers   Present
                                      required   size
----------------------------------------------------------

 .......    ...............              ....       ....
 .......    ...............              ....       ....
 .......    ...............              ....       ....
 .......    ...............              ....       ....
 .......    ...............              ....       ....
 .......    ...............              ....       ....
 .......    ...............              ....       ....
 .......    ...............              ....       ....
 .......    ...............              ....       ....


                TOTAL ------------>      ....


                 Page 1
```

REPORT 4.4 Communities with Less than Fifteen

And, there are other reports that show collection of data according to certain categories. REPORT 4.5 lists all the communities with total number of Baha'is under 25 years old.

REPORT 4.6 lists all the communities in the region--groups or Assemblies--with the names and telephone numbers of the secretaries. After having decided upon the kind of reports needed for the regional committee, we make them part of our computer system.

```
            HEAVENWAY REGION

                         Report Date : .........

List of Youth ( 15 to 25 )

Number     Name of Community        Youth
------------------------------------------


 .......   ...............           ....
 .......   ...............           ....
 .......   ...............           ....
 .......   ...............           ....
 .......   ...............           ....
 .......   ...............           ....
 .......   ...............           ....
 .......   ...............           ....
 .......   ...............           ....


                TOTAL ------------->  ....


                 Page 1
```

REPORT 4.5 List of Youth

```
              HEAVENWAY REGION
                             Report Date : .........

List of Communities in the Region


 Number   Community Name     Secretary name     Phone
 ----------------------------------------------------------


 ......  ............... .................. ..............
 ......  ............... .................. ..............
 ......  ............... .................. ..............
 ......  ............... .................. ..............
 ......  ............... .................. ..............
 ......  ............... .................. ..............
 ......  ............... .................. ..............
 ......  ............... .................. ..............
 ......  ............... .................. ..............

                    Page 1
```

REPORT 4.6 List of Communities

First, note that there are many similarities among these six reports. In addition to the title and page number, data such as community name and ID are common to all. One variable item in all of them is the information pertinent to each report, namely, teaching activities, declarants, and so on. Keeping this in mind, it makes writing programs for the reports very simple.

The programming language we are referring to is the one used by the report writer of your data base software. If you are not sure how to write the programs refer to the manual. See if there is any example that is similar to one of our applications.

Once you have implemented a system, and you are satisfied with the way it works, make a copy and modify it to meet the requirements of the other reports. Note, the title, heading, and footer (page number) should appear on each report page. The information in the body is extracted from either of the files (LOCALITY or TEACHING) of the data base.

We have five reports and an easy way to choose one of them is through the selection menu. SCREEN 4.3 is an example with report items and a selection entry field. To use it, the operator enters a report number (between 1 and 5) and then presses CARRIAGE RETURN. After the report is printed, control returns to this menu. Note, selection 6 is the exit to the Main Menu.

```
                    HEAVENWAY REGION

                      Report Menu


      1 -  Teaching activity

      2 -  Declarants in each community

      3 -  Volunteer pioneers

      4 -  List of communities with less than 15

      5 -  List of Communities in the region

      6 -  Exit to Main Menu

             SELECTION (1 to 6) : ..
```

SCREEN 4.3 Report Menu

Similarly, we need another menu for the system, to select one of the three main functions: Community Information Maintenance, Teaching Information Maintenance, and REPORT Menu. SCREEN 4.4 is an example of the Main Menu. To exit to the operating system (DOS), select 4 and press RETURN.

In implementing the interface screens, menus are done with the tools provided in your DBMS. They include application builder (generator), editor, and perhaps some programming. When building the interface screens, keep in mind that each handles one record of a file, and with function keys such as update, delete, and insert only one record is affected. However, the select key can retrieve (depending on how it is programmed) a group of records and show one at a time. The NEXT and PREVIOUS keys are used to browse forward or backward through the selected group. Not all the commands of the DBMS are alike, therefore implementing the function keys is possible to the extent that the software tool allows. In the Teaching Information Maintenance, the SELECT key should always retrieve a group of the teaching records for a community number or name, but show only one record at a time using either the NEXT or PREVIOUS keys.

```
                HEAVENWAY REGION

                TEACHING DATA BASE

                MAIN MENU
                *********


     1 - Community Information Maintenance

     2 - Teaching Information Maintenance

     3 - Reports

     4 - Exit to DOS

            SELECTION ( 1 to 4 ) : ..
```

SCREEN 4.4 Main Menu

To conclude this section, the application software of the teaching data base system has to go through the testing and validation phase. This means all the separate modules developed should be tested and proven to work according to specification. For example, consider any one of the information maintenance interface screens, each should perform all the functions listed at the bottom of the screen. Enter some data on the screen, use the function keys and see if the data base is affected exactly as you expect. If not, make appropriate changes to the program.

In the same way, print each report and verify all the data and the format. In all cases, check the calculations, such as the sum of any number of items.

4.5 COMPUTER BULLETIN BOARD SYSTEM

In Chapter 1, we introduced the computer Bulletin Board System (BBS), and briefly discussed the idea of using it in the Baha'i Community. As the requirement of the teaching data base calls for access of information through remote computers, we will explore how the BBS can be used to disseminate news, announcements, and other information quickly, and regionally.

To set up a BBS in conjunction with a data base system, let's first look at some of the software and hardware required. You will need a modem, a piece of an equipment that transmits and receives data between computer and telephone systems. The modem is connected to the computer by a cable at one end and hooked to a telephone jack at the other end. It runs at various speeds, such as 300, 1,200 and 2,400 bits per second (bps or baud). Over the normal telephone line the most common speeds are 300 and 1,200 bps. The modem with the BBS should have auto answer and auto dial features. As the names imply, it should be able to answer automatically an incoming telephone call and dial telephone numbers.

Next, there is the software to perform the bulletin board functions. As we have seen earlier, this software has many capabilities, and some of them are:

1. Loading messages, news, and text into the BBS,
2. Responding to a caller by automatically answering the telephone and connecting him/her to the system,
3. Controlling the various levels of access to the system,
4. Maintaining its own data base of users.

As you can see, it is complex software; if you are not familiar with it, do some reading about computer BBS in magazines, manuals, and books.

A commercially available BBS may cost you a lot (about $ 400.00). But, some good bulletin boards can be yours to use for a small fee ($ 10.00) from a public domain software outlet. These come with documentation on how to use them, and many computer hobbyists are fairly knowledgeable about their operation.

In a region, district, or state, a BBS can be used in many ways. One great advantage is the speed at which it works. Once the information is loaded, it is accessible to anyone within a region or a continent, and the transfer is completed within minutes.

In a region, the most common medium of communication is the newsletter, periodically prepared and mailed to all the believers. Among many others, the main focus of such newsletters is to inform Baha'is of current issues and events. The articles in such a newsletter are mainly about teaching activities and plans, ways to maintain and form Assemblies, and upcoming events. A computer bulletin board can indeed enhance the method of disseminating news. First, the newsletter can be prepared with a word processor, then loaded into the BBS. From that moment, the information is available to anyone who connects to this regional computer system.

Another important use is propagation of messages. Sometimes information in the form of a message, letter, or date about an event has to reach all communities in a short time. This depends on if there are enough computer users with data communication capabilities spread throughout the region. We are discovering that the growth of the Baha'i Faith is pressing its institutions and believers to act and respond more urgently than ever before. Perhaps, this will necessitate the use of BBS, as the use of microcomputers grows.

In addition to broadcasting newsletters and urgent documents, BBS is also useful for inquiries. It provides the means of communication between the regional committees and their associate institutions, or individual believers. If you have a query about a subject, just connect to the regional or district BBS and ask the question. The answer from the committee is placed in the mailbox of the inquirer. In this way, each is doing his job at his own convenience.

This idea can be extended to provide a forum. Let's say the committee is interested in gathering suggestions about a subject, say teaching among ethnic groups. In the BBS, a section can be devoted just for the discussion of this subject. Anyone interested can browse through what has already been said about it, and can add more ideas and comments. Thus this pool of information grows with the duration of time. In the same way, other issues can be selected as a point of discussion.

As the use of BBS grows among teaching committees across a country, there is also the possibility of tying all of them together into a network. Ideas will flow to more communities. This will also eliminate duplication of work, and no doubt ease the pain of growth in the Baha'i Faith.

In this area, we have to be wise and avoid publishing information that should not be seen by unwanted eyes. Any one with the access code and telephone number can reach the information of the bulletin board. But, some information may be intended to be confidential. To avoid embarrassing and damaging situations, the BBS provides different levels of security. The access allowed by a user can be controlled by the system operator of the BBS. In other words, you can choose who receives what information from the BBS. Also, you can deny permission to connect to the system at any time. BBS is discussed in more detail in Chapter 8.

4.6 USES AND MAINTENANCE

After having designed the teaching data base, created the data base files, implemented all the users interface screens, written programs to generate the reports, and finally tested the functions of the different software modules, it is time to think about the uses and maintenance of this system.

The first step in this process is to load the data base with the initial data of the region or district. From our software design, each community has a separate place in the computer to keep and maintain all its information. Each has two kinds of data; one grouped as information about the community, occupying only one record of the file while the other is organized as one record of data for each teaching activity in a locality. Obviously, there may be more than one teaching record for each community.

To prepare the community data, first collect all the relevant facts such as name, address, and so on, then fill all the fields of file "LOCALITY" (Table 4.1). If everything is not available during this operation, omitted information can be added at a later time. For each place in the region, it is essential to have at least the name, address, and a number. As for the number, you can use the code used at the National Center or assign your own.

After the data are ready, load one record at a time into the data base. SCREEN 4.5 is an example of a community called "UNITYVILLE." Note, Unityville is an Assembly where there are two volunteer pioneers.

```
                         Heavenly Region

                  Community Information Maintenance


Number : 9999    .        Name : UNITYVILLE

ADDRESS                                    Secretary :
                                            John Humble

Street      : 61 Carmel  Rd.
City        : Unityville                   Chairman  :
Prov/state  : Nova Scotia                   Mary Nice
Postal      : Y3Z-1V7                      Phone : 519-445-1121

Status      : A [ Assembly, Group or Other ]

Adults      :  1678   Youth : 201       Children : 51

Date established : Jan 2, 1951          New believers: 21

  |<-----   Pioneer Information -------->|

Residence : ...........................
      Job : ...........................

Pioneers Req"d : ....  Volunteer pioneers : 2

      <------  FUNCTION KEYS  ------->
F1 - SELECT  F2 - NEXT    F3 - PREVIOUS  F4 - INSERT
F5 - UPDATE  F6 - DELETE  F7 - EXIT TO MAIN MENU
```

SCREEN 4.5 A Community with Volunteers Pioneer

On the other hand, SCREEN 4.5a shows a community that is a group and needs 2 pioneers. Also, it provides information about residences and jobs.

```
                         Heavenly Region

               Community Information Maintenance


Number : 9911             Name : Gloryville

ADDRESS                                   Secretary :
                                           Henry Cunning
Street      : 34 Maple Grove Ave
City        : Gloryville                  Chairman  :
Prov/state  : Nova Scotia                  John Lam
Postal      : Y52-1Z8                     Phone : 519-427-2211

Status      : G [ Assembly, Group or Other ]

Adults      :  7      Youth : 2         Children : 2

Date established : Feb 2, 1986            New believers: 1

  |<-----   Pioneer Information -------->|

Residence : Houses / apartments    .....
      Job : Nursing, carpentry and mining

Pioneers Req"d : 2     Volunteer pioneers : ....

       <-------  FUNCTION KEYS  ------->
F1 - SELECT  F2 - NEXT   F3 - PREVIOUS  F4 - INSERT
F5 - UPDATE  F6 - DELETE F7 - EXIT TO MAIN MENU
```

SCREEN 4.5a A Group that Needs Pioneers

To enter records into the data base, first invoke this screen by selecting the "Community Information Maintenance" of the Main Menu. After typing the information, press the function key F4 to insert this record into the file "LOCALITY." Similarly, the rest of the community records are processed. To bring any one to the screen, type the number or name in the appropriate field and press the select key (F1). Make any change, if necessary, and press the update key (F5) to rewrite the record. And, if you want to remove a record, simply press the delete key (F6) after selecting it. Finally, the "NEXT" and "PREVIOUS" keys are used to browse through one record at a time, either forward or backward from a selected number of records.

SCREEN 4.6 shows an interface screen for the teaching side of the data base. Fill in the fields with community ID number, name and information about the teaching event.

```
                          HEAVENWAY REGION

                   Teaching Information Maintenance


Number : 9999          Name : Unityville


Method of teaching : Invitation to events/ one to one teaching
Initiated by (Institution) : National Teaching Committee
Participation : Zanjan Teaching Team
Activity      : To teach Ethnic groups and enroll
Starting Date : Apr 1, 87        Duration :  2 month

Coordinator   : Assembly of Unityville


     <-------  FUNCTION KEYS  ------->
F1 - SELECT  F2 - NEXT   F3 - PREVIOUS  F4 - INSERT
F5 - UPDATE  F6 - DELETE F7 - EXIT TO MAIN MENU
```

SCREEN 4.6 Teaching Event

The manipulation of data is done with the function keys as listed at the bottom of the screen. Here extra care is given to the name and number. As mentioned earlier, all teaching records of every locality are placed in the "TEACHING" file; and the distinction to which locality they belong is made by the name and number fields. If a record does not have one or both, it will be lost in the file or produce incorrect reports.

As part of maintenance, the teaching data base system also prints reports of various kinds. The Report MENU of SCREEN 4.3 provides a list of all the reports.

The first report is about the teaching activities in a district. In REPORT 4.7, all the teaching activities for each locality are printed for a period of time. Note, as part of heading, there is the name of region, date of the report, and the period between which activities occurred. Also REPORT 4.8 lists the number of declarants for each community within the same period.

HEAVENWAY REGION Date : Jan 30, 87

Teaching Activities from Apr 1 86 to Jan 30 87.

Number	Community Name	Activities
...9999	Unityville	To test ethnic groups
...1001	Gloryville	Hold public meetings at Pub. School
...1212	Collins	Public firesides
...4512	Bradford	Discussions on social issues
...1001	Gloryville	Mothers & tots
...6012	Claremont	Weekend deepening & teaching
...6012	Claremont	3 public talks on family life
...1001	Gloryville	Participate in religious discussion
...1001	Gloryville	Community services

Page 1

REPORT 4.7 Teaching Activities in a Region

HEAVENWAY REGION Date : Jun 30, 1987

List of New Believers

Number	Community Name	Declarants
...1001	Gloryville	21
...6012	Claremont	3
...4512	Bradford	1
...9999	Unityville	1
...1212	Collins	0
...9222	Fernwood	0
......	....	....
......	....	....
......	....	....

TOTAL ------------> 26

Page 1

REPORT 4.8 List of New Baha'is

The next two reports are about pioneering. REPORT 4.9 lists communities where pioneers are available, and REPORT 4.10 shows places where pioneers are needed. These two reports are used to match pioneer posts with volunteers.

HEAVENWAY REGION Date : Jun 30, 1987

List of Volunteer Pioneers

Number	Community Name	Number of Pioneers
...2062	Toronto	5
...4012	North York	20
...1012	Scarborough	5
...4217	Etobicoke	7
...5212	Markham	3
......	....	....
......	....	....
......	....	....
......	....	....

TOTAL ------------> 40

Page 1

REPORT 4.9 List of Volunteer Pioneers

A few words have to be said about the accuracy of these reports. They are printed with data extracted from the data base. To have the most up-to-date listings at all times, the data base should reflect the changes in the district. With localities in the district, new records should be created in the data base. If other changes, such as changes of address, chairman, secretary, and so on, take place in a community, the data should be updated as soon as available. Even minor details, such as number of declarants, youth, and adults, should be kept up-to-date. As the teaching work progresses, the file "TEACHING" must have current data. With routine maintenance, it will be possible to make the best use of this system by providing the most recent statistical reports of the region.

HEAVENWAY REGION Date : Jun 30, 1987

List of Communities with Less than 15

Number	Community Name	Pioneers required	Present number
...1225	Ajala Township	5	4
...9012	Tottenham	2	7
...6012	Claremont	1	8
...1212	Collins	2	7
...9622	Fernwood	7	3
......	....	....	....
......	....	....	....
......	....	....	....
......	....	....	....

TOTAL ------------> 17

Page 1

REPORT 4.10 List of Communities with Small Membership

In the same manner, the computer bulletin board requires maintenance. After every newsletter is completed the board should be loaded; and the operator should respond in a reasonable time to queries. Also, the users' ID number and name should be maintained. New events in any part of the region should be posted. Finally, REPORT 4.11 gives you the name, number, and secretary of each locality in the district.

```
            HEAVENWAY REGION          Date : Jan 30, 1987

List of Communities in the Region


  Number  Community Name   Secretary          Phone
 ------------------------------------------------------------

 ...9999  Unityville       John Humble........ 519-445-1121...
 ...1001  Gloryville       Henry Cunning...... 519-427-2211...
 ...1212  Collins          Lella Patel........ 416-447-3434...
 ...6022  Claremont        Kwong Lo........... 416-456-9643...
 .......  ................ ................... ...............
 .......  ................ ................... ...............
 .......  ................ ................... ...............
 .......  ................ ................... ...............
 .......  ................ ................... ...............



                           Page 1
```

REPORT 4.11 Community List

CHAPTER FIVE

FUND MANAGEMENT

In the Baha'i Faith, contributions to the Funds are considered vital and sacred. To emphasize its importance, the Fund is called the lifeblood of this religion. The Baha'i Fund, considered a divine institution, operates at different levels. The most common ones are the Local, National, International, and Continental Funds. Other Funds are formed for special projects such as building temples, teaching, pioneering, and so on. Any Baha'i in any part of the world can contribute to one or many of these Funds. Each Fund is directly associated to a particular institution of the Faith: the Local Fund to the Local Assembly, National Fund to National Assembly, and so on. Like blood flowing through the veins in a body, monies as contributions from many parts are channeled to other parts of these Funds for the promotion of the Baha'i Faith.

Given the levels of Funds and the flow from one to many, dealing with contributions and their transfer can be complex, as the number of the contributions and the types of the Funds increase.

Therefore, it requires a method of accounting that is easy to use, accurate, and up-to-date. Such a system should also provide the flexibility to accommodate growth in the Faith, as well as to handle complex accounting and statistical reports.

In this chapter, we will consider the capabilities of the computer software to achieve many of these accounting goals related to the Fund. No doubt computers can be suitable to manage the necessary transactions of any of these Funds. However, we will focus only on how treasury work can be done in a local community.

To understand the accounting aspect of the Local Fund, let's look into the kind of transactions that take place in regular situations. First, there are the contributions from individuals, which form the main source of income. Each contribution is sometimes divided into earmarked donation(s) to other levels of the Fund. Also, there are sometimes other means of income, such as sales of goods or funds raised by special activities. In addition to income, there are expenditures: the main one being the disbursement of earmarked contributions to various other Funds. Other expenses are payments of bills approved by the local Assembly. In a simple way, this describes the transactions related to the Fund at the local level.

The treasurer has to account for every contribution: disbursement of funds and payment of bills by the local treasury. In any system, manual or computerized, every receipt and payment must be recorded, and checks and balances must confirm the accuracy of the transactions. Further, the treasurer has to prepare reports on a regular basis for the Assembly and for the Feast. At the end of the year, a financial report is prepared. These different tasks of the treasurer provide us with some requirements when considering desirable features of part of the computerized Fund Management System (FMS). In this chapter, we will go through the different stages of design and implementation of the software, as well as provide some ideas for using it. We will provide one method of managing local funds, and similar approaches can be used to develop application software for any other fund.

```
         INCOME                                   EXPENSES
         ******                                   ********

                                .......
                                :     :
  ..................            :  T  :           .................
  :  CONTRIBUTIONS :----->:  R  :------->: PAYMENTS      :
  :................:            :  E  :           :...............:
                                :  A  :                          ....NATIONAL
                                :  S  :         ................:
                                :  U  :----->:EARMARKED      :...INTERNATIONAL
    ..................          :  R  :         :CONTRIBUTION   :
    : OTHER INCOME   :----->:  Y  :         :  TO            :...CONTINENTAL
    :................:          :     :         :...............:
                                :     :                          :...OTHERS
                                :     :
                                :     :                          ..NATIONAL
                                :     :     ................:
                                :     :--->:CONTRIBUTIONS  :..INTERNATIONAL
                                :     :     :FROM LOCAL FUND:
                                :     :     :    TO         :...CONTINENTAL
                                :.....:     :...............:
                                                                 :...OTHERS
```

Figure 5.1 Local Treasury

Figure 5.1 gives an overview of the different sources of income and expenditure, handled by the treasurer of a local Assembly.

5.1 SOME DESIRABLE FEATURES

First, we have to decide on the main categories of activities of a local Fund. We see three distinct divisions:

INCOME: Contributions from believers, and other revenues.

EXPENDITURES: Contributions to other funds, and payment of bills.

REPORT: Information given regularly to the community and to the local Assembly, and annual financial reports.

Obviously, this is just a sketch, and each division requires more detailed work. Let us describe all the different functions that this system should perform in order to accomplish all the activities in these categories.

1. The system maintains the name and address of each individual in the community. This is needed by the treasurer to process receipts.

2. The system allows every single contribution to be posted with the amount and date. Each such transaction must indicate all earmarked donations to any fund, an amount to the Local Fund, and a total. After posting many such contributions, a journal accounting for each month is printed. First, it is used to check the correctness of the posting when compared to the total amount of money received. Second, it is used to write official receipts for tax purposes.

3. Any income to the Local Fund from sources other than contributions is also posted. This may include such items as fund-raising events, sales of assets, and so on.

4. Similar to contributions, expenses are entered into the system. There are three types of expenses. One is the earmarked contributions transfered to other Funds. Then, there are the donations to other Funds from the local treasury. Finally, payments made for secretarial, teaching, or other expenses, and any other withdrawal from the local Fund. Again, this should show the details and a summary of the expenses for each month, to provide for checks and balances. In addition to amounts, each check number must be included for reconciliation purposes.

5. It is desirable to provide for a means to view an instantaneous status report of the Fund, showing the current bank balance with a summary of expenditures and income of the current month, as well as the contributions by individuals during the current Baha'i year.

6. In the whole system, there should be a global effect. Every transaction, income or disbursement, after it is posted, should affect the rest of the data to provide the most up-to-date status. For example, after entering any contribution, it should appear in both the journals and inquiries, thereby affecting the current balance.

7. Finally, there are the reports. Earlier we mentioned two reports, one for income and the other for disbursement, required during the time of posting the transactions. There is the treasurer's report to the Local Assembly to show the status of the Fund. This is a summary of contributions and expenditures, and the current balance. In addition, the community at the Nineteen Day Feasts should be given similar facts as well as trends of contributions, showing the participation of the community in the Fund and its relation to the budget as directed by the Assembly. At the end of the year, there are financial reports required at year-end and for tax reports.

This concludes the definition of the system required by the treasurer. Without any doubt, the computer is well suited to implement all the above ideas. Our next step is to translate these ideas into working software modules.

In implementing the Fund Management System, some thoughts have to be given in choosing appropriate software. In the previous two chapters, we used the DBMS as a software tool. But among the commercial software available, there are many programs that are specially designed for accounting to suit many different types of businesses. In principle, the Fund resembles business accounting; it is logical to look for some program already available and useful for the Faith, rather than "reinvent the wheel" so to speak. In fact, there are hundreds of accounting programs written for the personal computer. A general purpose program can be used to post contributions as part of accounts receivable, and make reports for the Feast and or Local Assembly. Similarly, the accounts payable side can be used to disburse the Funds and pay bills incurred as expenses.

If the goal is to computerize just the treasury work of a community, then perhaps an accounting program, written by the user or commercially bought, will satisfy all the needs of the treasury. But if the FMS is part of a greater computer system that handles membership, word processing, and data communication, then purchasing accounting software may not benefit the treasury fully. The main aspects to consider are flexibility and compatibility. Usually, an accounting software is designed to do accounting, and adding new features is absolutely impossible. The major disadvantage with such packaged software is that it never forms part of an integrated system which includes data communication, electronic spreadsheet, or word processing. In other words, it never allows you to import and export files among all these different kinds of programs.

In our case, we will use the DBMS to implement the Fund Management System for several reasons. One is that we have already used DBMS for membership and teaching data bases in the previous two chapters. Especially membership data base, a source for names and addresses of believers, is useful to the treasury, and should be integrated with the FMS. Therefore, it is logical to continue with it, as it is an adequate tool for our fund management ideas.

5.2 DEFINITION OF THE DATA BASE

Before creating a data base for the FMS, it is first necessary to decide the number of files and fields for each record. We assume the file and the programs related to membership of the community are already in operation as described in Chapter 3. As transactions of the Fund, there are three main categories: income, expenditures, and deposits to the bank, each needed to be part of the data base. These may be filed in separate files, with separate interface screens to manage the data. Or you may have just one file for all three, where one type is distinguished by a flag denoting the record as income, expenditure, or deposit. We chose the latter because it uses a simple design and is easier for the operator to use. Only one interface screen will suffice to manage all three types of data. The only disadvantage is that it requires more storage space.

The name of the file is "FUND," and Table 5.1 shows all fields with description, data type, and character length. The number field is for the I.D. number of the contributor. But, for payments or deposits this field is either left blank or a number is assigned to each transaction. This field can also identify a record with closing and opening balances of each month. Any such numbers should be unique and easily distinguished from numbers, payments, and deposits related to contributions from believers.

File name: FUND

FIELD NAME	DESCRIPTION	DATA TYPE	CHARACTER LENGTH
number	identification number	integer	
name	name of contributor	character	30
total	total amount per contribution	dollar	
local	to local fund	dollar	
national	to national fund	dollar	
international	to international fund	dollar	
continental	to continental fund	dollar	
other	to any other fund	dollar	
date	date of transaction	date	
comment	comment about contribution	character	25
type	type of transactions	character	1
month	the month number	integer	

Table 5.1 Fields for File FUND

The field "name" can be used in many ways. For contributions it consists of believers' names. For other transactions it shows a description. For example, "DEPOSIT" for deposits, "OPENING BALANCE" for opening balance, "SECRETARIAL EXPENSE" for payments, and so on.

The field "total" is for the total amount posted. It can be contributions from believers, transfer of payment to external funds, payment of bills, opening balance, and deposits.

The fields "national," "international," "continental," and "other" are strictly for contributions. The sum of these different amounts should always be the same as the total amount. They provide a breakdown of the contributions, partly for the local Fund and the rest earmarked to national, international, continental, and other Funds. The fields are also used for transfer of earmarked Funds from the local Fund to external Funds. The date field is for the date of the transaction.

The field "comment" gives extra information about a transaction. For example, it can be a description of the amount posted as "other." For example, "Temple Fund of India" in comment field may describe the earmarked donation corresponding to the amount in "other" field. It can describe single items under secretarial expense or income other than contributions, such as the sale of an asset. The "type" field simply shows the category of transactions: income, payments, or deposit, and, for each category, the name and comment fields provide further details.

The reporting of the treasury at the Feast and Assembly is based on the Baha'i calendar. Therefore, we need a way to group all the transactions according to one Baha'i month. The "month" field identifies all the records in the file "FUND" that belong to a particular Baha'i Fund. It is used for inquiry and for a few reports. Our next step is to use the definition of data base to create the screen interface.

5.3 SCREEN INTERFACE

One way to manipulate the data in the file "FUND" is to handle all the information for one record at a time. To do this, the operator has a screen layout consisting of the data and commands to insert, alter, or delete records. SCREEN 5.1 is an example of the screen interface that interacts with the data file. Note, that each of the dotted spaces represents a field, each having a description. At the bottom of the screen, there is a list of commands, each executed by pressing a function key on the keyboard. At the top, there is a heading with the title of this screen and name of the community. The "EXIT" command is used to terminate the posting session.

```
                              UNITYVILLE

                               Posting


Number :---------           Name : ------------------------------

Total amount : $ --------          Transaction date : -----------

Type : - (I - contribution , P - payments , D - deposit )

Comments      : -----------------------------      Month : --


DISBURSEMENTS :

               Local : $ --------

            National : $ --------

       International : $ --------

         Continental : $ --------

               Other : $ --------


<-------------------- Function keys ----------------->
F1. RETRIEVE     F2. NEXT      F3. PREVIOUS    F4. INSERT
F5. UPDATE       F6. DELETE    F7. EXIT TO MAIN MENU
```

SCREEN 5.1 To Post Transactions

Before going any further, a few words have to be mentioned about numbering the postings. In this system, there are many kinds of entries, such as:

1. opening balance for each Gregorian month
2. opening balance for each Baha'i month
3. different kinds of expenses
4. contributions of each believer
5. deposit of money to the bank

We must so choose a numbering system that it is easy to distinguish any category from any other. A well-chosen system will help in the routing work of the treasury. The following is one suggestion for numbering a system.

```
01 to 19  - opening  balances for Baha'i month
20        - anonymous contributions
21 to 49  - other income (noncontribution)
51 to 62  - opening balances for each Gregorian month
70 to 98  - different kinds of expenses

    e.g., 70 - summer teaching project
          80 - secretarial expenses
          90 - earmarked contribution
          92 - from local to other Funds

99          - deposit
100 to 2699 - membership ID numbers
```

5.4 REPORTS

Like the posting screen layout, we have to design the format of each report mentioned in the outline of the system. In addition to information extracted from the file "FUND," each should include appropriate titles and headings.

REPORT 5.1 is an example of an income journal. In this report the key is to select all income posted during a particular Baha'i month, indicated in the top left corner. For each revenue, the name description, total amount, and any earmarked contributions to National, Continental, or International Funds are printed. Remember, revenue can be in two forms: contributions from believers and any other kind of income. At the end of the report, it calculates the total amount summation for each column. On each page, there are the titles, headings, a page number, as well as the date of the report.

```
                              UNITYVILLE

                            Income Journal
Month : ...                                Date : ...........

                   |<---           FUNDS                --->|
 Name               Local   National  Int'l   Cont.     Other   Amount
------------------|-------|---------|-------|---------|-------|--------

 ................  ...... ......    ......  ......    ......  ........
 ................  ...... ......    ......  ......    ......  ........
 ................  ...... ......    ......  ......    ......  ........
 ................  ...... ......    ......  ......    ......  ........
 ................  ...... ......    ......  ......    ......  ........
 ................  ...... ......    ......  ......    ......  ........
 ................  ...... ......    ......  ......    ......  ........
 ................  ...... ......    ......  ......    ......  ........


      TOTALS --->  .............    ......  ......    ......  ........
                              Page 1
```

REPORT 5.1 Income Journal

The journal for expenses, as shown in REPORT 5.2, is similar in format to the previous report. It prints only the expenses, including transfer of earmarked donations. For each transaction, the name indicates the kind of expense. Each donation to other Baha'i Funds from the local treasury, or each earmarked transfer, is listed under the various Fund categories. Also, for each column a total amount is printed.

```
                              UNITYVILLE

                            Expense Journal
Month : ...                                Date : ...........

                    |<---         FUNDS              --->|
 Name               Local  National  Int'l  Cont.    Other  Amount
-------------------|-------|---------|-------|---------|-------|--------

 ................  ...... ......    ......  ......    ......  ........
 ................  ...... ......    ......  ......    ......  ........
 ................  ...... ......    ......  ......    ......  ........
 ................  ...... ......    ......  ......    ......  ........
 ................  ...... ......    ......  ......    ......  ........
 ................  ...... ......    ......  ......    ......  ........


      TOTALS --->  .............  ......  ......    ......  ........

                              Page 1
```

REPORT 5.2 Expense Journal

The treasurer's report to the Assembly provides the summary of the different types of transactions of a Baha'i month, as shown in REPORT 5.3. It starts with the opening balance of the current month; it prints, under the subheading "INCOME," the contributions with disbursement to all the different Funds, and any other income; a total of all the expenses is calculated. Finally, a closing balance as of the date shown on the report is also printed.

```
                              UNITYVILLE

                    Treasurer Report for Assembly

Month : ...                                   Date : ...........

                   |<---          FUNDS             --->|
Description         Local  National  Int'l   Cont.     Other   Amount
-------------------|-------|---------|-------|---------|-------|--------

 Opening balance                    ----------------------->  ........

 INCOME:
 ................   ....... ......    ......  ......    ......  ........
 ................   ....... ......    ......  ......    ......  ........
 ................   ....... ......    ......  ......    ......  ........
 ................   ....... ......    ......  ......    ......  ........
 ................   ....... ......    ......  ......    ......  ........
 TOTALS    ------>  ....... ......    ......  ......    ......  ........


EXPENSES:
 ................   ....... ......    ......  ......    ......  ........
 ................   ....... ......    ......  ......    ......  ........
 ................   ....... ......    ......  ......    ......  ........
 ................   ....... ......    ......  ......    ......  ........
 TOTALS    ------>  ....... ......    ......  ......    ......  ........


CLOSING BALANCE                                ---------->  ........



                               Page 1
```

REPORT 5.3 Treasurer Report for Assembly

The report for the Feast is an extension of the previous one. In addition to giving a summary of the transactions with a closing balance, it also provides information about participation. In REPORT 5.4, for example, the percentage of participation is printed with the total income of the current year compared with the budget.

```
                                  UNITYVILLE

                          Treasurer Report for Feast

Month : ...                                    Date : ...........

                   |<---          FUNDS                  --->|
Description         Local   National  Int'l   Cont.      Other   Amount
------------------|-------|---------|-------|---------|-------|--------

 Opening balance                      ----------------------->  ........

 INCOME:
 ................  ...... .....     .....  .....      .....   .......
 ................  ...... .....     .....  .....      .....   .......
 ................  ...... .....     .....  .....      .....   .......
 ................  ...... .....     .....  .....      .....   .......
 ................  ...... .....     .....  .....      .....   .......
 TOTALS     ------>  ...... .....     .....  .....      .....   .......


EXPENSES:
 ................  ...... .....     .....  .....      .....   .......
 ................  ...... .....     .....  .....      .....   .......
 ................  ...... .....     .....  .....      .....   .......
 ................  ...... .....     .....  .....      .....   .......
 TOTALS      ----->  ...... .....     .....  .....      .....   .......


CLOSING BALANCE                                   ---------->  .......

Number of contributions  :  .......
Participation            :  ...  %
Income year-to-date      :$ .......
Budget year-to-date      :$ .......

OVER (UNDER)             :$ .......


                                  Page 1
```

REPORT 5.4 Treasurer Report For Feast

The main purpose of the month-end report is to reconcile your accounting with the statement from the bank. This step is essential to detect any posting errors by the bank. REPORT 5.5 looks very similar to monthly bank statements, with credits and debits to the account. First, the report gives an opening balance. Then all the deposits to the bank and payments are listed in the order of the date of transaction. Also, check numbers are provided wherever applicable. With the closing balance, it provides total amounts of payments and deposits. When comparing this report to the bank statement, it will be easy to detect service charges and interest payments, and then make the adjustments in the FMS to produce correct reports. REPORT 5.6 is a year-end report, showing summary of revenue and expenditure during a fiscal year.

```
                                UNITYVILLE

                                Month-end Report

Date from .........    to   ...........

Description            Date           Check Number       Total
----------------------|-------------|----------------|----------

 OpeningBalance                    ---------->   ..........

DEPOSITS

 ....................  ............                   ..........
 ....................  ............                   ..........
 ....................  ............                   ..........
 ....................  ............                   ..........


PAYMENTS

 ....................  ............  .........        ..........
 ....................  ............  .........        ..........
 ....................  ............  .........        ..........
 ....................  ............  .........        ..........


TOTAL  DEPOSIT  : $ ..........

TOTAL  EXPENSES : $ ..........

                                Page 1
```

REPORT 5.5 Month-End Report

```
                              UNITYVILLE

                              YEAR-END REPORT

                                 Report Date: ............
REVENUE :

     General Contributions                            ..........
     Earmarked Contributions                          ..........
     Anonymous Contributions                          ..........
     Other Income                                     ..........

               TOTAL REVENUE    ----------->          ..........

LESS:
EXPENDITURE

     National Fund                          .........

     Teaching, consolidation and proclamation:

          Advertising              .........
          Children's classes       .........
          Education                .........
          Feast expenses           .........
                     TOTAL  --------------->  .........

     Earmarked contribution expenditures :

          National Fund            .........
          International Fund       .........
          Continental Fund         .........
          Other                    .........
                    TOTAL ----------------->  .........

     Bank Charges                                     ..........

     TOTAL EXPENSES                                   ..........

     EXCESS OF EXPENDITURES OVER REVENUE              ..........

     BANK BALANCE PER CASH BOOK, BEGINNING OF YEAR    ..........

     BANK BALANCE PER CASH BOOK, END OF YEAR          ..........
```

REPORT 5.6 Year-End Report

Thus we conclude the format design of all the reports necessary for the treasury work. Of course, we have given you suggestions for some of the reports, and it is important to remember that these may not satisfy the needs of every treasurer. From these ideas, you must decide on the format and the kind of reports that best meets your needs.

5.5 INQUIRY

One of the fascinating features of a computer system is the speed at which it can perform a task. It is possible to extract information from disk files, and after applying a few calculations and comparisons, you can see meaningful data on the screen within seconds. In our Fund Management System, there are two inquiries that are of particular interest to us. One is a listing of all the transactions of a month to give the treasurer a quick status report on the Fund. The other is a report of all contributions of any believer during a particular year.

In a transaction-type inquiry, as shown in SCREEN 5.2, the computer first calculates the opening balance of the month; then under the heading "INCOME," it lists all the income, including contributions and other revenues. For each column, a total amount of the Fund is also calculated and listed. Similarly, all the expenses, such as earmarked contributions, transfer and payments of bills are listed. Also, the total amounts are calculated and printed. Note, after each transaction, whether income or expense, a current amount is printed. Finally, the closing balance as of the current date is calculated.

It is possible that the transactions may be so numerous as to require more than one screen space. In other words, the list may be longer than 24 lines. To avoid the information being typed on the screen so fast that the eyes cannot catch it all, the program should print only one screen at a time. To move to the next page (screen), the user presses the "CARRIAGE RETURN." The function key F1 terminates the inquiry program. To use it, enter the Baha'i month number, and the information starts showing on the screen.

```
                                 UNITYVILLE

                                 Inquiry - Transactions

Month : ...

                    |<---          FUNDS             --->|  Current
Description          Local  National  Int'l   Cont.     Other   Amount
-------------------|-------|---------|-------|---------|-------|--------

 Opening balance                          ---------------------->  .......

 INCOME:
 ................   ....... ......    ......  ......    ......  ........
 ................   ....... ......    ......  ......    ......  ........
 ................   ....... ......    ......  ......    ......  ........
 ................   ....... ......    ......  ......    ......  ........
 ................   ....... ......    ......  ......    ......  ........
 TOTALS    ------>  ....... ......    ......  ......    ......  ........

EXPENSES:
 ................   ....... ......    ......  ......    ......  ........
 ................   ....... ......    ......  ......    ......  ........
 ................   ....... ......    ......  ......    ......  ........
 ................   ....... ......    ......  ......    ......  ........
 TOTALS     ----->  ....... ......    ......  ......    ......  ........

CLOSING BALANCE                                     ---------->  ........

  F1 - Exit to Main Menu      Press 'CARRIAGE RETURN' for next page
```

SCREEN 5.2 Transaction Inquiry

The screen interface for contribution inquiry of a member looks like SCREEN 5.3. After the number or name of a believer is entered, the program prints all the contributions, with the disbursements and date. At the end, totals of all the different kinds of contributions are given. Like the previous inquiry, only 24 lines are printed on one page and F1 is chosen to exit this program.

```
                                    INQUIRY

                              Contribution by Member


Number : .......           Name : ..............................


Amount     Local   National   Int'l          Cont.        Date
----------+--------+---------+------------+----------+----------

 ........  ........ ......    .......        .......     ...........
 ........  ........ ......    .......        .......     ...........
 ........  ........ ......    .......        .......     ...........
 ........  ........ ......    .......        .......     ...........
 ........  ........ ......    .......        .......     ...........
 ........  ........ ......    .......        .......     ...........
 ........  ........ ......    .......        .......     ...........
 ........  ........ ......    .......        .......     ...........


====================================================================
 ........  ........ ......    .......        .......  <---- TOTALS

====================================================================
F1 - EXIT Main Menu    Press 'CARRIAGE RETURN ' for next page
```

SCREEN 5.3 Inquiry of Contributions

5.6 IMPLEMENTATION

In the implementation phase, first we have to create the file "FUND." Again, for details about the steps necessary to define the name and data type of each field in a record, refer to the manual of the software you are using. Use Table 5.1 as an example or create a similar one to suit your application.

The next task is to build the user interface to interact with the data base. The Fund Management System is an integrated software, capable of five main functions: 1) posting transactions, 2) printing reports, 3) transaction inquiry, 4) believer contribution inquiry, and 5) existing operating system. When it is invoked, these five choices should be presented to the operator, which leads us to a Main Menu as shown in SCREEN 5.4.

```
                         UNITYVILLE


                         Main Menu


       1 -  Posting (income, expenses and deposit)

       2 -  Report Printing

       3 -  Transaction Inquiry

       4 -  Believer Contribution Inquiry

       5 -  Exit to DOS


         Selection ( 1 to 5 ) : -
```

SCREEN 5.4 Main Menu

The system, when completed and integrated, will execute any one of these five functions. After finishing any one of the first four tasks, the program returns to the Main Menu. For example, you select "1" from the Main Menu to do the posting: after exiting from posting, the control is passed to Main Menu. Then you select another task or exit to DOS.

When we select to do any reports, we have many choices. We have a selection menu for the reports, as shown in SCREEN 5.5. There are seven choices, the first six are for reports and the last to exit to the Main Menu.

```
                    UNITYVILLE

                    REPORT MENU

     1 - Income Journal

     2 - Expense Journal

     3 - Treasurer Report for Assembly

     4 - Treasurer Report for Feast

     5 - Month-End report

     6 - Year-End Report

     7 - Exit to Main Menu
```

SCREEN 5.5 Report Menu

We have so far five interface screens: two for menus, one to manage the data base, and two for inquiries. Again, to implement them, follow the rules of your data base software, explained in the manual.

To write programs to generate any of the five reports, use the language of your report generator. Remember, all these report programs are tied together by the Report Menu. After printing any of the reports, the program should go back to the Report Menu. In the given examples, the report formats are already defined.

Implementation is never over until all the modules are thoroughly tested to your satisfaction. In the posting screen interface, make sure all the functions, as listed at the bottom of the screen, work properly. It should affect the data in the file "FUND" as described without any error. Use some imaginary information and check the functions one by one. The programs should make the correct selections. The reports should print exactly as defined.

Like the posting screen, construct the two inquiry screens. In the transaction type, allow the operator to enter the month, then print the opening balance. Following that, retrieve from the file "FUND" only two income transactions of the chosen month and print all the details. Then calculate and print all the different totals.

Similarly, print all the expenses of the month and finally calculate the totals. The program keeps count of the number of lines printed. If it reaches 24, then it should pause until a "CARRIAGE RETURN" is pressed. The function key F1 (EXIT) terminates this program and goes to the Main Menu.

The contribution inquiry of a member first accepts either an ID number or name. The program should search the file "FUND" for all the contributions of this believer and show them on the screen with disbursements and total. As before, if line 24 is reached, it should stop printing until "CARRIAGE RETURN" is pressed. The "EXIT" function key returns the control to the Main Menu.

5.7 USES AND MAINTENANCE

Before attempting full installation and trying to use the FMS, make sure every function of the software, including reports, is thoroughly tested and the results are produced free of errors. As a designer of this system, you know that software is rarely free of bugs when running for the first time. It takes time for it to mature. As use increases, it will be put through severe tests, and any design defects will show. These of course, should be remedied as soon as possible.

It is important that the operator--the person who will be running the system regularly--be fully acquainted with its different features. It is not necessary for this person to become an expert before using it. To start, just go through the different stages of the various operations that occur periodically, say monthly. With time, the operator will gain more understanding.

To show the uses of this system, we will go through the different steps that will be normally required. We will post transactions, use the inquiry, and generate all the monthly and yearly reports. Before going any further, perhaps the use of calendar should be clarified. In this system, both Baha'i and Gregorian calendars are used. A major transaction of the local Fund involves the contributions at the Feast, which happens every nineteen days. Naturally, the treasurer's report at the Feast should coincide with the Baha'i month. Similarly, the report to the Assembly should follow the same pattern. Again, the fiscal year is based on the Baha'i system. In the FMS, the Baha'i calendar is followed throughout the system except for the month-end report. As mentioned before, it is necessary to check the accounting of the local Fund with the bank statement for possible errors. The bank statement is based on the Gregorian calendar, and therefore the month-end report produces transactions according to this cycle.

Now, let's prepare for the transition from the old to the new computerized system. From experience, it is not wise to forget about the old as soon as the new is put in place. Rather, both systems should be run in parallel for a period of time, say a few months. The reasons for this transition is to allow for training, to test the program, the programming, and to continue the work of the Fund with the least disruption.

To do the conversion, pick a Gregorian month that is most suitable. Reconcile the previous month's accounts with the bank statement, then calculate the balance forward for the current month. Since the system requires this balance forward, create a record using the SCREEN 5.6.

```
                          UNITYVILLE

                          Posting

Number : 54               Name : OPENING BALANCE

Total amount : $ 202.00        Transaction date : MAY 01,86

Type : -- (I - contribution , P - payments , D - deposit )

     Comments : STARTING APRIL 01, 86            Month : ----

DISBURSEMENTS :

               Local : $ --------

            National : $ --------

       International : $ -------

         Continental : $ -------

               Other : $ -------

<-------------------- Function keys ------------------->
F1. SELECT      F2. NEXT      F3. PREVIOUS     F4. INSERT
F5. UPDATE      F6. DELETE    F7. EXIT TO MAIN MENU
```

SCREEN 5.6 Gregorian Month Opening Balance

Similarly, calculate the balance forward as of the first day of the current Baha'i month then enter the amount with description and number into the system. In SCREEN 5.6, the record number of the opening balance for April 1986 is 54. And, SCREEN 5.7 shows an opening balance for Baha'i month of Light.

```
                              UNITYVILLE

                               Posting


Number : 01                  Name : OPENING BALANCE

Total amount : $ 325.75           Transaction date : MAY 01,86

Type : -- (I - contribution , P - payments , D - deposit )

     Comments : STARTING MONTH OF LIGHT   01, 141     Month : ----


DISBURSEMENTS :

               Local : $ --------

            National : $ --------

       International : $ -------

         Continental : $ -------

               Other : $ -------


<------------------ Function keys ------------------>
F1. SELECT      F2. NEXT     F3. PREVIOUS    F4. INSERT
F5. UPDATE      F6. DELETE   F7. EXIT TO MAIN MENU
```

SCREEN 5.7 Baha'i Month Opening Balance

INCOME PROCESSING

To enter income, there are two approaches. You can accumulate all the transactions and enter them in a batch, or enter them individually. The routine you choose depends entirely on you. After running the FMS program select "1" of the Main Menu for posting and enter an income transaction. SCREEN 5.8 is an example of income entry. It shows the ID number 0101, name as Adam, Alfred donated $100.00, and disbursed to five different Funds. The comment is used to describe the other Fund that is, in this case, to "TEMPLE FUND OF INDIA." Note, the month is 2 according to the Baha'i calendar, while the transaction was posted on "Apr 20, 1986."

```
                              UNITYVILLE

                              Posting


Number : 0101----              Name : Adam, Alfred--------------

Total amount : $ 100.00--            Transaction date :Apr 10,1986

Type : I- (I - contribution , P - payments , D - deposit )

Comments      : Temple Fund of India--              Month : 2---


DISBURSEMENTS :

                 Local : $ 60.00--

              National : $ 10.00--

         International : $ 10.00--

           Continental : $ 10.00--

                 Other : $ 10.00--


<-------------------- Function keys ----------------->
F1. SELECT       F2. NEXT      F3. PREVIOUS    F4. INSERT
F5. UPDATE       F6. DELETE    F7. EXIT
```

SCREEN 5.8 Income Entry

After typing information on the screen, enter it with the INSERT function key (F4). Similarly, after many have been posted, you may want to make a list for verification and writing official tax receipts. To run this report, in the Main Menu select "4" for Report then "1" for Income Journal. REPORT 5.7 is an income journal with one item as sale of a typewriter, and the rest as contributions with disbursements. The totals are very useful: the total amount is for deposit to the bank, while others (except for local) are totals for earmarked Funds. If you discover any mistake, make the changes and run this journal again. To keep a printed record, run this report every Baha'i month.

UNITYVILLE

Income Journal

Month : 2 Date : Apr 30, 1986

Name	Local	National	Int'l	Cont.	Other	Amount
	|<---		FUNDS		--->|	
Adam, Alfred	60.00	10.00	10.00	10.00	10.00	100.00
Adam, Joly	70.00	10.00	10.00	10.00	10.00	110.00
Typewriter sale						230.00
Loyo, Jim	10.00	2.00	2.00	2.00		16.00
Puffy, John	10.00					10.00
TOTALS --->	150.00	22.00	22.00	22.00	20.00	466.00

Page 1

REPORT 5.7 Income Journal

To enter a payment, invoke the posting screen, as shown earlier, and type the information. SCREEN 5.9 is a payment example for pamphlets. Here, the name is "Summer Teaching Project" and under this number it is possible to make several entries to keep expenses together and keep track of certain activity costs. To store it in the system, press insert key (F4).

```
                              UNITYVILLE

                              Posting

Number : 70                 Name : Summer Teaching Project

Total amount : $  15.23          Transaction date :Apr 15, 1986

Type : P  (I - contribution , P - payments , D - deposit )

Comments       : Pamphlets                          Month : 2


DISBURSEMENTS :

               Local : $

            National : $

       International : $

         Continental : $

               Other : $

<------------------- Function keys ----------------->
F1. SELECT       F2. NEXT     F3. PREVIOUS    F4. INSERT
F5. UPDATE       F6. DELETE   F7. EXIT TO MAIN MENU
```

SCREEN 5.9 Posting Transaction

Similarly, payments such as transfer of earmarked donations, contributions from local Fund to other Funds, and so on, are entered, as shown in SCREEN 5.10.

```
                              UNITYVILLE

                              Posting

Number : 90                 Name : Earmarked contributions

Total amount : $ 86.00       Transaction date : Apr 15, 1986

Type : P  (I - contribution , P - payments , D - deposit )

Comments      : month of Jamal                  Month : 2


DISBURSEMENTS :

               Local : $

            National : $

       International : $

         Continental : $

               Other : $

<------------------ Function keys ------------------->
F1. SELECT      F2. NEXT     F3. PREVIOUS   F4. INSERT
F5. UPDATE      F6. DELETE   F7. EXIT TO MAIN MENU
```

SCREEN5.10 PostEarmarked Contributions

To print an expense journal, choose "2" of the Report Menu. As shown in REPORT 5.8, there are three types of expenses: payments of bills, earmarked transfer of funds and donations from the local Fund. And, for every column a total is printed.

UNITYVILLE

Expense Journal

Month : 2 Date : Apr 30, 1986

Name	|<---	|<--- National	FUNDS Int'l	Cont.	--->| Other	Amount
Summer Teaching Project						15.23
Summer Teaching Project						110.00
Secretarial Expenses						25.00
Earmarked Contr.		22.00	22.00	22.00	20.00	86.00
From local Fund		50.00	10.00	10.00		70.00
TOTALS --->		72.00	32.00	32.00	20.00	306.23

Page 1

REPORT 5.8 Expense Journal

We should not forget to post another kind of transaction, which is deposits to the bank. SCREEN 5.11 is a deposit, note under comment it shows both contributions and sales. You can use one number for all the deposits. Unlike income and payments, there is no journal for deposits. However, these transactions will appear on the month-end report, as we will see later.

```
                              UNITYVILLE

                               Posting


Number : 99                 Name : Deposit

Total amount : $ 466.00         Transaction date :Apr 16, 1986

Type : D  (I - contribution , P - payments , D - deposit )

     Comments : Contribution/sale                    Month : 2


DISBURSEMENTS :

                Local : $

             National : $

        International : $

          Continental : $

                Other : $

<----------------- Function keys ------------------>
F1. SELECT       F2. NEXT      F3. PREVIOUS    F4. INSERT
F5. UPDATE       F6. DELETE    F7. EXIT MAIN MENU
```

SCREEN 5.11 Post Deposit to Bank

INQUIRY

After having a few transactions in the file "FUND," let's try the inquiries. Choose "2" in the Main Menu for transaction inquiry, then enter month "2." The information will appear as shown on SCREEN 5.12. This is a quick way of glancing at all the different transactions of a month. Note, information is divided into three types: income, deposits and expenses. Normally, the total income and deposits should be equal. And if they are not, it is time for some investigation. It provides you with the opening and closing balances, a help for keeping the accounting in order.

UNITYVILLE

Inquiry - Transactions

Month : 2

Description	Local	National	Int'l	Cont.	Other	Amount
	|<---		FUNDS		--->|	
Opening balance					---------------------->	325.75
INCOME:						
Adam, Alfred	60.00	10.00	10.00	10.00	10.00	100.00
Adam, Joly	70.00	10.00	10.00	10.00	10.00	110.00
Typewriter sale						230.00
Loyo, Jim	10.00	2.00	2.00	2.00		16.00
Puffy, John	10.00					10.00
TOTALS ------>	150.00	22.00	22.00	22.00	20.00	466.00
DEPOSIT						
TOTAL ------>						
EXPENSES:						
Summer Teaching Project						15.23
Summer Teaching Project						110.00
Secretarial Expenses						25.00
Earmarked		22.00	22.00	22.00	20.00	86.00
From Local Fund		50.00	10.00	10.00		70.00
TOTALS ------>		72.00	32.00	32.00	20.00	306.23
CLOSING BALANCE					----------->	485.52

F1 - Exit   Press 'CARRIAGE RETURN' for next page

SCREEN 5.12 Transaction Inquiry

You can also check the contributions for a person year-to-date. To do so, select "2" on the Main Menu, and when the screen for the inquiry appears, enter the number or name of the member. SCREEN 5.13 is an inquiry for Adam, Alfred. It gives the details of each contribution and a total amount donated up to the current date.

UNITYVILLE

Inquiry - Contribution of member

Number : 0101 Name : Adam, Alfred

Amount	Local	National	Int.	Cont.	Other	Date
100.00	100.00					Jan/10/87
120.00	100.00	20.00				Feb/01/87
150.00	100.00	30.00	10.00	10.00		Mar/01/87
						<-- TOTALS
370.00	300.00	50.00	10.00	10.00		

Press 'CARRIAGE RETURN' for next page

SCREEN 5.13 Contribution Inquiry

ASSEMBLY REPORT

Depending on the Assembly, the treasurer has to provide a financial report at every meeting. This report shows the most up-to-date status of the local fund. In the FMS, choose "1" from the Report Menu to print the treasurer's report, an example is shown in REPORT 5.9. It summarizes all the income and expense transactions and calculates the closing balance. In the income category, both total contributions and other revenues are shown. For any more details, refer to the journals.

UNITYVILLE

Treasurer Report for Assembly

Month : 1 Date : ....

Description	|<--- Local	National	FUNDS Int'l	Cont.	--->| Other	Amount
Opening balance			---------------------->			325.75
INCOME:						
Contribution	150.00	22.00	22.00	22.00	20.00	236.00
Other Incomes						230.00
TOTALS ----->	....	......	......	......	......	466.00
Total expenses	72.00		32.00	32.00	20.00	306.23
CLOSING BALANCE					----------->	485.52

Page 1

REPORT 5.9 Treasurer's Report For Assembly

FEAST REPORT

The Feast report is really an extension of the previous one. As in REPORT 5.10, in addition to a summary and closing balance, the number and percentage of participation, as well as a comparison with the budget, are given. With a graphic printer, you can even demonstrate the level of contributions with bars, graphs, and charts. Note, the donations are over the budget in this case.

UNITYVILLE

Treasurer Report for Feast

Month : 1 Date : ....

Description	|<--- Local	National	FUNDS Int'l	Cont.	--->| Other	Amount
Opening balance			-------	-------	-------	-----> 325.75
INCOME:						
Contribution	150.00	22.00	22.00	22.00	20.00	236.00
Other Incomes						230.00
TOTALS ------>	....	......	......	......	......	466.00
Total expenses	72.00		32.00	32.00	20.00	306.23
CLOSING BALANCE					---------->	485.52

Number of contributions : 4
Participation : 80 %
Income year-to-date :$ 486.00
Budget year-to-date :$ 460.00

OVER (UNDER) :$ 26.00

Page 1

REPORT 5.10 Treasurer's Report for Feast

MONTH-END REPORT

The month-end report follows the Gregorian calendar. In REPORT 5.11, it is from April 1, 1986 to April 30, 1986. Here, the details and summary of the expenses and closing balance are given. While comparing this report with the bank statement, watch for errors in either of them. Also, make sure the computer system includes such items as interest and service charges. If any account in not correct, then make the proper adjustment.

UNITYVILLE

Month-end Report

Date from Apr 01, 86 to Apr 30, 86.

Description	Date	Check Number	Total
Opening Balance		----------->	202.00
DEPOSITS			
	April 3, 1986		250.00
	April 15, 1986		466.00
PAYMENTS			
Summer Teaching Project	April 4	201	-126.25
Summer Teaching Project	April 3	202	- 15.23
Summer Teaching Project	April	203	-110.00
Secretarial Expense	April	204	- 25.00
Earmarked	April	205	- 86.00
From Local Fund	April	206	- 70.00

TOTAL DEPOSIT : $ 716.00

TOTAL EXPENSE : $ 432.48

Page 1

REPORT 5.11 Month-End Report

YEAR-END REPORT

At the end of a fiscal year, the treasurer must produce a financial report for the annual meeting. These figures can also be used for filing tax forms. REPORT 5.12 shows an example of a year-end report with different revenues, expenditures, and finally the cash at the end of the year.

```
                           UNITYVILLE

                           YEAR-END REPORT

REVENUE :

     General   Contributions                             766.99
     Earmarked Contributions                             770.00
     Anonymous contributions                              21.37
     Other income                                          9.73

               TOTAL REVENUE    ------------>           1568.09

LESS:
EXPENDITURE

     National Fund                              267.00

     Teaching, consolidation and proclamation:

          Advertising             460.16
          Children's class         80.00
          Education                33.00
          Feast expenses          .........
                    TOTAL   ---------------->  573.16

     Earmarked contribution expenditures :

          National Fund           587.00
          International Fund       69.50
          Continental Fund         44.50
          Other                    85.75
                   TOTAL ------------------>  786.75

     Bank Charges                                         15.16

     TOTAL EXPENSES                                     1642.07

     EXCESS OF EXPENDITURES OVER REVENUE                  -73.96

     BANK BALANCE PER CASH BOOK BEGINNING OF YEAR        451.80

     BANK BALANCE PER CASH BOOK END OF YEAR              377.82
```

REPORT 5.12 Year-End Report

CHAPTER SIX

DISTRIBUTION SERVICES

At this stage of the development of the Baha'i Faith, when its membership is growing throughout the world, easy access to literature describing the essential principles and teachings is one of the most important elements in promoting its expansion. Within the Baha'i Administration, there are distribution services established at different levels. And, one of their main functions is to disseminate literature without interruption. This is a great responsibility and a challenge. To be effective, it requires constant examination and improvement of the methods of distributing literature.

To understand better, it is important to look at the different activities of distribution services at local and regional levels. In the local community, there is a distribution service representative or a Baha'i librarian who takes responsibility for supplying Baha'i literature or other Baha'i materials to the believers. This task is accomplished in many ways, and we will consider the three most common ones.

First, the representative or librarian simply takes one or more orders from Baha'is combines them, and sends one order with payment to the National Distribution Service or any other company. After a period of time, the goods arrive and are distributed. This process is fairly straightforward, and works quite well for small communities.

An alternative to this method of ordering from the National Center is to keep a stock of books and materials locally. The stock can be either purchased or given on consignment by the National Distribution Service. Therefore, community members buy directly from this local stock. For the sake of our discussion, let's call such an arrangement a "distribution outlet." In some ways this method operates like your corner grocery or book store, following the principle of supply and demand. Routinely the stock is checked and replenished.

Last, book sales at Baha'i gatherings such as conventions and conferences are common. Normally, the books are supplied on consignment by the National Distribution Service or some other company to their representative or to a committee that ensures a good variety of books is available at these gatherings. After the sale, the unsold books or materials are returned with proper report.
Of these methods, the latter two are the most complicated because the volume of sales is large; therefore, we will focus our discussion on the distribution outlet and on consignment orders. Within the outlet system, there are two main areas of activity: inventory control of the materials and order processing with accurate accounting. To serve the members well, the inventory should consist of a variety of material with high quantities of those items that are in constant demand. The caretaker of the outlet has to check the stock of each item regularly and make timely purchases. In addition, the order processing side of this business requires making sales records, adjusting the inventory after sales, and keeping track of the cash received.

On the other hand, consignment orders require the handling of a large volume of books in a short time. They involve three main steps: 1) a selection of books to be sold at an event, 2) thorough check of the incoming goods, and 3) making note of any damaged or missing items. After the sale, you have to balance the number of books and materials received with the quantities sold and remaining. Also, the cash collected from sales is matched with prices and quantities. Finally, unsold materials are returned with payments of goods sold, and perhaps with an explanation of discrepancies in transactions. This is only a simplified description of these distribution outlets and sales of the Baha'i literature at conventions and conferences. However, it shows us briefly the areas where most activities take place.

In this chapter, we will describe in detail the requirements of both the distribution outlet and consignment sale. As done in previous applications of the computer to the Baha'i community, we will design the different building blocks with ideas of how to implement them, then show you the steps needed to use it in real life situations.

6.1 REQUIREMENTS

We will first deal with the requirements of the distribution.

DATA BASE: The data base, a place for keeping information in an organized fashion, must have a record of each stock item, with stock number, title, prices, quantities, and so on. All the records collected together should form part of the inventory control file. In another file, each record must show all the data necessary for an order such as stock number, item description, prices, quantity, number, and date. The system must provide the human interface to manage information in both files, such as:

Inserting a record.

Deleting a record.
Updating data of a record.

With a function called "NEXT," following records of a selected group can be viewed.

With a function called "PREVIOUS," previous records of a selected group can be viewed.

Selecting any record, using the stock code in inventory control, and invoice number in order processing.

ORDER PROCESSING: In this distribution outlet system, order processing is the hub of all activities. An order is made when the user enters all the necessary data, such as stock codes, date, prices, quantities, and the like to the system data base through an easy to use screen interface. The operator can do further processing using the following capabilities:

Recall any order and make changes to it,

Enter cash received for an order,

Cancel any order,

Produce a printed copy of an order.

For one order, the screen interface should allow up to twenty items, each with prices, quantities, and a total amount. While processing an order, the inventory information for each stock, when entered as part of an order, should show at the bottom of the screen.

INVENTORY CONTROL: An interface screen allows the operator to store all information for each stock item as part of the inventory control. Routinely, new items are added, prices and quantities are updated, reports are run to check reorder points and quantity on hand. Every time an order is processed, the quantity of the item on hand is decreased by the quantity sold. If an order is canceled the quantity is in reverse. Remember, this quantity can never be less than zero.

6.2 CHECK POINTS

As mistakes are likely to happen, we have to build into the system a mechanism to detect errors and make corrections once they are found. One effective way is to have printed copy of the information for verification. On paper, it is easier to check for spelling mistakes, notice total quantities seemingly wrong, or prices that are out of date. Here is a list of reports and listings that can be helpful.

1. A detailed listing of each order to check if it was properly processed;
2. A summary of all the orders during a period of time, say one month, showing the sales and cash received. This will allow you to check, at a glance, any unpaid invoice or discrepancies between your accounting and the orders processed;
3. A list of all the materials sold during a period;
4. A list of all the inventory items with quantity on-hand below the reorder point. This is to ensure that the stock is regularly updated, thus providing a better service to the community;
5. A yearly sales report shows the trend of the sales. It gives an opportunity to plan the stock for the following year.

6.3 CONSIGNMENT

There are three main activities related to sale of literature on consignment.

1. Receiving of the consignment and verification of the stock,
2. Sales of the materials at a Baha'i event,
3. Return of unsold goods with payment and report.

The system provides a storage space in the data base for title, quantity arrived, quantity sold, and price of each item on consignment. After its arrival, these facts are entered with the help of screen interface and keyboard. After the sale, the quantity sold is entered for each item, then a report shows both quantities with the unit price and the total amount of each item as well as the grand total sales, which is the amount of money to be sent with returned materials.

The distribution service system will have both the capability to handle the outlet arrangement and consignment. Both consignment and inventory item information can be kept in one file. Each record will have some common fields, such as stock code and title that apply to both kinds. Some fields, such as prices and quantities should be kept separate for each category.

6.4 DEFINITION OF DATA BASE

From the outline, the data base is made of two files: one for inventory and consignment information, and the other to store all information of orders. Let's call the former "STOCK" which is defined in detail in Table 6.1. One record of this file contains information related to one item of the stock.

Filename: STOCK

FIELD NAME	DESCRIPTION	DATA TYPE	LENGTH
code	code of the stock item	character	10
name	name of the item	character	30
publisher	publisher name	character	30
selling-price	suggested retail price	dollar	
cost-price	cost price	dollar	
consignment-price	retail price (consignment)	dollar	
Q-on-hand	quantity in stock	integer	
Q-on-order	quantity on order	integer	
Q-cons-received	quantity received on consignment	integer	
Q-cons-returned	quantity returned (consignment)	integer	
Q-sold	quantity sold year-to-date (distribution outlet)	integer	
reorder point	quantity below which ordering is required	integer	

Table 6.1 Record Definition of "STOCK" File

Note, the name of the fields has been abbreviated to conform with the length restrictions of the software. Check the number of characters allowed in your DBMS and change them as required. Also notice, all the different prices in the record have data-type dollar and quantities as integers. The description briefly explains each field. There are three kinds of information. Some are either for consignment or distribution outlets, and the rest are common to both. The following shows how these fields are used to store consignment and inventory (outlet) information:

CONSIGNMENT	INVENTORY
code	code
name	name
publisher	publisher
consignment-price	selling-price

q-cons-received	cost-price
q-cons-returned	q-on-hand
	q-on-order
	q-sold

The next file is to store data for every order processed. It is called "DETAILS." Table 6.2 defines the field name, data type and character length of the record. Each record contains information about one item of an order.

Filename: DETAILS

FIELD NAME	DESCRIPTION	DATA TYPE	LENGTH
Number	order number	integer	
Code	stockcode number	character	10
Description	description of an item	character	30
Unit_price	unit price of an item	dollar	
Amount	cost amount of an item	dollar	
Quantity	quantity of item purchased	integer	

Table 6.2 Record Definition of "DETAILS" File

But, we know there may be up to twenty items in an order; all items of an order are stored in the "DETAILS" file with the number field as the link among all of them. Each order has a unique number, found in all the records of the same order.

Associated with the order processing, there is another file called "ORDER," that contains the header information. Table 6.3 provides details of each field in this record.

Filename: ORDER

FIELD NAME	DESCRIPTION	DATA TYPE	LENGTH
Number	order number	character	10
Name	name of purchaser	character	30
Date	date of processing	date	
Total	total amount of order	dollar	
Payment	payment received	dollar	

Table 6.3 Record Definition of "ORDER" File

In addition to the order number and name of the purchaser, it also stores the date of the purchase, total amount of the order and payment. Unlike the "DETAILS" file, it holds only one record for each order.

6.5 SCREENS

To manage the data base, we need an easy-to-use interface for the operator. One method is to provide a screen layout with part or all information of a file record, then allow changes to the data base through the keyboard using the alpha-numeric and function keys. Since there are many tasks, such as inventory control, order processing, and reports, it is necessary to provide a screen layout in the form of a menu for the operator to select and execute any of these tasks. Such menu screens do not interact with any data base files. In this section, we will design all the screen layouts necessary for an integrated system.

SCREEN 6.1 is an example of screen interface called INVENTORY CONTROL, and it is used with the file STOCK. While defining this file, the record was made wide enough to contain both outlet and consignment information. Note, this screen shows only those fields for the outlet; therefore, using it you can manage only data about outlet stock and not consignment materials. As part of the body, it contains the stock code, name of the item, two different prices, and three quantities. Also, at the bottom of the screen the function keys are labeled. The function key F7 is to exit from this program to the Main Menu (which will be designed later in this section).

```
                      UNITYVILLE


                INVENTORY CONTROL


Stock code : ........     Name  : ..............................
                      Publisher : ..............................

PRICES                               QUANTITIES


Retails   :  $  ...........         On hand : .........

   Cost   :  $  ...........        On order : .........

Binding   :  ........          Year to date : .........

                              Reorder point : ...

<---------------------- FUNCTION KEYS ---------------------->

      F1 - SELECT   F2 - NEXT     F3 - PREVIOUS   F4 - INSERT
      F5 - UPDATE   F6 - DELETE   F7 - EXIT MAIN MENU
```

SCREEN 6.1 Inventory Control

In SCREEN 6.2, called CONSIGNMENT PROCESSING, all the fields related to consignment are shown. This interface is also linked to the STOCK file, but only stores information about consignment items. It also displays the stock code and name of the material. Again, the function keys and the operations are listed at the bottom.

```
                    UNITYVILLE


              CONSIGNMENT PROCESSING


Stock code : ........          Name  : ..........................


                                   |<--   QUANTITY  -->|
Unit price :  $  ...........       Received : .........

                                   Returned : .........

<--------------------- FUNCTION KEYS ---------------------->

     F1 - SELECT   F2 - NEXT      F3 - PREVIOUS   F4 - INSERT
     F5 - UPDATE   F6 - DELETE    F7 - EXIT MAIN MENU
```

SCREEN 6.2 Consignment Processing

The next screen interface is for order processing, and it is not as straightforward as the previous two. In this case, there are two files "ORDER" and "DETAILS" to manage. Logically, we should provide two screen layouts, one for the header information and the other for different items of the order, and both working together to enter one order into the system. In SCREEN 6.3, the title is "ORDER PROCESSING", and the subtitle is "HEADER INFORMATION," indicating this is a screen for entering header data for the order only.

```
                    UNITYVILLE

                    ORDER PROCESSING

|<---------   HEADER INFORMATION   ---------->|

Sold to : .............................  Order number : .......

Date    : ..............         Total amount : $ ..........

                                  Payment     : $ ..........

                                  Balance     : $ ..........


<-------------------- FUNCTION KEYS --------------------->

F1 - SELECT   F4 - INSERT  F5 - UPDATE   F6 - DELETE
F7 - EXIT MAIN MENU        F8 - ENTER DETAILS
```

SCREEN 6.3 Order Processing (Header)

First, there is the field for name of the person to whom the material is sold; then, there are other fields such as order number and date of transaction. In addition to the total amount of an order and payments, the balance is included. But, it is not a field in the record "ORDER." The balance is to provide for an amount owing, which is simply a difference between total due and payments. The program for this screen makes this calculation, thus at a glance the operator can see the balance. The list of the function keys is provided to change the data base. The key F8 takes you to the Main Menu, while F7 presents you with SCREEN 6.4, titled ORDER PROCESSING - DETAILS.

```
                      ORDER PROCESSING - DETAILS
Number :.......... Sold to: ..........................

 STOCK            DESCRIPTION       QUANTITY    UNIT       AMOUNT
 CODE                                          PRICE
=================================================================
1  .......  ......................    ....   ......      .........
2  .......  ......................    ....   ......      .........
3  .......  ......................    ....   ......      .........
4  .......  ......................    ....   ......      .........
5  .......  ......................    ....   ......      .........
6  .......  ......................    ....   ......      .........
7  .......  ......................    ....   ......      .........
8  .......  ......................    ....   ......      .........
9  .......  ......................    ....   ......      .........
10 .......  ......................    ....   ......      .........
                                 TOTAL ------------>     .........
            <-------   STOCK INFORMATION   --------->
Unit price  : .......     On hand : .........    On order : ........
Cost price  : .......     reorder point : ......

            <------------   FUNCTION KEYS  -------------->
F1-SELECT    F2-NEXT 10 ITEMS   F3-PREVIOUS 10 ITEMS    F4-INSERT
F5-UPDATE    F6-DELETE          F7-BACK TO HEADER
```

SCREEN 6.4 Order Processing (Details)

When this screen is shown, the order number and the buyer's name are automatically displayed from the "HEADER SCREEN." Up to ten items, each with stock code, description of the material, quantity purchased, unit price and amount, are entered. The function key F2, when pressed, clears the area where item information is entered and allows the user to type up to ten more. If F3 is pressed, the previous ten items are shown.

To enter all these items into the file "DETAILS," press the insert key (F4), and the update key (F5) writes the records into file with changes. When this screen first comes up, you can recall the details of an order, if it already exists, by pressing the "SELECT" key (F1). The "DELETE" key is to remove all the items of an order. Finally, the F7 key takes you back to the "HEADER SCREEN," where you can enter the total amount and payment. In SCREEN 6.4, stock information is shown every time a new item is entered. It provides the operator with the current status of the stock that is useful while processing orders. This concludes the interface to the data base.

In the menu category there are two screens: the Main Menu, mentioned earlier, is the first screen layout shown when the Distribution Service System program is up and running. As in SCREEN 6.5, there are four main tasks that can be performed.

```
                 UNITYVILLE

                 DISTRIBUTION SERVICE SYSTEM


                 MAIN MENU

     1 - Inventory Control

     2 - Consignment Processing

     3 - Order Processing

     4 - Reports

     5 - Exit to DOS

         SELECTION : (1 TO 5 ) ..
```

SCREEN 6.5 Main Menu

When the selection is made, control is passed on to the program selected. And, when it is terminated, the control is switched back to this menu. To go to DOS, select item 5. Another menu type interface is needed for reports, as shown in SCREEN 6.6. In this case, after a selection is made any one of the reports is printed. After one printing is over, you can select another one. To go back to Main Menu select item 6. This concludes the design of the layout of the screen interface of this system.

```
                    UNITYVILLE


                    REPORT MENU

   1 - Stock Check

   2 - Order Printing

   3 - Month-End Report

   4 - Year-End Report

   5 - Consignment

   6 - Exit to Main Menu

        SELECTION (1 TO 6 ) ..
```

SCREEN 6.6 Report Menu

6.6 REPORTS

In this section, we will design the reports needed in all three categories: inventory control, order processing, and consignment. The design shows the general format of each page with labels and information extracted from the data base. These examples give only general ideas of how reports of a distribution service will look. During this phase of designing reports you should also pay attention to some of the information that is necessary in your own particular application.

A computerized inventory control software can be quite complex, but we have chosen to keep our example very simple and straightforward to use. Therefore, there is only one report to print, as shown in REPORT 6.1. As the title indicates, it is a list of all items, and is used for the purpose of checking the stock. In addition to the stock and description, it prints the quantity on hand, quantity on order, and to-date sales. Also included is the cost of one item and the total amount. It prints an asterisk (*) beside the description to show any quantity below the reorder point. This is useful in order to decide whether or not to place a new order.

```
                  UNITYVILLE

           STOCKCHECKING           DATE : .........

STOCK            DESCRIPTION          ON   ON  REORDER  UNIT   TOTAL
CODE                           SOLD HAND ORDER POINT   PRICE AMOUNT
====================================================================

...... ......................* .... .... .... ....    ...... .......
...... ......................* .... .... .... ....    ...... .......
...... ......................* .... .... .... ....    ...... .......
...... ......................* .... .... .... ....    ...... .......
...... ......................* .... .... .... ....    ...... .......
...... ......................* .... .... .... ....    ...... .......
...... ......................* .... .... .... ....    ...... .......
...... ......................* .... .... .... ....    ...... .......

                                 GRAND TOTAL --------->    ........

                  Page 1
```

REPORT 6.1 Stock Report

Another important use of this report is to judge the stock. For example, if the quantity sold to date is very low but quantity on hand is high, that will capture your attention. And if this item is not selling as expected, maybe some decision needs to be made. The total amount gives you an idea where most of the capital is tied up in your inventory, similarly, the grand total amount keeps you informed of the total stock value.

After an order is processed, you may want to include a printed copy of the invoice when delivering the goods to the purchaser. The example, in REPORT 6.2, looks similar to the screen interface for order processing. It is intended to fit on one page with the header information and the details of the order. Also, it gives the total amount, payment, and balance.

```
                    UNITYVILLE

                    INVOICE


Sold to: ........................      Date : ...........

                                    Order number : .........


  STOCK      DESCRIPTION          QUANTITY  UNIT      AMOUNT
  CODE                                      PRICE
============================================================
1  .......  .................... ....    .....    .........
2  .......  .................... ....    .....    .........
3  .......  .................... ....    .....    .........
4  .......  .................... ....    .....    .........
5  .......  .................... ....    .....    .........
6  .......  .................... ....    .....    .........
7  .......  .................... ....    .....    .........
8  .......  .................... ....    .....    .........
9  .......  .................... ....    .....    .........
10 .......  .................... ....    .....    .........


                              TOTAL ----------->    .........

Payment : $ .........          Balance  : $ ..........
```

REPORT 6.2 Packing Slip

At the end of the month, as an operator of the distribution outlet you might like to know how the business is performing, how sales compare with cost of goods, and if there is any invoice not fully paid. This is exactly what REPORT 6.3 does. First, for a particular month, it lists all the orders with cash receipts and balance owing. At the end of the report, it calculates and prints the total sales, cash, and outstanding amounts.

```
                    UNITYVILLE

      Month-end  report for the month of ............

                                               Date : .............

ORDER    DATE         NAME                AMOUNT   PAYMENT   BALANCE
NUMBER                                    OWING
=================================================================

 .....  ..........  ...............    .....   ......   .......
 .....  ..........  ...............    .....   ......   .......
 .....  ..........  ...............    .....   ......   .......
 .....  ..........  ...............    .....   ......   .......
 .....  ..........  ...............    .....   ......   .......
 .....  ..........  ...............    .....   ......   .......
 .....  ..........  ...............    .....   ......   .......
 .....  ..........  ...............    .....   ......   .......
 .....  ..........  ...............    .....   ......   .......


     TOTAL SALE   : $  ..........
     TOTAL CASH   : $  ..........
TOTAL AMOUNT OWING: $  ..........


                    Page 1
```

REPORT 6.3 Month-End Report (Cont.)

```
                      UNITYVILLE

        Month-end  report for the month of ............

                                         Date : .............


STOCK    DESCRIPTION              QUANTY. |<-UNIT PRICE->|<--TOTAL-->|
CODE                                SOLD    COST  RETAIL   COST  RETAIL
=======================================================================

 .....  ......................... ....  ......  ......  ...... ......
 .....  ......................... ....  ......  ......  ...... ......
 .....  ......................... ....  ......  ......  ...... ......
 .....  ......................... ....  ......  ......  ...... ......
 .....  ......................... ....  ......  ......  ...... ......
 .....  ......................... ....  ......  ......  ...... ......
 .....  ......................... ....  ......  ......  ...... ......
 .....  ......................... ....  ......  ......  ...... ......

                       GRAND TOTAL SALES ------> $ ..........

                       GRAND TOTAL COST  ------> $ ..........

                            PROFIT(LOSS) ------> $ ..........

                      Page 2
```

REPORT 6.3 Month-End Report

As you see, this allows you to see any unpaid or partially paid orders. Second, the report summarizes sales according to the stock item. In other words, a total quantity for every single book or material sold during a month is calculated, along with the cost amount. When all the items are listed, it also gives a grand total that is the cost of goods for the month. These amounts can be used to calculate profit or loss. Remember, this amount does not include any operating costs.

Similarly, a year-end report should provide a total sales and cost of goods for the year. For each item, REPORT 6.4 lists the total quantity sold, unit cost, and retail price, and prints the total cost and selling amounts. The profit or loss is different between the two grand totals: sale and cost of goods.

```
                    UNITYVILLE


YEAR-END REPORT FOR THE YEAR ENDING ..........

STOCK  DESCRIPTION                QUANTY. |<-UNIT PRICE->|<--TOTAL-->|
CODE                                SOLD    COST  RETAIL   COST  RETAIL
======================================================================

 .....  ........................  ....   ......  ......  ......  ......
 .....  ........................  ....   ......  ......  ......  ......
 .....  ........................  ....   ......  ......  ......  ......
 .....  ........................  ....   ......  ......  ......  ......
 .....  ........................  ....   ......  ......  ......  ......


                       GRAND TOTAL SALES  ------> $ ..........

                       GRAND TOTAL COST  ------> $ ..........

                            PROFIT(LOSS) ------> $ ..........

                      Page 1
```

REPORT 6.4 Year-End Report

Finally, there is the consignment order. It is most appropriate to send a report after the sale of the material on consignment. For each item, the quantity being returned is entered into the system REPORT 6.5 shows a description of the items, and quantities received or returned. Also, the unit price, and the total amounts are included. At the end of this report the totals of quantities and amount are calculated and printed.

```
                    UNITYVILLE


                    CONSIGNMENT   SALE   REPORT

                                     Date : ............

STOCK     DESCRIPTION            |<-QUANTITY->|   UNIT     AMOUNT
CODE                           RECEIVED RETURNED  PRICE
========================================================================

......  ......................... ....  ....     ......   .........
......  ......................... ....  ....     ......   .........
......  ......................... ....  ....     ......   .........
......  ......................... ....  ....     ......   .........
......  ......................... ....  ....     ......   .........
......  ......................... ....  ....     ......   .........


                  TOTALS ------>  ....  ....     ......   .........

                    Page 1
```

REPORT 6.5 Consignment Sale Report

6.7 IMPLEMENTATION

After having finalized the definition of files, screen layouts and report formats, the next step is to build these software modules, and put them together into a working system. To implement them requires the various software utilities of your data base.

First, create the files in the data base. Make sure the data base already exits. In the distribution service system, we require three files, which are STOCK, ORDER, and DETAILS. Earlier, we defined the record of each file; therefore, refer to Tables 6.1 to 6.3 for details about names and data types of each field.

Next, we have to consider the screen interfaces. They consist of two phases: One is the layout with labels, and spaces where information is typed. The other is the software that actually links the data base, screen, and keyboard together. In other words, the screen and keyboard are used to manage the data base. In this system there are four screens, namely:

1. Inventory Control
2. Consignment Processing
3. Order Processing - Header
4. Order Processing - Details

In each of these screens, the function keys are also programmed to provide easy management of the data base. Therefore, give attention to all the different details of each of the screens, already described in the design section. After programming these parts, do adequate testing until you are satisfied that all the different functions work as intended in the outline of the design. The software tools required in this process depend on the DBMS you are using.

On the other hand, the two menu screens do not interact with the data base; their main function is to provide "walkways" from one task to another. Each is connected to the different stand-alone software parts. The two menus required in this system are:

Main Menu
Report Menu

Remember, the only way to go in or out of the system is through the Main Menu. Build these two menus and ensure the switching of control between programs is correctly done.

As mentioned earlier, in DBMS the report is produced using the report writer, a utility to extract data from the data base and print it in a formatted manner. For each report, write a program using the layout as shown in the design section. Some of the dotted spaces are for information from the data base and others are for date of the report, calculated amounts, and so on. Also, pay attention to the headings and labels that make the report meaningful and useful.

The list of reports is:

Stock Check
Order
Month-End Report
Consignment Sale Report
Year-End Report

Implementation is not really over until the different parts of the software are integrated and thoroughly tested. When running, they should be free of errors. Therefore, carefully verify the interface screens by entering some data. Test all the functions such as insert, update, delete, exit, and so on. After you have loaded the data base with test data, make a copy of each report, and again verify the calculations, data, and labels.

6.8 INVENTORY CONTROL

In this section, we will discuss the steps necessary to do all the different steps of processing. Before we can use the system for order processing or printing reports, the STOCK file has to be loaded with real to life information. You have to decide on a list of items that the distribution outlet will stock. Then, a stock code is assigned to each item. You can use the code from the National Distribution Service or make your own code system. When choosing your code, pay attention to all the different types of books. For instance, there are books by the Central Figures of the Faith, the Guardian, Universal House of Justice, and from other sources. Also, each book can be in different languages and bindings. An effective method would be to determine the categories by the code number. Also, collect other data such as title, quantities, prices, and reorder points.

Once the inventory data is organized, enter one item (one record) at a time into the data base. On the Main Menu, select "1" for the Inventory Control screen. Enter as shown in SCREEN 6.7, which is an example of book information called Hidden Words. During this process, you can modify an existing record, delete unnecessary data, recall a record, update it with changes, and so on. After the inventory information is loaded into the data base, return to the Main Menu by pressing function key "F7" to exit.

```
                    UNITYVILLE

                    INVENTORY CONTROL

Stock code : 00112       Name    : Hidden Words
                    Publisher : BPT-VS

       PRICES                  QUANTITIES

Retails   :  $  6.50          On hand : 20

   Cost   :  $  5.00         On order :  0

Binding   : paper        Year to date :  3

                         Reorder point: 10

<----------------- FUNCTION KEYS ------------------->

F1 - SELECT    F2 - NEXT     F3 - PREVIOUS    F4 - INSERT
F5 - UPDATE    F6 - DELETE   F7 - EXIT TO MAIN MENU
```

SCREEN 6.7 Process Inventory Item

For reports, select "4" from the Main Menu, then choose "1" from the Report Menu for stock check report. REPORT 6.6 is a list of all the items. Note, the asterisk (*) indicating the quantity on hand is below the reorder point. Reorder point is a combination of quantity on-hand and quantity on-order.

UNITYVILLE

STOCK CHECKING DATE : Nov 30, 85

STOCK CODE	DESCRIPTION		SOLD	ON HAND	ON ORDER	REORDER POINT	UNIT PRICE	TOTAL AMOUNT
CAL220	Date Book (85)	*	30	10	0	10	3.00	30.00
PER050	Book of Certitude (c)		7	3	10	5	13.50	40.50
00112	Hidden Words		25	26	0	10	5.50	130.00
00193	Prayers of Baha'u'llah	*	75	15	0	15	6.00	90.00
00193	Tablets of Baha'u'llah		12	11	0	10	10.00	110.00
01021	Six Thousands Words	*	16	0	5	10	11.00	0.00
01129	Glorification & Praise		15	25	0	10	5.00	125.00
01334	Some Baha'is to Rememb		25	12	0	10	8.00	96.00
01999	A Gift of Love		15	2	12	10	3.00	6.00
02000	The Baha'i Proof		3	3	0	3	13.00	39.00
H-25	Well Spring of Guid(c)		16	12	0	10	15.50	186.00
H-26	Well Spring of Guid(p)		26	15	0	10	7.75	116.25

GRAND TOTAL ---------> 968.75

Page 1

REPORT 6.6 Checking Stock

Check each item, especially prices and quantities, to ensure correct information is in the data file. If you discover any mistake go back to the Inventory Control screen and make the changes.

6.9 ORDER PROCESSING

In this system, order processing is the most used part. Before we show an example of how to enter an order, let's give some thought to routine operations. It is a fact of life that errors are likely to occur, either through the program (bugs), typing mistakes by the operator, or by the purchaser giving you the wrong facts about an order. In any case, if there is suspicion of anything improper, there should be a method of detecting it, and then an easy way to correct the mistake.

If it is a software problem, then it should be fixed by the person doing the implementation. In other situations, if a few rules are applied to the routine operation, detecting and fixing errors should not be an agonizing experience. Here are few a suggestions:

1. Always process one order at a time; do not combine several orders from different persons into one. Combining orders may initially

seem like a time saving idea, but a lot of time can be spent fixing errors if anything goes wrong.

2. Always have a sequential and unique number for each order. Again, it makes backtracking orders easier. If an order is canceled, void that number instead of reusing it.

3. After an order is processed, make two copies of the order; one for the customer and the other for your own file. Finally, have the order checked by the purchaser to ensure the quantity, amount, and payment are correct.

4. Do regular backups of data.

Of course, these are only a few suggestions. During your own routine operations, you may want to add a few of your own.

To enter an order into the system, select "2" from the Main Menu. Then type the header information as shown in SCREEN 6.8. Insert this record into the file by pressing F4. To enter the details touch F7 and you have SCREEN 6.9, with the order number and purchaser's name. For each item, enter the stock code, description, quantity, unit price, and amount. Note, every time a stock code is typed, the inventory information is shown at the bottom of the screen. Press F4 to insert the details into the file DETAILS. Go back to the header screen and then exit to the Main Menu.

```
                      UNITYVILLE

                      ORDER PROCESSING

|<---------    HEADER INFORMATION    ---------->|

Sold to : Goodwill, Dave................  Order number : 0121...

Date : Nov 16, 1986...    Total amount : $ 73.05

                               Payment: $ 70.05

                               Balance: $  3.00


<----------------- FUNCTION KEYS ------------------>|
F1 - SELECT    F4 - INSERT  F5 - UPDATE    F6 - DELETE
F7 - EXIT      F8 - ENTER DETAILS
```

SCREEN 6.8 Enter Header Information

```
                        ORDER PROCESSING - DETAILS
Number :0121     Sold to: Goodwill, Dave

  STOCK      DESCRIPTION          QUANTITY   UNIT       AMOUNT
  CODE                                       PRICE
=================================================================
1  CAL220..  DATE BOOK............. 10..    ..3.00    ....30.00
2  CAL230..  POCKET CALENDAR....... 10..    ....25    .....2.50
3  PER050..  BOOK OF CERTITUDE (C).. 3..    .13.50    ....40.50
4  .......   ...................... ....    ......    .........
5  .......   ...................... ....    ......    .........
6  .......   ...................... ....    ......    .........
7  .......   ...................... ....    ......    .........
8  .......   ...................... ....    ......    .........
9  .......   ...................... ....    ......    .........
10 .......   ...................... ....    ......    .........
                               TOTAL ----------->     ....73.00
         <-------   STOCK INFORMATION    --------->
Unit price  : .......   On hand : ......... On order : ........
Cost price  : .......   Reorder point : ......

      <-----------   FUNCTION KEYS  ------------->
F1-SELECT    F2-NEXT 10 ITEMS  F3-PREVIOUS 10 ITEMS  F4-INSERT
F5-UPDATE    F6-DELETE         F7-BACK TO HEADER
```

SCREEN 6.9 Enter Details of Order

Thus an order is entered. If you want to make any change, recall this order by going to the HEADER INFORMATION SCREEN, then type the order number and press "F1." Similarly, you can see the details of that order. Use the function keys (F5) or (F6) to update or delete.

Next, go to the REPORT MENU and select "1" to print the order, and it looks like REPORT 6.7.

UNITYVILLE

ORDER

Sold to: Goodwill, Dave   Date : Nov 16, 1986

Order number : 0121

	STOCK CODE	DESCRIPTION	QUANTITY	UNIT PRICE	AMOUNT
1	CAL220	DATE BOOK	10	3.00	30.00
2	CAL230	POCKET CALENDAR	10	.25	2.50
3	PER050	BOOK OF CERTITUDE (C)	3	13.50	40.50
4	....	....	....	......	....
5	....	....	....	......	....
6	....	....	....	......	....
7	....	....	....	......	....
8	....	....	....	......	....
9	....	....	....	......	....
10	....	....	....	......	....

TOTAL -----------> 73.00

Payment : $ 70.00   Balance : $ 3.00

REPORT 6.7 Process Order

Every month, to do the month-end report select "3" of the Report Menu. REPORT 6.8 gives the sales, cash received, and stock report.

UNITYVILLE

Month-end-report for the month of Dec 1985

Date : January 15, 1986

ORDER NUMBER	DATE	NAME	AMOUNT OWING	PAYMENT	BALANCE
91	12/2/85	Humble, Joe	70.00	70.00	0.00
92	12/12/85	Gracious, Mary	56.00	50.00	6.00
93	12/18/85	Careful, Henry	60.00	59.00	1.00
94	12/19/85	Merciful, Habib	31.00	31.00	0.00
95	12/22/85	Radiant, Pierre	76.00	76.00	0.00
96	12/28/85	Joyeux, Chantalle	90.00	90.00	0.00

TOTAL SALE : $ 383.00
TOTAL CASH : $ 376.00
TOTAL AMOUNT OWING: $ 7.00

Page 1

REPORT 6.8 Month-End Report (Cont.)

```
                     UNITYVILLE

      Month-end-report for the month of Dec 1985

                           Date : Jan 15, 1986


STOCK  DESCRIPTION              QUANTY.  |<-UNIT PRICE->|<--TOTAL-->|
CODE                            SOLD      COST  RETAIL   COST  RETAIL
=====================================================================

 0112 Dawn Breakers                1     60.00   70.00  60.00  70.00
 0193 Prayers of Baha'u'llah       8      6.00    7.00  48.00  56.00
 1123 Tablets of Baha'u'llah       4     10.00   15.00  40.00  60.00
 1021 Six Thousand Words           2     11.00   15.50  22.00  31.00
 1129 Glorification and Praise    10      5.00    7.60  50.00  76.00
 1334 Some Baha'is to Remember    10      8.00    9.00  80.00  90.00

                   GRAND TOTAL SALE  ------> $  383.00

                   GRSND TOTAL COST  ------> $  300.00

                      PROFIT(LOSS)   ------> $   83.00

                   Page 2
```

REPORT 6.8a Month-End Report

Finally, the year-end report is shown in REPORT 6.9.

UNITYVILLE

YEAR-END REPORT FOR THE YEAR ENDING Dec 1985

STOCK CODE	DESCRIPTION	QUANTY. SOLD	UNIT PRICE COST	UNIT PRICE RETAIL	TOTAL COST	TOTAL RETAIL
0112	Dawn Breakers	10	60.00	70.00	608.00	700.00
0193	Prayers of Baha'u'llah	25	6.00	7.00	150.00	175.00
1123	Tablets of Baha'u'llah	40	10.00	15.00	400.00	600.00
1021	Six Thousand Words	26	11.00	15.50	286.00	403.00
1129	Glorification and Praise	30	5.00	7.60	150.00	228.00
1334	Some Baha'is to Remember	13	8.00	9.00	104.00	117.00
1999	A Gift of Love	40	3.00	4.40	120.00	176.00
2000	The Baha'i Proofs	30	13.00	18.00	390.00	540.00

GRAND TOTAL SALES ------> $ 2939.00

GRAND TOTAL COST ------> $ 2200.00

PROFIT(LOSS) ------> $ 739.00

Page 1

REPORT 6.9 Year-End Report

6.10 CONSIGNMENT PROCESSING

On the consignment side of the distribution service system, the process is simple and direct. After receiving the consignment, for each item enter the stock code, name, unit price, and quantity received as shown in SCREEN 6.10.

```
                    UNITYVILLE


                    CONSIGNMENT PROCESSING


Stock code : 193...         Name      : Prayers of Baha'u'llah
                          Publisher   : Baha'i Publishing Trust

                             |<--    QUANTITY   -->|
Unit price :  $    7.00...    Received :     10....

                              Returned :      5....

<---------------- FUNCTION KEYS ------------------>
F1 - SELECT   F2 - NEXT   F3 - PREVIOUS   F4 - INSERT
F5 - UPDATE   F6 - DELETE F7 - EXIT TO MAIN  MENU
```

SCREEN 6.10 Consignment Processing

Remember, it is possible an item may already exists in the data base. To verify enter the code, and use function "SELECT" F1. If it exists just enter price and quantity received, otherwise create a new record.

After the sales are over, enter the quantity to be returned. To do so, call the CONSIGNMENT PROCESSING screen by selecting "3" of the Main Menu, and enter the quantities. Then select "5" of the REPORT MENU to produce REPORT 6.10.

UNITYVILLE

CONSIGNMENT SALE REPORT

Date : Dec 1985

STOCK CODE	DESCRIPTION	QUANTITY RECEIVED	QUANTITY RETURNED	UNIT PRICE	AMOUNT
0193	Prayers of Baha'u'llah	10	5	7.00	35.00
0112	Dawn Breakers	1	1	70.00	00.00
1123	Tablets of Baha'u'llah	20	10	15.00	150.00
1021	Six Thousands Words	30	11	15.50	294.50
1129	Glorification and Praise	10	2	7.60	60.00
1334	Some Baha'is to Remember	25	6	9.00	171.00
1999	A Gift of Love	50	2	4.40	211.20
2000	The Baha'i Proofs	20	10	180.00	180.00
	TOTALS ------>	166	47		1101.70

Page 1

REPORT 6.10 Consignment Report

This report is used to verify the amount of money to be sent with the returning goods.

6.11 TELECOMMUNICATION

In the outline of the distribution service system, we mentioned uses of telecommunication. But so far we have avoided its discussion because it needs separate attention. Data communication requires extra hardware and software; therefore it is not necessary while implementing this computerized distribution service. As we will see, it is a useful tool and in the future it will become a necessity.

Before going any further we have to assume that the National Distribution Service has a computer system that allows remote computers to connect to it to extract information. If so, we can use it to down- load inventory information such as code, titles, and prices from the National Distribution Service to the local outlet. This can happen in different situations; if a new outlet computer system is installed, there is no need to type hundreds of items. Through the telephone line, it can be transferred to your own data base, and occasionally an update of prices can be sent. In both cases, the transition is accomplished within minutes.

With many outlets having this facility, the National Distribution Service can use telecommunication as an advertising media. New titles or material can automatically be passed on whenever a connection is made. Similarly, special sales of material and messages can be broadcasted to all the outlet services.

From the outlets, orders can be placed through data communication. In this case, a format of the electronic order form is first decided upon by the administrator of the National Distribution Service. To use it, prepare the order using a word processor, and after making the connection, send it. It reaches the destination much faster than the mail, and you can even ask for an acknowledgment. (For more details about setting up on-line telecommunication, see Chapter 8.)

CHAPTER SEVEN

SCHOOL MANAGEMENT

Institutions providing education are an integral part of the growth and development of the Baha'i Faith. Among these institutions, the summer and winter schools are popular in most parts of the Baha'i world. Some of these seasonal schools, after years of service, find permanent homes, such as Louhelen Baha'i School in the United States. The main purpose of such schools is to encourage the participants to acquire a better understanding of the Baha'i Teachings and their application in our individual and collective lives. To achieve this goal successfully, many administrative activities, although they take place in the background, are essential in supporting these educational objectives. Some of these activities are:

1. Maintaining special mailing lists,
2. Encouraging contributions to endowments and scholarship funds,
3. Registration,
4. Managing kitchen and book sales,
5. Providing accurate financial account for all activities.

In all these areas, managing information efficiently is important because human and financial resources in the Baha'i Faith are limited.

In this chapter, we have taken the above-mentioned areas and applied the use of the microcomputer to them in the hope of improving the management of Baha'i schools. By no means do we cover every possible situation of every school. However, our examples will give an idea of computerizing the most active areas of school management.

In each section, we will first explain each area of activity, noting desirable features of a computer software. Then we will discuss the data requirements of the application. Next, we describe the design of each piece of program that will handle information. Because the level of activities in one school is different from the next, we have made this design flexible, thus making it easy to modify depending on the needs of the community.

The design includes screen interfaces for the user to interact with the computer. These are of two kinds: one is to select the tasks of a particular area and the second manages the data base. Each screen has a heading, and is followed by the body, with fields marked by dotted lines, where the operator enters the data. At the bottom of the screen, the functions to manage the data base and the transfer to other programs are listed. You will also find report formats, with dotted lines where the program prints the information extracted from the data base.

Before going further, we should establish what you will need to know to implement these ideas. In previous chapters, we suggested using a software tool called the data base management system (DBMS). If you feel the need for background knowledge about this software, refer to Chapter 3, which explains some of the functions of DBMS. We will be using these functions in this application. As mentioned earlier, this tool is recommended for its convenience, flexibility, and low cost. However, to translate these ideas into working programs, you can also use computer languages such as BASIC, PASCAL, or COBOL. Finally, if you are interested in producing programs, the implementation is left up to you. However, we have made suggestions, wherever necessary, to help you in this task.

We start with a screen interface that lists a school's main tasks. By making a selection it enters that particular module of the program. For example, in SCREEN 7.1, if you choose 1, Special Mailing List, it prompt the program to find the mailing list from the data base. Or, if the selection is item 7, the control goes to DOS. In the rest of this chapter we will discuss similar menus for each area of the school management system.

```
                    NEW DAY BAHA'I SCHOOL

                    MAIN MENU

   1 - Special Mailing List

   2 - Special Contributions

   3 - Registration

   4 - Kitchen Operation

   5 - Inventory Control

   6 - General Ledger / Financial Statement

   7 - To DOS
                  Selection  ( 1 to 7) : ..
```

SCREEN 7.1 Main Tasks Menu

7.1 SPECIAL MAILING LIST

Mail is most common means of advertising a school's upcoming events, and also a popular method of conducting business with other Baha'i institutions. An inexpensive way of having up-to-date mailing labels of a region or state is to get them from your Baha'i National Center, if its record is computerized automatically. However, sometimes, the school administration has to keep a SPECIAL MAILING LIST, with names and addresses of customers who are randomly scattered all over the globe. Our concern is to computerize this list, which consists of the following types:

1. Baha'is outside a region,
2. Baha'i agencies,
3. Non-Baha'is,
4. Suppliers of goods.

Let's explain these four types. It is likely that Baha'is at a given school are from out of state, but attend and support the programs regularly. To encourage this, the staff should include their names in the program's mailing list. Since these names are relatively few and from different parts of the country or world, we include this category in the special mailing list.

Also, the staff of the school may communicate with Baha'i institutions in many different countries, such as Baha'i National Centers, committees, other schools, and so on. Therefore, each school maintains its own list of such names and addresses.

Another kind of special mailing list is a list of all the suppliers that sell goods to the school. Later, we will see how this supplier information is useful when processing purchase orders of books and materials.

In this application, one screen interface is sufficient to maintain information, stored in the data base, of all these types. Information such as names, addresses, and telephone numbers are common to all. To distinguish among them, there is a flag. Through this interface screen, the user is able to do the following operations:

1. Select a record,
2. Insert a record,
3. Update an existing record,
4. Delete a record,
5. Show the next record,
6. Show the previous record.

The other function of the software is to print mailing labels with names and addresses for any particular type chosen. Also, the operator selects whether to print one, two, or three columns of labels.

DATA BASE

TABLE 7.1 gives a sample of the file for mailing list, called "NAMES," showing a typical entry in this file. Associated with each field name is a description explaining its use. Also, the data type of each field and the length needed for any character type are listed. Note that under the field TYPE, we have suggested only four kinds, but more can be easily added.

File name: NAMES, Special mailing list file

Field Name	Description	Data Type	Length
ID	Baha'i identification number	character	10
name	name of person or business	character	30
address1	name of street	character	30
address2	apartment or suite number	character	30
city	name of the city	character	30
state	name of state	character	30
country	name of country	character	30
postal	postal or zip code	character	10
phone_h	home phone number	character	10
phone_b	business phone number	character	10
note	comment, or name of contact if business	character	30
type	type of mailing address 1 - outside region 2 - Baha'i Agency 3 - non-Baha'i 4 - suppliers of goods	integer	

TABLE 7.1 Record of File NAME

DESIGN

After defining the data file, we devote the rest of this section to the design of the programs, explaining how to manage the data of the mailing list through the screen interfaces and how to print the mailing labels.

SCREEN 7.2 is an interface screen of the special mailing list. Through the functions listed at the bottom of the screen, the user maintains the data of the file NAMES. Note that the field TYPE takes values ranging from one to four, a way of distinguishing the kind of list. The field NOTE (shown as Contact/comment on the screen) is to insert the name of a person if the record is for a supplier. Otherwise, it is used for comments or notes.

```
                    NEW DAY  BAHA'I SCHOOL

                    SPECIAL MAILING LIST

                    Maintenance


ID number : ........       Name : ..............................

Street       : .................................
Suite/Apt    : .........................
City         : .........................
State        : .........................
Country      : ........................
Postal Code  : ...........

Telephone :(H)...-...-....   (W) ...-...-....

Contact/comment : ...........................................

                  ............................
Type      : .. -->| 1 - Outside a region     |
                  | 2 - Baha'i Agency        |
                  | 3 - Non-Baha'i           |
                  | 4 - Suppliers            |
                  |..........................|

<-------------------- FUNCTIONS ------------------------>
F1 - SELECT     F2 - NEXT    F3 - PREVIOUS    F4 - INSERT
F5 - UPDATE     F6 - DELETE  F7 - EXIT MAIN MENU
```

SCREEN 7.2 Interface to Maintain Mailing List

To print labels, we use the SCREEN 7.3, which provides a selection of the type of list and the number of columns. After making the choices, the user presses function key F1 to generate the labels, as shown in REPORT 7.1.

```
                NEW DAY BAHA'I SCHOOL

                PRINT MAILING LIST




                ............................
Selection : ..  --->|  1 - Outside a region     |
                    |  2 - Baha'i Agency        |
                    |  3 - Non-Baha'i           |
                    |  4 - Suppliers            |
                    |...........................|


                 ............................
   Column : .. ->:                           :
                 :  1 - One Column           :
                 :  2 - Two Columns          :
                 :  3 - Three Columns        :
                 :...........................:

-----------------------------------------------------------------
F1 - PRINT                F7- EXIT TO SPECIAL MAILING LIST
-----------------------------------------------------------------
```

SCREEN 7.3 Select and Print Mailing Labels

```
Kalimat Press                 Glory Baha'i Youth Magazine
1600 Sawtelle Boulevard       P.O. Box 19,
Suite 34                      Panchgani 412805
Los Angeles, CA 90025-3114    Maharashtra
U.S.A                         INDIA

Spiritual Mothering Journal   Dialogue
18350 Ross Ave.               P.O Box 24B21
Sandy, OR 97055               Los Angeles, CA 90024
U.S.A.                        U.S.A
```

REPORT 7.1 Mailing Labels

7.2 SPECIAL CONTRIBUTIONS

The next task in our computer application is to manage the special contributions to various funds, received at a Baha'i school. To take care of such donations, there are three main concerns--maintaining membership information, entering amounts of contributions into the system, and printing mailing lists and income reports.

The kinds of contributions are numerous and differ at each place. However, to illustrate managing special contributions, we have chosen only three different types, which are as follows:

1. Friends,
2. Endowments,
3. Scholarships.

Note that more funds can be added to this list. The next few paragraphs briefly describe each category.

There are many Baha'is who are interested in the growth and development of a particular school. These Baha'is are called "FRIENDS" of the school. To participate, one pays a yearly or lifetime membership fee and subscribes to a special newsletter about the progress and development of the school.

Next, the National Assembly will occasionally set up an endowment fund for the development of a particular aspect of the Baha'i school. If such a fund is directly related to the school, then Baha'is can make donations to such a fund during a session.

Finally, the school may decide to set up a scholarship fund to promote education. Again, the administration has to account for such contributions.

To produce adequate accounting of the funds, the computer can provide a means for the user to access the data base where personal data and all transactions are kept. First, it maintains the name, Baha'i ID number, address, and phone number, with a flag to distinguish the three different types of membership. All these data are kept on one record of a file.

When a contribution is made, the operator enters the data into the system. Both personal information and contributions are regularly maintained through such functions as selection, addition, deletion, or changes. One example of contribution information would consist of Baha'i ID, name of the person, date, amount, and the type of fund to which they contribute. Also, there is space for any comment to be made about any particular contribution.

Finally, the computer program prints mailing labels according to any one of the three types of membership. Again, the user has the choice of printing labels in one, two, or three columns, and an income report of all the contributions to different funds during a given period of time.

DATA BASE

We need one file as a profile of each member having personal and membership information. This is called "CONNAME," as shown in TABLE 7.2. This table shows the name of each field, description of its use, data type, and length of characters. Note that the lengths of the file names are no more than eight characters, as sometimes required by DOS.

File name: CONNAME, profile of membership (contribution)

FIELD NAME	DESCRIPTION	DATA TYPE	LENGTH
id	Baha'i identification number	character	10
name	name of person or business	character	30
address1	name of street	character	30
address2	apartment or suite number	character	30
city	name of the city	character	30
state	name of state	character	30
country	name of country	character	30
postal	postal or zip code	character	10
phone_h	home phone number	character	10
phone_b	business phone number	character	10
friends	membership type in the category of FRIENDS. 1 - adult ($ 20) 2 - family ($ 30) 3 - student ($ 13) 4 - life time ($ 500)	integer	
endowment	types of contribution for endowment funds. 1 - monthly 2 - yearly 3 - one time	integer	
scholarship	types of contribution for scholarship fund. 1 - monthly 2 - yearly 3 - one time	integer	
date	date when membership starts	date	
amount_c	amount of contribution for endowment fund	dollar	
amount_s	amount of contribution for scholarship fund	dollar	

TABLE 7.2 Record of File CONNAME

The other file, called "CONTRIB," is to place all the contributions in certain categories, as shown in TABLE 7.3.

File name: CONTRIB, contribution transaction file

FIELD NAME	DESCRIPTION	DATA TYPE	LENGTH
ID	Baha'i identification number	character	10
name	name of person contributing	character	20
type	type of contribution 1 - Friend 2 - Endowment 3 - Scholarship	integer	
posting_date	date of contribution	date	
amount	amount of contribution	dollar	
comment	any note about the contribution	character	30

TABLE 7.4 Record of File CONTRIB

DESIGN

As seen earlier, we need a selection menu for the special contributions. SCREEN 7.4 provides four functions, three for special contributions and one to exit the operation.

```
            NEW DAY BAHA'I SCHOOL

            SPECIAL CONTRIBUTIONS

    1 - Maintain Membership Information

    2 - Post Contributions

    3 - Print Mailing Label/Income Report

    4 - Exit to Main Menu

         Selection (1 to 4) : ..
```

SCREEN 7.4 Contribution Task Menu

To maintain the information about a member, we have SCREEN 7.5. Notice that after the personal data such as name, ID, address, and telephone number, there are three kinds of contributions listed. Each kind is divided into subcategories and the amount of donation pledged. Also, the function keys F1 through F7 perform the operations as listed on the screen, to manage data.

```
                       NEW DAY BAHA'I SCHOOL

                       SPECIAL CONTRIBUTIONS

                       Information   Maintenance

ID : .......      Name : .............................

Street     : .................................
Suite/Apt  : .........................
City       : .........................
State      : .........................
Country    : .........................  Postal Code : ...........

   Telephone:(H)...-...-....   (W) ...-...-....


 |<-- Friends -->|     |<-- Endowments -->|  |<-- Scholarships -->|

 Choice : ..             Choice : ..             Choice : ..
 .................................................................
 | 1 - Adult     $  20 | 1 - Monthly           | 1 - Monthly       |
 | 2 - Family    $  30 | 2 - Yearly            | 2 - Yearly        |
 | 3 - Student   $  15 | 3 - One time          | 3 - One time      |
 | 4 - Lifetime  $ 500 |                       |                   |
 |.....................|.......................|...................|

          MMDDYY
   Date : ......      Amount :$ .........    Amount :$ ..........
<------------------ FUNCTIONS ------------------------------->
F1 - SELECT      F2 - NEXT     F3 - PREVIOUS     F4 - INSERT
F5 - UPDATE      F6 - DELETE   F7 - EXIT TO CONTRIBUTION MENU
```

SCREEN 7.5 Interface to Maintain Membership Information

The donations are recorded into the system through SCREEN 7.6. It requires data such as type of contribution, name, ID, and so on. In the field "COMMENT" the operator types any remark while processing a contribution.

```
                         NEW DAY BAHA'I SCHOOL

                         POST CONTRIBUTIONS


ID : .............         Name : ..............................

      MMDDYY
Date : ......           Amount : $ ..........

                              ..................................
                              |                                |
Type of contribution : .. --->| 1 - Friend                     |
                              | 2 - Endowment                  |
                              | 3 - Scholarship                |
                              |................................|

Comment : ..........................


<--------------------< FUNCTIONS >------------------------->
F1 - SELECT      F2 - NEXT    F3 - PREVIOUS      F4 - INSERT
F5 - UPDATE      F6 - DELETE  F7 - EXIT TO CONTRIBUTION MENU
```

SCREEN 7.6 Interface to Post Contributions

There are two listings: mailing labels and income report. SCREEN 7.7 provides the choices to print any one.

```
                    NEW DAY BAHA'I SCHOOL

                    PRINT MAILING LIST/CONTRIBUTION INCOME

                         ....................
Choice of report : ..-->| 1 - Labels         |
                        | 2 - Income Report  |
                        |....................|

                          MMDDYY        MMDDYY
          Date   from :  ......  to  :  ......

                     ...........................
Selection : .. -->|  1 - Outside a region     |
                  |  2 - Baha'i Agency        |
                  |  3 - Non-Baha'i           |
                  |  4 - Suppliers            |
                  |...........................|


                      ..........................
      Column : .. ->:                          :
                    :  1 - One Column          :
                    :  2 - Two Columns         :
                    :  3 - Three Columns       :
                    :..........................:

------------------------------------------------------------
F1 - PRINT                 F7- EXIT TO SPECIAL CONTRIBUTION
------------------------------------------------------------
```

SCREEN 7.7 Interface to Select and Print Labels

The label is the same as in previous section (see REPORT 7.1). The income report consists of contributions within a given period of time, say one week or month. Note that in REPORT 7.2, in addition to donations, the program prints the total income.

```
                         NEW DAY BAHA'I SCHOOL

                         CONTRIBUTION INCOME REPORT

From : ..........        to : ............


 ID       NAME                 DATE   TYPE  AMOUNT  COMMENT
=========!=================!======!=====!=======!==============


 ........ ................. ......   .    ....... ............
 ........ ................. ......   .    ....... ............
 ........ ................. ......   .    ....... ............
 ........ ................. ......   .    ....... ............
 ........ ................. ......   .    ....... ............
 ........ ................. ......   .    ....... ............


                        TOTAL  ---------->   ........

                         Page 1
```

REPORT 7.2 Contribution Report

7.3 REGISTRATION

Registration is fairly simple if participants are only enrolled in sessions. But if a school provides lodging, meals, linen, and other facilities, then this task becomes complicated. Usually, for any session, most of the guests arrive within a short period of time. During this time, the person responsible for registration provides keys, receives payments, and handles all the irregularities such as cancellations and changes. Obviously, it is a demanding process.

Considering these demands, our objective is to make registration less timeconsuming by using the computer for the repetitive work. A suitable program can easily keep all the information about guests from preregistration until the time they leave. This process involves (1) managing registration, (2) printing confirmation letters, and (3) balancing the account at check-out time. Also, during a slower time the staff can print an income report of a session or a period of time and a statistical report whenever required.

This registration software will have an interface screen through which the user manages all the information found on the registration form filled out by the guest. In addition to data such as name, address, and phone number, the operator enters discounts, meals, linen, deposits, and balance owed. In this system, guests are enrolled according to a registration generated by the system, thereby making it possible to include more than one person for one registration. Information about accompanying participants is entered by the same interface screen and stored in the data base. At check-in time, the operator assigns rooms and enters payment.

At check-out time, the guest pays the amount owed, bringing the registration account to a close. Although the system is registration specific, with one account number given to one or a group of persons, the program selects from the data base according to a room number or name of the guest, making any inquiry easier. Also, this portion of the software performs normal data-management chores.

Another important aspect of the registration is a confirmation letter. Its content, decided by the registrar, acknowledges the receipt of the preregistration form along with any deposit. It also confirms the requested facilities such as linen or special meals, and it provides the balance of payment due. If any of the requested facilities are unavailable, the software selects the appropriate text to be printed on this letter.

The income report gives a detailed account of the revenue from registration. It prints the registration number along with the number of persons attending a session. For each number, it gives total payment and a breakdown according to the facilities provided, such as room, linen, discount, meals, and so on. Also, it gives a grand total of all payments received. This report is printed according to a session or a particular period of time, say one month, for instance.

Many Baha'i schools are required to send a statistical report of the attendance to their National Centers. This report includes the many different categories of attendants. Each school has its own interest in this area, and so on in each case such a report takes a different form. Considering this, we are giving one format that includes age, race, and non-Baha'i participants. The age group is made up of adults, youths and children, while the race categories consist of Asian, black, Hispanic, native and white.

DATA BASE

In this application the amount of information we have to store is much more than the two previous cases. First, there is the registration of a person and family, which involves recording personal information, facilities requested by the guest, the session to be attended, payments and so on. TABLE 7.4 gives the details of a record for a file called "REGISTRA." Next, with each registration there may be more than one person, and we have chosen to store the data of the accompanying participants in the file "ACCOMPAN," as shown in TABLE 7.5.

File name: REGISTRA - Registration information file

Field Name	Description	Data Type	Length
registration	registration number	character	10
name	surname	character	30
address1	street name	character	30
address2	apartment number	character	30
city	name of city	character	30
state	name of province or state	character	30
country	name of country	character	30
postal	postal or zip code	character	10
phone_h	home phone number	character	10
phone_b	business phone number	character	10
session	name of session	character	30
session_date	starting date of the session	date	
checked-in	checked-in ? y - yes n - no	character	1
checked-out	checked-out ? y - yes n - no	character	1
age	age of the guest	integer	
sex	sex of the guest m - male f - female	character	1
race	race of the guest p - Persian w - White b - Black h - Hispanic	character	1
Baha'i	Baha'i ? y - yes n - no	character	1
discount_type	any discount ? 0 - Assembly 1 - family 2 - senior citizen	integer	
lodging	type of lodging 1 - dormitory 2 - double 3 - single	integer	
days	number of days of attendance	integer	
breakfast	breakfast ? (y/n)	character	1
dinner	dinner ? (y/n)	character	1
lunch	lunch ? (y/n)	character	1
facility	facility ? (y/n)	character	1
linen	linen ? (y/n)	character	1
deposit	amount of deposit	dollar	

key_deposit	deposit for keys	dollar
discount	amount of discount	dollar
balance	amount owing	dollar
date_arr	arrival date	date
room	room assigned	character 5

TABLE 7. 4 Record of File REGISTRA

File name: ACCOMPAN - Accompanies information file

Field Name	Description	Data Type	Length
registration	registration number	character	10
name	name of accompany	character	30
sex	sex of accompany m - male f - female	character	1
age	age of accompany	integer	
race	race of accompany a - Asian b - Black h - Hispanic w - White	character	1

TABLE 7.5 Record of File ACCOMPAN

DESIGN

To accomplish all the registration tasks, as mentioned earlier, we need a menu such as SCREEN 7.8. It contains four functions for registration and one to exit to the MAIN MENU.

The registration file interacts with files REGISTRA and ACCOMPA. For example, in SCREEN 7.9, the upper part is about registration, while the lower section is about the accompanying attendants. This screen is used from the preregistration until the guest checks out. Also, the operator can inquire about rooms or quests of each attendant, and this can be done using the name or registration number fields.

```
                NEW DAY BAHA'I SCHOOL

                REGISTRATION

        1 - Registration

        2 - Print Confirmation

        3 - Print Income Report

        4 - Print Statistical Report

        5 - EXIT TO MAIN MENU
```

SCREEN 7.8 Registration Menu

In this interface, we have added two functions, one to process check-ins (F1) and the other for check-outs. In either case, these functions are used to verify the correctness of data and to stamp each registration with a flag (preregistration, checked-in, or checked-out). For example, verification may include seeing whether or not there is an outstanding balance at check-out time, or if rooms are properly assigned during check-in time.

```
                    NEW DAY BAHA'I SCHOOL
                    REGISTRATION

Registration # : .......          Discount type: ..
Name   : ......................   Lodging       : ..
Address: ......................   Days          : ..
       : ......................   Persons       : ..
City   : ......................   Breakfast (y/n): .
State  : ......................   Lunch     (y/n): .
Country: ............... Zip:.......  Dinner    (y/n): .
Phone(H) : ... ... ....           Facility  (y/n): .
Phone(W) : ... ... ....           Deposit        : $
............
Session  : .......................  Key deposit    : $...........
Session date  : ...... (mmddyy)     Discount       : $ ...........
Checked-in (y/n) : .                Balance        : $ ...........
Checked-out(y/n) : .               Arrival date   : ......(mmddyy)
Age : ...     Room  : .....   Sex :  .... Race : .... Baha'i (y/n) : .
|<----------             ACCOMPANIES      ----------------------->|
  NAME                         SEX   AGE BAHA'I(y/n)  RACE    ROOM
  ....................          .    ...     .         .      ....
  ....................          .    ...     .         .      ....
  ....................          .    ...     .         .      ....
  ....................          .    ...     .         .      ....
<--------------------- FUNCTIONS ----------------------->
F1 - SELECT    F2 - NEXT    F3 - PREVIOUS    F4 - INSERT
F5 - UPDATE    F6 - DELETE F7 - CHECKED-IN F8 - CHECKED-OUT
F9 - EXIT TO REGISTRATION MENU
```

SCREEN 7.9 Interface to Maintain Registration

After the preregistration, the guest receives a confirmation letter, such as in REPORT 7.3. The staff decides the final content, but the computer can be programed to select an appropriate text according to the meals or facilities requested and insert it in the body of the letter. Further, name, address, and other data are pulled from the registration file.

```
                    NEW DAY BAHA'I SCHOOL
                   <ADDRESS>


June 22, 1986

<name>

<address>



Dear Friend:


The New Day School is pleased to confirm your reservation for the session : Upon
your arrival, we will have room with linen and a crib ready for you. In your group
there will be 2 adults, one child and one infant. Also, you have requested all meals
during this session.

Thank you for your reservation deposit of $ .... , and the balance due is $ ......

As a preparation for your stay at New Day School, we are enclosing an information
sheet for you to read. We look forward to receiving and serving you at New Day
School, hoping your stay with us will be a memorable one.


Best loving greetings,


Registrar
```

REPORT 7.3 Confirmation Letter

The next task is to print an income report. There are two kinds of selections. One prints data for a particular session and the other prints all registration during a specified period of time. In REPORT 7.4, for each registration it shows the number of persons and of amounts received through rooms, linen, facility, and meals. In addition, it includes any discount. Finally, the program adds amounts to print the total for each column of numbers.

NEW DAY BAHA'I SCHOOL

INCOME REPORT   Date : ....

FROM : ....   TO : ....

SESSION : ....

REG #	PERSON	ROOM $	LINEN $	MEALS $	TOTAL $	DISC $	AMOUNT $
......	...	......	......	......	......	.....	......
......	...	......	......	......	......	.....	......
......	...	......	......	......	......	.....	......
......	...	......	......	......	......	.....	......
......	...	......	......	......	......	.....	......
......	...	......	......	......	......	.....	......
......	...	......	......	......	......	.....	......
......	...	......	......	......	......	.....	......
......	...	......	......	......	......	.....	......
TOTALS ---->		......	......	......	......	.....	......

PAGE 1

REPORT 7.4 Registration Income Report

When enough data are collected, the staff prints a statistical report for the administration. REPORT 7.5 is a simple example of attendance numbers extracted from files, in three categories: age, race, and non-Baha'i. The age group has adults, youths and children, while the race is made of Asian, black, Hispanic, native and white.

7.4 KITCHEN

In this section, let's look at some of the steps taken in the kitchen to supply the guests with meals. Following this, we'll consider the requirements needed to automate some of these steps. During a session, lasting either a weekend or week, the guests are served three meals as well as an occasional snack. In simple terms, one of these meals includes three main steps: buying the food, preparation, and serving the guests.

```
                    NEW DAY BAHA'I SCHOOL

              STATISTICAL REPORT    Date : ...........



SESSION  |<--  AGE  -->|<--    RACE     -->|  NON
           A  Y  C     A  B  H  N  W    BAHA'I
 ......   .. .. ..    .. .. .. .. ..     ...
 ......   .. .. ..    .. .. .. .. ..     ...
 ......   .. .. ..    .. .. .. .. ..     ...
 ......   .. .. ..    .. .. .. .. ..     ...
 ......   .. .. ..    .. .. .. .. ..     ...
 ......   .. .. ..    .. .. .. .. ..     ...
 ......   .. .. ..    .. .. .. .. ..     ...

 TOTALS -> .. .. ..   .. .. .. .. ..     ...

                    PAGE 1
```

REPORT 7.5 Attendance Statistical Report

Since computer technology is not developed enough to be a practical tool in preparation or serving of meals, we'll only focus on planning of meals for any session, printing goods required, and accounting of the cost of food.

Now, let's determine some features of this system. One approach is to have menus, each containing items of only one of the meals or a snack. For example, a breakfast menu called "Bacon and Eggs" will have scrambled eggs, bacon, coffee, tea, and fruit salad. All except the fruit salad require only one item. A fruit salad needs apples, oranges, grapes, and mixed nuts. Similarly, you can have menus for different meals, such as dinner, lunch, breakfast, or a snack.

From a pool of menus, the kitchen staff selects the meals for one day, or for a weekend or week-long session. They can change this selection anytime or make up new ones. It is possible to omit a meal or skip a day while making the selection, adding flexibility to the planning stage. A list shows what food is required to prepare a meal covered by any of the selections.

Regularly, say once a week, the kitchen staff tallies all the purchases and submits a report to the accounting department. All these activities continue on a cyclical basis. Thus this simple process gives us a basis to develop the requirements of the computer programs.

Among the tasks, an obvious one is to maintain menus stored in the data base. Each menu consists of ingredients satisfying one of the four categories:

1. Breakfast,
2. Lunch,
3. Dinner,
4. Snack.

Each menu record is made of an identification and description of the menu such as "Bacon and eggs," "Rice pudding," and so on. Next, there are up to six items. In each item, the number of ingredients is different, varying from one to six.

After these menus are entered in the data base, you select a menu for the week including breakfast, lunch, dinner, and a snack. This selection is identified by a number and a description. The menu selection screen format is arranged to have the days (up to 7) lined up in a row and the meal set in columns. An ID is chosen that best describes the selection, for instance, it can be the number of a week, abbreviated session name, or any other form.

Another requirement is to print a food list. Given the number of guests expected, a selection ID, and a code to identify a week or weekend, the user can print a list that shows the food and quantity needed for each selected meal. Also, a space is allowed to enter manually the unit and total prices, and the quantity purchased. The numbers are added together to produce the total expense for a week, weekend or a day.

Finally, the system lets you enter expenses, for the purpose of accounting, for a period of time, for example, a week or weekend. This record of data contains the week code, number of guests, and a space for comment by the operator. Again, through the interface screen you can recall any old entries, add new ones, or modify any existing one.

DATA BASE

To satisfy the data storage requirements of the kitchen operation, we require three files. One is "MENU," as shown in TABLE 7.6, to collect menus for different meals. Each record is made up of menu identification, description, and ingredients of each item.

The next file, called "SELECT," shown in TABLE 7.7, is a group of menus described previously, arranged according to the meals for a particular day. In addition, one can have selection of meals for seven days.

File name: MENU - file to keep menus

Field Name	Description	Data Type	length
menu_Id	identification of a menu	character	10
menu	description of a menu	character	20
item_one	description of item one	character	20
item_1	quantity of item one	integer	
item_two	description of item two	character	20
item_2	quantity of item two	integer	
item_three	description of item three	character	20
ingr_three_a	description of ingredient one	character	20
ingr_3_a	quantity of ingredient one	integer	
ingr_three_b	description of ingredient one	character	20
ingr_3_b	quantity of ingredient one	integer	
ingr_three_c	description of ingredient one	character	20
ingr_3_c	quantity of ingredient one	integer	
item_four	description of item four	character	20
ingr_four_a	description of ingredient one	character	20
ingr_4_a	quantity of ingredient one	integer	
ingr_four_b	description of ingredient two	character	20
ingr_4_b	quantity of ingredient two	integer	
ingr_four_c	description of ingredient three	character	20
ingr_4_c	quantity of ingredient three	integer	
item_five	description of item five	character	20
ingr_five_a	description of ingredient one	character	20
ingr_5_a	quantity of ingredient one	integer	
ingr_five_b	description of ingredient two	character	20
ingr_5_b	quantity of ingredient two	integer	
ingr_five_c	description of ingredient three	character	20
ingr_5_c	quantity of ingredient three	integer	
ingr_five_d	description of ingredient four	character	20
ingr_5_d	quantity of ingredient four	integer	
item_six	description of item six	character	20
ingr_six_a	description of ingredient one	character	20
ingr_6_a	quantity of ingredient one	integer	
ingr_six_b	description of ingredient two	character	20
ingr_6_b	quantity of ingredient two	integer	
ingr_six_c	description of ingredient three	character	20
ingr_6_c	quantity of ingredient three	integer	
ingr_six_d	description of ingredient four	character	20
ingr_6_d	quantity of ingredient four	integer	
ingr_six_e	description of ingredient five	character	20
ingr_6_e	quantity of ingredient five	integer	

TABLE 7.6 Record of File MENU

File name: SELECT

Field Name	Description	Data Type	length
selection_id	identification of a selection	character	20
description	description of a menu selection	character	20
one_breakfast	menu ID for breakfast meal, day 1	character	10
one_lunch	menu ID for lunch meal, day 1	character	10
one_dinner	menu ID for dinner meal, day 1	character	10
one_snack	menu ID for snack meal, day 1	character	10
two_breakfast	menu ID for breakfast meal, day 2	character	10
two_lunch	menu ID for lunch meal, day 2	character	10
two_dinner	menu ID for dinner meal, day 2	character	10
two_snack	menu ID for snack meal, day 2	character	10
three_breakfast	menu ID for breakfast meal, day 3	character	10
three_lunch	menu ID for lunch meal, day 3	character	10
three_dinner	menu ID for dinner meal, day 3	character	10
three_snack	menu ID for snack meal, day 3	character	10
four_breakfast	menu ID for breakfast meal, day 4	character	10
four_lunch	menu ID for lunch meal, day 4	character	10
four_dinner	menu ID for dinner meal, day 4	character	10
four_snack	menu ID for snack meal, day 4	character	10
five_breakfast	menu ID for breakfast meal, day 5	character	10
five_lunch	menu ID for lunch meal, day 5	character	10
five_dinner	menu ID for dinner meal, day 5	character	10
five_snack	menu ID for snack meal, day 5	character	10
six_breakfast	menu ID for breakfast meal, day 6	character	10
six_lunch	menu ID for lunch meal, day 6	character	10
six_dinner	menu ID for dinner meal, day 6	character	10
six_snack	menu ID for snack meal, day 6	character	10
seven_breakfast	menu ID for breakfast meal, day 7	character	10
seven_lunch	menu ID for lunch meal, day 7	character	10
seven_dinner	menu ID for dinner meal, day 7	character	10
seven_snack	menu ID for snack meal, day 7	character	10

TABLE 7.7 Record of File SELECT

Finally, there is a file, called "EXPENSES," to record the summary of kitchen expenditures as described in detail of each field in TABLE 7.8. Also, these data can be used for the financial report.

File name: EXPENSES - Kitchen expense file

Field Name	Description	Data Type	length
number	a number to identify the expense	character	10
comment	any note related to this expense	character	20
guests	number of guests served	integer	
cost	cost of the food	dollar	
date	date of expense	date	

TABLE 7.8 Record of File EXPENSE

DESIGN

The first screen interface in this design is a selection of kitchen tasks, as shown in SCREEN 7.10

```
                    NEW DAY BAHA'I SCHOOL

                    KITCHEN


    1.  Menu Maintenance

    2.  Menu Selection

    3.  Print Foods Required for a Selection

    4. Enter Food Expenses

    5. Exit to Main Menu
```

SCREEN 7.10 Kitchen Task Selection

SCREEN 7.11 is a screen interface that maintains the menus stored in the file MENU. The field "MENU ID" gives each record a unique identification for retrieval. This always starts with either B for breakfast, L for lunch, D for dinner, or S for snack. The next field describes the menu. The rest of the fields are used to describe the ingredients and quantities of items required. Notice, that some items use only one ingredient while others may require several.

After collecting many such menus, you may select the meal for any time of the week using SCREEN 7.12 . You will notice that it has its own identification code and a description. Arranged in rows (days) and columns (meals), you insert the selection, which is the menu ID, described earlier. Among the functions, you will notice F7 gets the name of a menu from the file "MENU." For example, let's say you chose menu "BB&E" for breakfast on the first day. You type this menu ID and press F7, which will print the name "Bacon and Eggs," one line below. As mentioned earlier, make a selection from one meal to all the meals for a given session.

```
                    NEW DAY BAHA'I SCHOOL

                    MENU MAINTENANCE


                     .......................
                     | B - Breakfast       |
Menu ID : ......... -->| L - Lunch         |
                     | D - Dinner          |
                     | S - Snack           |
                     |.....................|

Menu   : ........................................


Item          Description                       Quantity

 1. .............................               ......

 2. .............................               ......

 3. .............................
Ingredients (a)............................       ......
            (b)............................       ......
            (c)............................       ......

 4. .............................
Ingredients (a)............................       ......
            (b)............................       ......
            (c)............................       ......

 5.  .............................
Ingredients (a)............................       ......
            (b)............................       ......
            (c)............................       ......
            (d)............................       ......

 6. .............................
Ingredients (a)............................       ......
            (b)............................       ......
            (c)............................       ......
            (d)............................       ......
            (e)............................       ......

<-------------------- FUNCTIONS ---------------------->
F1 - SELECT  F2 - NEXT     F3 - PREVIOUS  F4 - INSERT
F5 - UPDATE  F6 - DELETE   F7 - EXIT TO KITCHEN MENU
```

SCREEN 7.11 Interface to Maintain Menus

```
                    NEW DAY BAHA'I SCHOOL

                    MENU SELECTION

Selection ID : .......   ..........................................

    BREAKFAST        LUNCH       DINNER        SNACK
1   ..........       ..........  ..........    ..........
   ................ ........... ............  ...............

2   ..........       ..........  ..........    ..........
   ................ ........... ............  ...............

3   ..........       ..........  ..........    ..........
   ................ ........... ............  ...............

4   ..........       ..........  ..........    ..........
   ................ ........... ............  ...............

5   ..........       ..........  ..........    ..........
   ................ ........... ............  ...............

6   ..........       ..........  ..........    ..........
   ................ ........... ............  ...............

7   ..........       ..........  ..........    ..........
   ................ ........... ............  ...............

<-------------------- FUNCTION -------------------->
F1 - SELECT  F2 - NEXT     F3 - PREVIOUS  F4 - INSERT
F5 - UPDATE  F6 - DELETE   F7 - EXIT TO KITCHEN MENU
F7 - GET MENU NAME
```

SCREEN 7.12 Interface to Select Menus for Meals

After the kitchen staff makes a menu selection, he/she prints the list of food required, such as REPORT 7.6. This program requires two pieces of information--one is the number of guests expected and the other is the code to identify a day, session, weekend or week. This ID is only to show when a menu selection is used. Given the number of guests, the staff has to come up with a multiplying factor to produce the quantity of each ingredient. To be economical, this program prints only the meals and days chosen. Also note, under the heading "quantity bought," and "prices," the space is left empty to be filled out while purchasing the necessary items.

```
                         NEW DAY BAHA'I SCHOOL
                         FOOD  REQUIRED

Number of guests : ..........    Week ID : ..............
                                               |<  Quantity >|<--Price-->|
Day  Meal time  ID      Food                  Reqr'd  Bought Unit    Total
-------------------------------------------------------------------------------
1. Breakfast  ...... ...................... ....  .....  ...... ......
                     ...................... ....  .....  ...... ......
                     ...................... ....  .....  ...... ......
   Lunch      ...... ...................... ....  .....  ...... ......
                     ...................... ....  .....  ...... ......
                     ...................... ....  .....  ...... ......
   Dinner     ...... ...................... ....  .....  ...... ......
                     ...................... ....  .....  ...... ......
                     ...................... ....  .....  ...... ......
   Snack      ...... ...................... ....  .....  ...... ......
                     ...................... ....  .....  ...... ......
                     ...................... ....  .....  ...... ......

2. Breakfast  ...... ...................... ....  .....  ...... ......
                     ...................... ....  .....  ...... ......
                     ...................... ....  .....  ...... ......
   Lunch      ...... ...................... ....  .....  ...... ......
                     ...................... ....  .....  ...... ......
                     ...................... ....  .....  ...... ......
   Dinner     ...... ...................... ....  .....  ...... ......
                     ...................... ....  .....  ...... ......
                     ...................... ....  .....  ...... ......
   Snack      ...... ...................... ....  .....  ...... ......
                     ...................... ....  .....  ...... ......
                     ...................... ....  .....  ...... ......

3. Breakfast  ...... ...................... ....  .....  ...... ......
                     ...................... ....  .....  ...... ......
                     ...................... ....  .....  ...... ......
   Lunch      ...... ...................... ....  .....  ...... ......
                     ...................... ....  .....  ...... ......
                     ...................... ....  .....  ...... ......
   Dinner     ...... ...................... ....  .....  ...... ......
                     ...................... ....  .....  ...... ......
                     ...................... ....  .....  ...... ......
   Snack      ...... ...................... ....  .....  ...... ......
                     ...................... ....  .....  ...... ......
                     ...................... ....  .....  ...... ......

                                  Page 1
```

NEW DAY BAHA'I SCHOOL
GOODS REQUIRED

Number of guests : .... Week ID : ....

Day	Meal time	ID	Food	Quantity Reqr'd	Quantity Bought	Price Unit	Price Total
4.	Breakfast	......	....	....	.....	......	......
			....	....	.....	......	......
			....	....	.....	......	......
	Lunch	......	....	....	.....	......	......
			....	....	.....	......	......
			....	....	.....	......	......
	Dinner	......	....	....	.....	......	......
			....	....	.....	......	......
			....	....	.....	......	......
	Snack	......	....	....	.....	......	......
			....	....	.....	......	......
			....	....	.....	......	......
5.	Breakfast	......	....	....	.....	......	......
			....	....	.....	......	......
			....	....	.....	......	......
	Lunch	......	....	....	.....	......	......
			....	....	.....	......	......
			....	....	.....	......	......
	Dinner	......	....	....	.....	......	......
			....	....	.....	......	......
			....	....	.....	......	......
	Snack	......	....	....	.....	......	......
			....	....	.....	......	......
			....	....	.....	......	......
6.	Breakfast	......	....	....	.....	......	......
			....	....	.....	......	......
			....	....	.....	......	......
	Lunch	......	....	....	.....	......	......
			....	....	.....	......	......
			....	....	.....	......	......
	Dinner	......	....	....	.....	......	......
			....	....	.....	......	......
			....	....	.....	......	......
	Snack	......	....	....	.....	......	......
			....	....	.....	......	......
			....	....	.....	......	......

Page 2

```
                        NEW DAY BAHA'I SCHOOL
                        GOODS REQUIRED

Number of guests : ..........    Week ID : ..............

                                            |< Quantity >|<-Price-->|
Day  Meal time  ID       Food               Reqr'd  Bought Unit Total
--------------------------------------------------------------------

6. Breakfast  ...... ..................... ....  .....  ...... ......
                     ..................... ....  .....  ...... ......
                     ..................... ....  .....  ...... ......
   Lunch      ...... ..................... ....  .....  ...... ......
                     ..................... ....  .....  ...... ......
                     ..................... ....  .....  ...... ......
   Dinner     ...... ..................... ....  .....  ...... ......
                     ..................... ....  .....  ...... ......
                     ..................... ....  .....  ...... ......
   Snack      ...... ..................... ....  .....  ...... ......
                     ..................... ....  .....  ...... ......
                     ..................... ....  .....  ...... ......

                              Page 3
```

REPORT 7.6 Food Requirement Report

Finally, you add the food expenses and the number of guests served for each session and enter these numbers into the system for accounting. SCREEN 7.13 is an example of a screen used to post the food expenses. In addition, it requires a posting date, week number, and comments if necessary.

```
                    NEW DAY BAHA'I SCHOOL

                    ENTER FOOD EXPENSES

Week Number : ..........    Comment : .........................


Guests Expected : ...............   Cost of food : $ .........

              MMDDYY
Date entered : ......

<---------------- FUNCTIONS >--------------------->
F1 - SELECT  F2 - NEXT     F3 - PREVIOUS  F4 - INSERT
F5 - UPDATE  F6 - DELETE   F7 - EXIT TO KITCHEN MENU
```

SCREEN 7.13 Interface to Enter Food Expenses

Then print a list, such as REPORT 7.7.

```
                    NEW DAY  BAHA'I SCHOOL

FOOD EXPENSES         DATE : ..............

FROM : .........    TO :  ...........

WEEK # OF     COST OF     DATE      COMMENT
NUM  GUESTS    FOOD
-------!-------!----------!---------!----------------------

 ...... ...... $.........  ........  .........................
 ...... ...... $.........  ........  .........................
 ...... ...... $.........  ........  .........................
 ...... ...... $.........  ........  .........................
 ...... ...... $.........  ........  .........................
 ...... ...... $.........  ........  .........................
 ...... ...... $.........  ........  .........................
 ...... ...... $.........  ........  .........................

 TOTALS ...... $........
```

REPORT 7.7 Food Expense Report

7.5 INVENTORY CONTROL

In many Baha'i schools, sales of books and other materials are very much a part of the usual business. This discussion of inventory control not only covers regular stock but also handles consignments, both outgoing and incoming. Here, our task is to define the requirements in the following three areas:

1. Regular stock material,
2. Consignment received,
3. Outgoing consignments of material.

Before delving into more details, let's explain the two kinds of consignments. The incoming consignment consists of materials given by an individual or institution of the Faith and to be sold at the school. Usually an agreement between the supplier and the school dictates the terms, for example: the profit margin, the time after which unsold goods are returned, and so on. On the other hand, the outgoing consignment is a package of material the school lends an individual or institution, which they then sell for the school. The regular stock consists of books and materials made by the school.

Considering this scope, we derive a list of tasks that an integrated inventory control system should have, and they are as follows:

1. Inventory maintenance,
2. Supplier information,
3. Transfer of goods,
4. Purchase of goods,
5. Print purchase orders,
6. Consignment (outgoing),
7. Print consignment orders,
8. Enter sales of goods,
9. Transaction reports,
10. Stock report,
11. Consignment (incoming).

DATA BASE

Among all the sections of the school management system we have looked at, the inventory control needs the largest amount of files. The most important one is the inventory file called "INVENTO." TABLE 7.9 gives a detailed description of each field.

File name: INVENTO - Inventory master file

Field Name	Description	Data type	length
stock_code	stock code of a material in inventory	character	10
description	description of material or title of a book	character	30
binding	binding of a book e.g. cloth, paper back, etc	character	10
language	language of a book	character	10
location	location where stock is stored	character	10
cost	cost price of material	dollar	
retail	retail price of material	dollar	
q_on_hand	quantity on hand at a particular location or quantity received as consignment	integer	
q_on_order	quantity on order or quantity sold as consignment	integer	
q_back_order	quantity on back order	integer	
consignment	is this item on consignment ? y - yes n - no	character	1
consign_from	place from where consignment is received	character	30

TABLE 7.9 Record of File INVENTO

In this system there are many warehouse locations, some within the school premises, others destination for materials to be sold on consignment. Obviously, we have to track all the transfers. The file to store these data is "TRANSFER," as shown in TABLE 7.10. Note that each item of a consignment order occupies one record.

File name: TRANSFER - File to store transfers and consignments

Field Name	Description	Data type	length
stock_code	stock number of a material or book	character	10
description	description of a material or book	character	20
from_location	the source location of transfer	character	10
to_location	the destination location of transfer	character	10
quantity	quantity transferred	integer	
type	type of transfer c - consignment r - regular stock	character	1
consign_num	ID number of consignment	character	10
consign_name	name of the place where consignment is going to	character	30

TABLE 7.10 Record of File TRANSFER

Also, we want to process all the purchasing for the school store. The file for this is called "PURCHASE." Each item of a purchase order needs one record, as described in TABLE 7.11.

Finally, we store the sales data in file "SALES." As shown in TABLE 7.12, the fields serve many purposes. In addition to keeping a record of sales during a given period of time, its data are used for sales analysis, to calculate cost of goods, and show profit margin.

File name: PURCHASE - File to store purchase orders

Field Name	Description	Data type	length
po_number	purchase order number	character	10
date	processing date	date	
amount	total amount for the order	dollar	
supplier_num	code number of the supplier	character	10
supplier_name	name of the supplier	character	30
product_code	product code of supplier	character	10
stock_code	the stock number of the material	character	10
description	description of the material ordered	character	10
binding	binding if it is a book	character	10
language	language if it is a book	character	10
q_ordered	quantity ordered	integer	
q_received	quantity received for this order	integer	
q_bo	quantity on back order	integer	
retail	retail price of the item	dollar	
cost	cost price of each item	dollar	
total	total amount of each item	dollar	

TABLE 7.11 Record of File PURCHASE

File name: SALES - File to store sales data

Field Name	Description	Data type	length
batch	batch of posting	character	5
type	type of sales 1 - consignment 2 - store	integer	
date	date of sales	date	
stock_code	stock code of material or book	character	10
description	description of material or title of book	character	30
quantity	quantity sold	integer	
price_retail	unit retail price	dollar	
price_cost	unit cost price	dollar	
amount	total sale amount	dollar	

TABLE 7.12 Record of File SALES

DESIGN

In the inventory, the design of all the screen interfaces, menus, or tools to manage a data base are perhaps more complicated and therefore more interesting. In this section, we will not only discuss the screen formats and reports, but also offer some ideas and logical steps (algorithms) to make any inventory control operation more fruitful. SCREEN 7.14 , the inventory control menu, provides a selection of tasks.

```
             NEW DAY BAHA'I SCHOOL

             INVENTORY CONTROL

     1 - Inventory Maintenance
     2 - Supplier Information
     3 - Transfer of Goods
     4 - Purchase Orders
     5 - Print Purchase Orders
     6 - Consignment (Outgoing)
     7 - Print Consignment Orders
     8 - Enter Sales of Goods          ......................
     9 - Transaction Reports ------->| Sales/Cost of Goods  |
                                     | Consignments         |
                                     | Back Orders          |
                                     | Transfer of Goods    |
                                     |......................|
     10 - Stock Report
     11 - Consignment (Incoming)
     12 - EXIT TO MAIN MENU
```

SCREEN 7.14 Interface to Select Inventory Control Tasks

INVENTORY MAINTENANCE: SCREEN 7.15 is the inventory maintenance menu. Along with the functions, the format is divided into categories such as quantity, consignment, warehouse location, and prices and descriptions of stock items. With a little creativity, we can make the stock code and warehouse location work in our favor. The location is unique but the code is not, for it is possible to have items at more than one location. First, choose the stock code so that it reflects a variety of things such as language in which the book is written, materials made in-house or consignment stock from another source. For example, "HPI0022" can mean a Hispanic book published in-house, while "CDS222" could be a consignment item from the distribution service.

```
                    NEW DAY BAHA'I SCHOOL

                    INVENTORY CONTROL

Stock code : ........ Description : .........................
Binding :  .......... Language    : ..................

|<--  PRICES   --->|  |<--------       WAREHOUSE      ----------->|

Cost   : $ ........    No. : ....... Locations : .................
Retail : $ ........

|<-- QUANTITY ---->|  |<--------      CONSIGNMENT     ----------->|

On hand    : ........  (Y/N) : ......
On Order   : ........  From  : ................................
Back Order : ........

<-------------------- FUNCTION ------------------->
F1 - SELECT  F2 - NEXT    F3 - PREVIOUS  F4 - INSERT
F5 - UPDATE  F6 - DELETE  F7 - EXIT TO INVENTORY MENU
```

SCREEN 7.15 Interface for Inventory Maintenance

SUPPLIER INFORMATION: As the supplier information has already been discussed in the section covering the special mailing list, use the same screen interface for choosing item 2 of the inventory control menu.

TRANSFER OF GOODS: The user interface to process a transfer of goods looks like SCREEN 7.16, which shows the stock code and destination of the transfered goods. In addition, it has the date of transfer, quantity, and a choice of flags to delineate whether goods are consignment or regular stock. Note, we can process only one transfer at a time.

```
                    NEW DAY BAHA'I SCHOOL


                    TRANSFER OF GOODS

Stock code  : ........                 |<--  Warehouse    ---->|

Description : ........................ From : .....  To : ......

      MMDDYY                     .....................
Date : ......      Type : . -->| C - Consignment     |
                               | R - Regular stock   |
                               |.....................|
Comment : ...........................       Quantity : ...

<--------------------- FUNCTIONS --------------------------->
F1 - SELECT  F2 - NEXT     F3 - PREVIOUS  F4 - PROCESS TRANSFERS
F5 - UPDATE  F6 - DELETE   F7 - EXIT TO INVENTORY MENU
```

SCREEN 7.16 Interface to Process Transfers

Now, let's look at the procedure for moving stock from one place in the computer system to another.

The steps are:

1. Check if the stock exists in the inventory file. If it does not, warn the operator and do not proceed.

2. Check if a record exists for source and destination locations. If not, warn the operator and do not proceed.

3. Press key F4 to process the transfer. This will take the following steps: It will adjust the quantities in both source and destination stock of INVENTO file, and place a record in TRANSFER file.

4. Continue with the transfer or exit.

Note, similar verification of stock items in the file will be done in many of the screens discussed later.

PURCHASE ORDER: To create a purchase order, the operator uses SCREEN 7.17. It has a unique purchase order number, the date, and the total amount of the order. In addition, the supplier information such as number, name, and product code if necessary can be entered. After following these steps, the stock code and destination of the item, and other data such as quantity ordered, prices (retail and cost) and amount will be recorded.

```
                    NEW DAY BAHA'I SCHOOL


                    PURCHASE ORDER

                                 MMDDYY
PO Number : .......  Date : ......   Total Amount : $ .........


|<-------     SUPPLIER INFORMATION     ------------->|

Number : .........    Name : ...................................
Product code : .........



Stock code : .......   Description : ...........................

Language : .................Binding : ............

|<----------     Quantities      -------------->|
Ordered : ......    Received : .......  B/O : ........

|<----------                 Prices                    --------->|

Retail : $ ........   Cost  : $ .........     Amount : $ ........

<-------------------- FUNCTION ------------------->
F1 - SELECT  F2 - NEXT     F3 - PREVIOUS  F4 - INSERT
F5 - UPDATE  F6 - DELETE   F7 - EXIT TO INVENTORY MENU
```

SCREEN 7.17 Interface to Process Purchase Order

Using this screen, you can add as many items as the order requires. When the goods arrive the same interface is used to call the purchase order and fill in the quantity received. If necessary, you can also fill the back order quantity and change the prices.

Any purchase order can be printed according to a number. When finished it will look like REPORT 7.8.

```
                    NEW DAY BAHA'I SCHOOL


FROM :  ..........................    TO: .........................
        ..........................        .........................
        ..........................        .........................
        ..........................        .........................
        ..........................        .........................

-------------------------------------------------------------------
DATE : ..........          |       P/O : .............
-------------------------------------------------------------------

 STOCK         DESCRIPTION        ORDERED     PRICE        AMOUNT
 CODE

 .......  .....................    .....   $ .......   $ ........
 .......  .....................    .....   $ .......   $ ........
 .......  .....................    .....   $ .......   $ ........
 .......  .....................    .....   $ .......   $ ........
 .......  .....................    .....   $ .......   $ ........
 .......  .....................    .....   $ .......   $ ........

                                    TOTAL ----------->  $ ........
```

REPORT 7.8 Purchase Order Report

CONSIGNMENT (OUTGOING): The next step is to process goods that are sent out on consignment. Until they are sold they are considered property of the school that is stored outside the school premises. This is similar to a transfer of goods, discussed earlier, except that with each unique consignment number there are one or more items packaged together. To do this, use SCREEN 7.18. Note that through key F7 the user enters the returned quantity.

```
                      NEW DAY BAHA'I SCHOOL

                      CONSIGNMENT (OUTGOING)

Consignment number : ........   Name : ......................

        MMDDYY
Date :  ......

|<------ WAREHOUSE   LOCATION-------->|

From : ........      TO : ........

Stock code    Description                     Quantity Returned

 .........    ..............................  .....    .....



<------------------- FUNCTIONS ------------------->
F1 - SELECT  F2 - NEXT     F3 - PREVIOUS  F4 - INSERT
F5 - UPDATE  F6 - DELETE   F7 - RETURNED
F8 - EXIT TO INVENTORY MENU
```

SCREEN 7.18 Interface to Process Consignment (Outgoing)

After preparing a consignment order, the operator prints it. It will look like REPORT 7.9.

```
                      NEW DAY BAHA'I SCHOOL

                   CONSIGNMENT ORDER (OUTGOING)


From :  ......................    To : ......................
        ......................         ......................
        ......................         ......................
        ......................         ......................

-------------------------------------------------------------
Date : .........    Consignment No. : ................
-------------------------------------------------------------

 Stock        Description         Quantity    Price      Amount
 Code

 ......   .....................   ......  $ ........ $ .........
 ......   .....................   ......  $ ........ $ .........
 ......   .....................   ......  $ ........ $ .........
 ......   .....................   ......  $ ........ $ .........
 ......   .....................   ......  $ ........ $ .........
 ......   .....................   ......  $ ........ $ .........

                        TOTALS ---->  .......    $ .........
```

REPORT 7.9 Consignment Order

SALES: A sale, either through the store or on consignment, is posted by the system using the SCREEN 7.19. It has a field to enter a code for a batch of sales. Function key F7 pulls the location, description, and prices from the inventory file of a given stockcode. This will speed up this process by not having to type this information. Also, functions such as INSERT, UPDATE, or DELETE must be used to adjust the quantities in the INVENTO file.

```
                    NEW DAY BAHA'I SCHOOL

                    POST SALES

Batch :.........
Type  : .. 1 - consignment (outgoing)    Date : .............
           2 - store             Consignment # : .........

-------------------------------------------------------------------
 STOCK LOCATION DESCRIPTION       QUANTITY |<-     PRICES        ->|
 CODE                                      COST    RETAIL     AMOUNT

 ....... ...... ................ ..... ....... ....... ..........


<-------------------- FUNCTIONS ---------------------------->
F1 - SELECT F2 - NEXT F3 - PREVIOUS F4 - INSERT F5 - UPDATE
F6 - DELETE F7 - PULL STOCK INFO.   F8 - EXIT TO INVENTORY MENU
```

SCREEN 7.19 Interface to Enter Sales

STOCK: To print the stock transaction report, make the choices, such as date and type, shown on SCREEN 7.20.

```
                    NEW DAY BAHA'I SCHOOL

                    INVENTORY TRANSACTION REPORTS

Date  from : ..............
        to : ..............


                      Choices : .....

                                   1 - All
                                   2 - Consignment/Transfer
                                   3 - Purchase orders
                                   4 - Sales
                                   5 - EXIT to INVENTORY MENU
```

SCREEN 7.20 Interface to Select Inventory Transaction

In REPORT 7.10, quantity applies to all three categories, while type shows whether it is on consignment or regular stock.

```
                        NEW DAY BAHA'I SCHOOL

                  STOCK TRANSACTION REPORT  DATE : ..........


STOCK DESCRIP-  DATE  TYPE  QUNT'Y <CONSIGNMENT      |<--  SALES    -->|
CODE  TION                         TRANSFER  <PURCHASES>
                                   FROM TO    P/O  B/O RETAIL COST  AMOUNT

 ..... ........ ..... .... ..... ...   ...   .... ....$......$.....$.....
 ..... ........ ..... .... ..... ...   ...   .... ....$......$.....$.....
 ..... ........ ..... .... ..... ...   ...   .... ....$......$.....$.....
 ..... ........ ..... .... ..... ...   ...   .... ....$......$.....$.....
 ..... ........ ..... .... ..... ...   ...   .... ....$......$.....$.....
 ..... ........ ..... .... ..... ...   ...   .... ....$......$.....$.....

                              TOTALS------------>   $......$.....$.....
```

REPORT 7.10 Transaction Report

At any given time, REPORT 7.11 gives the status of each item in stock. It gives the quantity in stock and the amounts ordered and on back order. In addition to prices (cost and retail), it lists the warehouse location.

```
                        NEW DAY BAHA'I SCHOOL

                          STOCK REPORT         DATE: ..........

STOCK   DESCRIPTION  LOC BINDING      COST               |< QUANTITY >|
CODE                      LANGUAGE            RETAIL    O/H  O/O  B/O

 ..... ............ ...  .... ....  ........ ......... .... .... ....
 ..... ............ ...  .... ....  ........ ......... .... .... ....
 ..... ............ ...  .... ....  ........ ......... .... .... ....
 ..... ............ ...  .... ....  ........ ......... .... .... ....
 ..... ............ ...  .... ....  ........ ......... .... .... ....

                             Page 1
```

REPORT 7.11 Stock Report

CONSIGNMENT (INCOMING): Finally, we have an account of all goods received on consignment. SCREEN 7.21 is a selection menu.

```
                    NEW DAY BAHA'I SCHOOL

                    CONSIGNMENT FROM OUTSIDE


        1 - Enter all consignments
        2 - Enter Sales
        3 - Print report
        4 - EXIT TO INVENTORY MENU
```

SCREEN 7.21 Interface to Select Consignment (Incoming) Tasks

You can enter information about each item through SCREEN 7.22. The information goes to the INVENTO file. Note that in defining the record for the INVENTO file, there are two fields (consign_num and consign_name) for consignment items from other sources.

To enter the quantity sold, recall all the records belonging to a consignment order and make an update after entering the quantity. At any time REPORT 7.12 will show all items on consignment along with the quantities received and sold. This concludes the inventory control computer system.

```
                    NEW DAY BAHA'I SCHOOL

                   ENTER CONSIGNMENT

From : ..............            Date : ............



STOCK   DESCRIPTION       COST    RETAIL |<     QUANTITY     >|
CODE                                      RECV.   SOLD    DIFF.


 ......  ................. $.....  $.....  .....   .....   ......

<------------------- FUNCTIONS ------------------->
F1 - SELECT  F2 - NEXT     F3 - PREVIOUS  F4 - INSERT
F5 - UPDATE  F6 - DELETE   F7 - EXIT TO INVENTORY MENU
```

SCREEN 7.22 Interface to Process Consignment

```
                    NEW DAY BAHA'I SCHOOL

               PRINT CONSIGNMENT REPORT        DATE : .........


SRCE.  STOCK  DESCRIPTION       COST    RETAIL        |< QUANTITY    >|
       CODE                                   AMOUNT  RECV. SOLD DIFF.


....  ......  .................$..... $.....$.....    .... .... .....
....  ......  .................$..... $.....$.....    .... .... .....
....  ......  .................$..... $.....$.....    .... .... .....
....  ......  .................$..... $.....$.....    .... .... .....


                      TOTAL AMOUNT ----> $ .......
```

REPORT 7.12 Consignment Report

7.6 ACCOUNTING/FINANCIAL REPORT

The level accounting, discussed in this chapter, is restricted to only general ledger and financial report. These allow the accounting staff to make entries to any account. The postings are grouped according to batches and specified periods (months) of the year. One or more batches are printed to balance the accounts or correct any mistakes. Also, a summary of each account gives the total credit or debit for a selected range of periods. Finally, from the accounts stored in the system, various financial reports can be generated.

DATA BASE

Since we are interested only in the transactions of general ledger accounts, two files will suffice. One is the account master file, called "GLMAST," as shown in TABLE 7.13.

File name: GLMAST - General ledger master file

Field Name	Description	Data type	Length
gl_number	general ledger account number	integer	
gl_name	the description of the account	character	30
gl_type	type of account 1 - revenue 2 - expenses 3 - asset	integer	
gl_balance	the current balance of the account	dollar	
glper1	balance of period 1	dollar	
glper2	balance of period 2	dollar	
glper3	balance of period 3	dollar	
glper4	balance of period 4	dollar	
glper5	balance of period 5	dollar	
glper6	balance of period 6	dollar	
glper7	balance of period 7	dollar	
glper8	balance of period 8	dollar	
glper9	balance of period 9	dollar	
glper10	balance of period 10	dollar	
glper11	balance of period 11	dollar	
glper12	balance of period 12	dollar	
glclose	year-end closing balance	dollar	

TABLE 7.13 Record of File GLMAST

The other file called "GLTRAN," contains only transactions of all the accounts. It is described in TABLE 7.14.

File name: GLTRAN - General ledger transaction file

Field Name	Description	Data type	Length
p_date	posting date of transaction	date	
period	period of transaction	integer	
entry	journal entry number	integer	
flag	credit or debit 1 - credit 2 - debit	integer	
note	any particulars about a transaction	character	30
gl_number	the general number to which transaction is posted	integer	

TABLE 7.14 Record of File GLTRAN

DESIGN

Let's start a discussion of the design of the accounting and financial reports program by first considering SCREEN 7.23. It lists all the tasks necessary to print financial reports.

```
                    NEW DAY BAHA'I SCHOOL

                    GENERAL LEDGER  MENU

    1 - Account Maintenance
    2 - Post to G/L accounts
    3 - Print G/L Entry
    4 - Summary of Accounts
    5 - Financial Report
    6 - EXIT TO MAIN MENU
```

SCREEN 7.23 Account Task Menu

We need an interface screen to maintain the master file (GLMAST) of each account. It looks like SCREEN 7.24.

```
                          NEW DAY BAHA'I SCHOOL

ACCOUNT MAINTENANCE

G/L Number : ........ Name: ...............................
Type :  .. ( 1 - Revenue, 2 - Expenses, 3 - Asset )

Current Balance        : $ ............
Last year-end Balance  : $ ............

Balance by period :

1. $ .................              7.$ ......................
2. $ .................              8.$ ......................
3. $ .................              9.$ ......................
4. $ .................             10.$ ......................
5. $ .................             11.$ ......................
6. $ .................             12.$ ......................

<----------------- FUNCTIONS ------------------->
F1 - SELECT  F2 - NEXT     F3 - PREVIOUS  F4 - INSERT
F5 - UPDATE  F6 - DELETE   F7 - EXIT TO G/L MENU
```

SCREEN 7.24 Interface to Maintain G/L Account Data

Transactions are posted to any account, already entered into the master file using SCREEN 7.25. A group of transactions is given an entry number and the total debit and credit amounts should be verified before posting, as this program does not do such verification automatically. However, if you desire, you can add this feature to your particular design.

```
                    NEW DAY BAHA'I SCHOOL

                    POSTING


Entry : .......   Period : ........    Date : .......

      Amount to post : $ ........

Account      Name                    Debit     Credit

 .......   ........................  .......   .........


<------------------- FUNCTIONS ----------------------->
F1 - SELECT   F2 - NEXT     F3 - PREVIOUS     F4 - INSERT
F5 - UPDATE   F6 - DELETE   F7 - GET ACCOUNT NAME
F8 - EXIT TO G/L MENU
```

SCREEN 7.25 Interface to Enter Account Transactions

After entering the account number, press key F7 to show the name of the account by retrieving it from the master file. After checking the type the system moves the cursor to either the debit or credit position. However, the user has the choice of entering a debit or credit amount regardless of the type. By pressing function key F4, the information goes to the GLTRAN file and the closing and period amounts of selected accounts are updated in the GLMAST file.

Another program extracts the entry data from GLTRAN and prints a journal according to a range of entry or period. An example of the printout by entries is given in REPORT 7.13.

```
                    NEW DAY BAHA'I SCHOOL

     G/L ENTRY JOURNAL          DATE : ..........


Entry   Period Date     Account    Name         Debit   Credit

 .....  ..... .......  ......  .............  ......  ......
        ..... .......  ......  .............  ......  ......
        ..... .......  ......  .............  ......  ......

                      TOTALS --------->       ......  ......

 .....  ..... .......  ......  .............  ......  ......
        ..... .......  ......  .............  ......  ......
        ..... .......  ......  .............  ......  ......

                      TOTALS --------->       ......  ......

                GRAND TOTALS --------->       ......  ......
```

REPORT 7.13 Journal Entry Report

REPORT 7.14 shows a format for a summary of accounts. For one or more accounts, the operator chooses a specified period (1 to 12) and the program prints out the total debit or credit amount for that period. It also gives the closing balance for each period. For this report, the data come from file GLMAST.

```
                      NEW DAY BAHA'I SCHOOL

            SUMMARY OF ACCOUNTS     DATE : .........

FROM PERIOD : ....    TO PERIOD : ....

PERIOD      ACCOUNT       NAME                     DEBIT     CREDIT

 ......   .......... ......................  .......   .......
          .......... ......................  .......   .......
          .......... ......................  .......   .......
          .......... ......................  .......   .......
          .......... ......................  .......   .......

                          TOTALS  ------>    .......   .......

 ......   .......... ......................  .......   .......
          .......... ......................  .......   .......
          .......... ......................  .......   .......
          .......... ......................  .......   .......
          .......... ......................  .......   .......

                          TOTALS  ------>    .......   .......

                    GRAND TOTALS  ------>    .......   .......

                    PAGE 1
```

REPORT 7.14 Summary of Accounts Transactions

FINANCIAL STATEMENT

Finally, we print the financial report .

New Day Baha'i School

BALANCE SHEET FOR THE PERIOD ENDING November 1987

ACCOUNT TITLE	ACTUAL	LAST YEAR	%
ASSETS			
ACCOUNTS RECEIVABLES	550.00-		
PETTY CASH	492.00		
CURRENT BANK ACCOUNT	4,699.00		
PAYROLL BANK ACCOUNT	50,000.00		
BANK	2,260.00		
SERVICE CHARGES	1,758.78		
INVENTORY GDS IN HAND	20,000.00		
MACHINERY & EQUIPMENT	34,000.00		
OFFICE EQUIPMENT	4,000.00		
TOTAL ASSET ---------->	116,659.98		
LIABILITIES			
BANK LOAN PAYABLE	1,215.16		
ACCOUNTS PAYABLE	3,568.38		
TOTAL LIABILITIES	4,783.54		
SALARY & WAGES			
SALARY & WAGES PAYABLE	5,500.78		
TOTAL SALARY & WAGES	5,500.78		
TAXES PAYABLE			
FEDERAL TAXES	982.75		
TOTAL TAXES PAYABLE	982.75		
TOTAL LIABILITY	105,393.69-		

REPORT 7.15 Financial Report

CHAPTER EIGTH

TELECOMMUNICATIONS AND COMPUTERS

In Chapter 1, we saw a parallel between the growth of the Baha'i Faith and the development of telecommunication's--both born on the same day (May 23, 1844) in opposite hemispheres of the globe. Abdu'l- Baha and Shoghi Effendi used telegrams extensively during their ministries to convey messages and directives to friends throughout the world. Currently, Baha'i Centers in Haifa and throughout the planet, routinely use the most modern communication technology such as E-MAIL, telegrams and Telex to transfer information.

The administrative structure of the Baha'i Faith, with a World Center as well as national and local administrative bodies spread throughout the world, is indeed a global organization, tied together to form an extensive network. To maintain a healthy operation at all three levels of administration requires an uninterrupted flow of both incoming and outgoing information. For instance, at the World Center the staff constantly sends out mail in the form of documents to hundreds of national centers, individuals, agencies, and pioneers. In return, the staff gets feedback from many of these recipients that is vital to their work at the World Center. At the national level, similar mail flow exists from any national center to local assemblies (thousands in some cases), to committees, and to other parts of the world. Similarly, among the institutions associated with the International Teaching Center, it is vital that reports and memos are promptly delivered to promote and protect the Cause of God. Imagine the traffic of mail at all these different levels of Baha'i institutions. As the Faith expands, the volume of information transfer will likely grow.

Our traditional mail system is adequate only if the delivery of information is not time sensitive. But if messages or information have to reach their destination within a day or an hour, then this system is not fast enough. This type of situation is not unusual, and in fact is becoming increasingly common as the Baha'i Faith grows in numbers and complexity.

To demonstrate a different kind of delivery system, here are two scenarios. Imagine the Baha'i Publishing Trust of India has just published a book, and is ready to advertise it throughout the world. At its disposal is an electronic mail system with a list of all the national distribution services and other agencies. To promote this book it prepares an information sheet, and sends a copy to all the members of a distribution list, using the electronic mail (E-MAIL). Within minutes this information reaches every single member, and within a day or less the Baha'i Publishing Trust of India starts receiving orders for this book from all over the world.

Let's take a different situation. On the continent of Africa there is a major economic development project. Experts in this field are invited from different parts of the world: China, Australia, South America, and Finland, where a similar project has succeeded. After a few days of consultation, these experts return to their respective countries. But the work continues while using a computer conferencing system. With this communication tool, every member of the team is informed about the most current development of the project. Everyone participates by making comments and suggestions and is kept aware of contributions from other members. Among many benefits, problem solving happens through timely consultation among members scattered throughout different continents.

These two examples may sound like futuristic fables but, in fact they are not. Both of these technologies, the electronic mail system (EMS) and computer based conferencing (CBC), have existed for many years and are used extensively to enhance communication in engineering, agriculture, medicine, corporate management, sales, and so on. Many worldwide corporations have their own communications network, connecting people in many places, while many others buy such services from public companies.

In this chapter, we will discuss four services: bulletin boards, electronic mail, computer conferencing, and data bases (data banks). All of them are products that combine computers with modern communication to provide on-line services. We'll describe the functions of these services and will also suggest applications relevant to the growth and expansion in the Baha'i Faith.

8.1 ON-LINE

Before going any further, let's explain what on-line is. It is one of the most common "buzz words" among computer users. Simply put, it means interacting with any computer through a terminal or microcomputer, in order to use its facilities. In some cases, the computer is nearby and therefore the connection can be direct, while in other instances it may be some distance away, requiring telephone lines, or other kinds of connection.

But, in cases of EMS, CBC, or data bases, the computer is located far away from the user, perhaps in another city, country, or continent. If you go "on-line" to such computer services using a normal telephone line, the expense can be astronomical, especially if one must go across an ocean. To avoid such high-cost activity, there are communications networks. In most cases, they provide a local phone number to their users, amounting to a negligible phone charge (if any), and you can connect to mail, conferencing, or any other on-line services.

To illustrate communications networks, Figure 8.1 shows a simple diagram where network "A" is linked to three commercial services on two continents, each having different kinds of on-line capabilities. While in another continent, the user can, through a local telephone call, participate in any of these services. Here, the user is in Israel and is able to connect to on-line services in Sweden, the United States, and Canada through network "A." There are many such networks worldwide, some serving as many as forty-five countries. A few are listed in Figure 8.2.

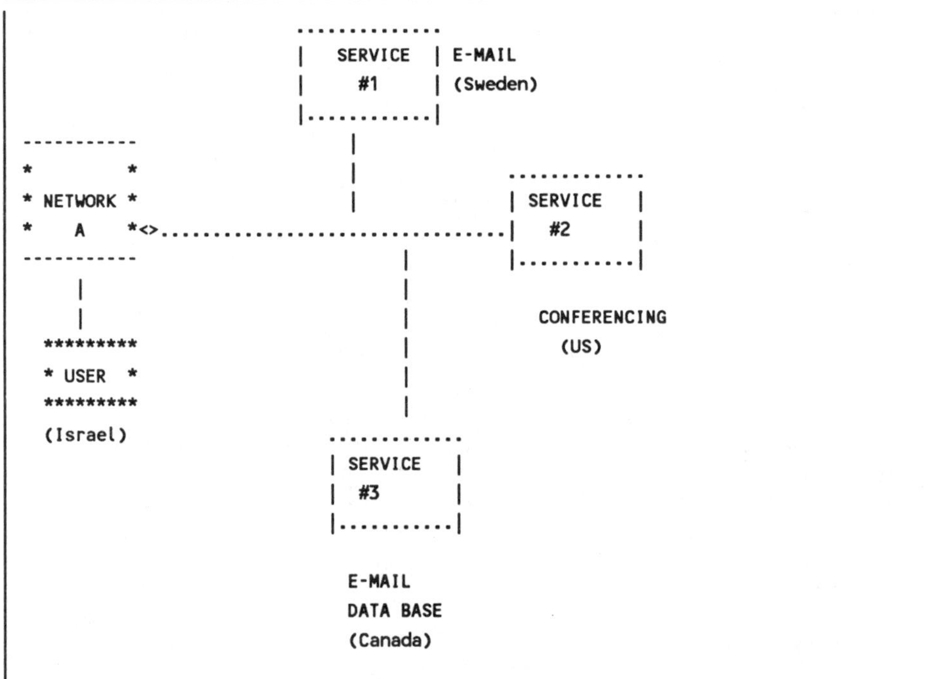

Figure 8.1 Data Communications Network

Many on-line services, for instance, MCI Mail, Compuserve, and Western Union, have their own network. To access their services, they allow users to go through their own network or other commercial systems. Each public network is linked to a selected number of messaging and/or data base computers, so therefore they are restricted within a country or continent. But, if a user wants to access a service outside a region of the network, it is sometimes possible to do so by using a gateway. A gateway, as shown in Figure 8.3, serves as a switching post to connect a user to several networks. In this example, Network 1 is in South America, and Network 2 is in Australia. A user in Europe can access any of these networks through a gateway. This gateway makes E-MAIL, computer conferencing, and data bases truly international, and heightens possibilities of accessing far distant data bases or communicating with any subscriber.

Name	Country	Telephone
Tymnet	US	1-800-336-0149
Telenet	US	1-800-336-0437
Datapac	Canada	N/A
UNINET	US	N/A
Dialnet	England	N/A

Figure 8.2 List of Networks

One gigantic network is Porta/COM, a Swedish network and vendor of on-line services. Its reach is so extensive that it is possible to connect through it to any on-line subscriber in the world. It acts as a gateway to many worldwide computer mail and conferencing systems, or any data bases.

```
          conference
data base     *                                           data base
  *                                   e-mail                *
     (Network 1)   e-mail              *
                    *                         (Network 2)    * e-mail
      *    ------------------------------
     e-mail                 |                   *
     conference             |                 e-mail
                            |
  ( South America )         |                ( Australia )
                            |
                            |
                      --------------
                      * GATEWAY  1 *
                      --------------
                            |
                      **************
                      *   USER     *
                      **************
                        ( Europe )
```

Figure 8.3 Data Communication Gateway

8.2 COMPUTER BULLETIN BOARD SYSTEM

A short history will help us appreciate the life and development of the computer bulletin board system (CBBS). During the early days of personal computers (mid 1970s), a desire to share ideas, programs, and text grew among users by using ordinary telephone lines and MODEM (computer communications equipment). Such data communication was not new, as it was routinely done in time-sharing mainframe computers. However, the early microcomputer users discovered that a protocol was required, to transmit or receive data without losing any pieces. A protocol is information associated with each transfer of data which checks if the data have arrived at their destination in the original form. It is like a packing slip with an order you receive from a store. It tells you exactly what was shipped, and if the slip does not match with the items in the package, then the appropriate action can be taken. In data transfer, the receiving party sends an acknowledgment to indicate whether the data are good or bad. In case of a bad transfer, the sender transmits another copy of the information. A particular protocol was used in a program called "MODEM" (an unwise choice of program name as a standard piece of equipment has the same name), which later became very popular and went through several stages of revision.

Several computer hobbyists joined forces to improve this MODEM program, which could transfer files only from one point to another. The next step was to produce another program with functions that could work like a message system or bulletin board. This allowed callers using MODEM (or improved versions) to access this computer-based bulletin board and leave messages for other callers. Soon both the idea of computer messaging and the protocol used in MODEM became well-known among computer hobbyists, and this lead to new developments and improvements of CBBS functions. It was possible not only to post and remove bulletins but also to leave a copy of programs for anyone to use. These programs are known as public domain software. User clubs for computers such as Atari, Commodore, IBM-PC, Apple, and others set up their own CBBS to help their members exchange ideas, problems, or solutions related to hardware or software.

It took the devotion of many computer afficionados to develope and install the new CBBS. Currently, there are about 500 to 600 installed across the North American continent. New ones are constantly emerging, replacing old ones. The lifetime of a board can be a few hours or it can last many months. During the last few years, CBBS has become popular among different kinds of computer users, and apparently it appeals to many because it hides the real identity of the user. The age, color, or sex of the operator is not obvious unless one volunteers such information.

When we look at the current CBBS, it has developed over a short period of time, and today it has far more sophisticated functions. Also, its expanded use extends far beyond the hobbyists. It is used at radio stations to receive requests for songs; at service stations, allowing workers to retrieve messages at the office after working hours; at mail order outlets to place orders; and in many more contexts. Also, there are many specialized boards that serve church goers and dating services, agriculturists and psychologists alike.

In earlier chapters, we mentioned uses of CBBS such as in placing book orders with National Centers as well as establishing a teaching network. To use one is easy, but it is definitely involved if you want to operate one. In this section, we'll first look in more detail at some of the recent capabilities added to CBBS and will also discuss more uses for CBBS for the Baha'i Faith. Then we'll describe some of the important tasks of a bulletin board operator (sometimes called "SYSOP"). This will give any prospective SYSOP a good idea whether or not committing to such a task would be advisable.

FUNCTIONS

With all the latest development in the CBBS software, the most outstanding improvement has probably been in the area of automation. You can have one operating in a corner of a room during all hours of the day or night. During this time, it can answer many calls; it can transfer and receive numerous files, programs, messages, and memos; and it can accommodate many protocols and transmission speeds.

Since the first CBBS, the MODEM, operators have used many protocols to transmit and receive data safely. KERMIT, CIS (CompuServe), and XON/OFF are a few of these. Some CBBS programs provide one or more of these protocols. Therefore, as a user, you need one compatible protocol to connect to a bulletin board system.

Usually, the functions are either to benefit the user or to make maintenance easier for the SYSOP. First let's look at the capabilities available to the user. We should keep in mind that in both cases functions vary from one product to next; however, we will give some of the most common and useful ones. Once a CBBS is up and running, it has a MODEM to answer telephone calls of the user automatically. Many of these MODEMs with answer mode work on various speeds, namely, 300, 1,200 and 2,400 baud (bits per second), and they also have the "intelligence" to detect the speed of the incoming signal and to adjust their own baud rate. If it is an open system, the user can enter anywhere permissible in the bulletin board, then browse, download, or post any message. However, there are others that are closed, requiring therefore that each user have some form of identification to log in to the bulletin board. In its files, it has an index of all the users and when a caller comes on-line, it verifies the name and password. Also, it allows the SYSOP to maintain the information about all the users.

In some of these closed systems, the built-in security can be quite complex. Therefore, the CBBS program allows privileged users to see the user ID or password, both of which can be given, taken away, or changed by the SYSOP. It's a good way of controlling access to information.

Also, many who log-in to a CBBS as a member of a computer club or interest group routinely receive newsletters, and messages, or post comments and notes for other users. If a system supports mailbox, then you would examine your box and perhaps read the messages. Also, you can post private mail in any user's box. If the SYSOP is around, you can also directly communicate with him/her. Or, you can leave a note in case SYSOP is not on-line.

The SYSOP has control over the activities of any user. The CBBS comes with the facility to maintain user's information such as the ID, password, and privileges to view information. The sophisticated program keeps a record of the activity of every caller. It keeps track of the time logged as well as sending messages or browsing any other posted information.

In most computer bulletin boards, only one user can connect at a time. It is possible that a user is overly interested in a session and will spend a long time on the board, preventing any one else from accessing it. To avoid such a situation, SYSOP can either politely ask the caller to disconnect or limit each session to a fixed time.

STATING YOUR OWN

For reasons mentioned earlier, you may decide to set up your own computer bulletin board. You will need a computer such as an Apple, Commodore, Atari, IBM-XT, or any other brand. The hardware should have enough local memory, permanent storage (floppy or hard disk), and communication ports to run the CBBS software. Also, a MODEM that has both answer and dial features with variable speed of data transfer is required. Of course, a telephone line to connect to the outside world is also necessary.

When choosing the software, see that it has all the capabilities that you need. In addition to some basic functions, the security of the system is sometimes important. Above all, you want to know how easy it is to set up a board and maintain it afterwards. In case of obscene calls or improper materials posted on the board, you want a CBBS that will edit and filter out any undesirable material. Not every software has all these features, therefore it is your responsibility to ensure that the product you purchase will satisfy your needs.

Before setting up any system, it is wise to reflect upon the responsibilities of a SYSOP. It is realistic to assume that your time spent managing a CBBS will be anywhere from 5 hours to 20 hours a week. This will include such tasks as :

1. Gathering information to put on the board,
2. Maintaining the user's data base.
3. Monitoring the transactions on your board regularly and eliminating any suspicious messages or programs,
4. Answering queries from callers,
5. If it is a system that is widely open, it is important to warn your users that you are not responsible for the inaccuracy of the information. It will help you legally, if for some reason the information from your board causes any harm to anyone,
6. Equiping yourself to filter any obscene and unwanted information,
7. Discouraging distribution of copyrighted programs.

There are CBBSs dying and being born every week. Some survive for only months and some for years. Two factors contribute to prolonging the life of the board. First, a diversity of material will attract a wide variety of users. One way to teach the Faith using a CBBS is to attract callers by offering a variety of services, one of which could be religion. Generally, people tend to avoid discussion about religion. However, some are interested in social, cultural, or philosophical issues. On computer bulletin boards these issues can provide an opportunity to share Baha'i perspectives and principles with callers. The other factor prolonging the life of the board is the personality of the SYSOP. An orderly board in which complete control of the material is kept, and a little bit of entertainment can be very effective in keeping present users as well as attracting new ones.

AS A USER

If your interest is as a user and you have all the necessary equipment and software, then there are benefits to be derived from CBBS. There may be as many as 30 boards in your region, especially if you reside in a large city.

One benefit is to collect public domain software. Some of them have up to 600 programs of all kinds. You can get word processors, computer languages, communications tools, software for accounting, data base, computer-aided learning, and many more. In fact, many of the software tools discussed earlier can be obtained from these boards. Among such programs, the quality of the product and documentation varies from good to poor. Furthermore, if you encounter any problem while using one, you have to depend on your own resources, since the kind of help you can get from a software store is not available. However, sometimes the only way to know about the quality of a public domain software is by taking a jump into the unknown and using it. If you encounter any problem, that cannot be resolved after using your own resources, post a message on a computer bulletin board describing the situation. Sometimes it can bring help from someone who has solved similar problems or knows how to fix it.

It is interesting to explore the special-interest group boards. Anonymity makes discussions of ideas and beliefs much easier, and can provide an opportunity to contribute Baha'i points of view on many current issues. Where do such boards exist? The computer community is always helpful and generous, and you can get help by posting messages on the board. Another place to find a live CBBS is in a local computer newspaper. Some devote entire sections to updates and news about boards.

CBBS is definitely one of the ways of communicating ideas and information inexpensively in this computer age. This is true only if the user does not have to pay for long-distance calls. CBBS runs fairly well at a regional scale. However, at national or international levels, other systems of communication, such as electronic mail and computer conferencing, are more appropriate and economical.

8.3 ELECTRONIC MAIL

In the Baha'i Faith, the increase of membership and the expansion of various levels of administration have created a surge in the flow of information. At the same time, outside the Baha'i world there is an explosion of information taking place, due mainly to more uses of personal computers. One of the outcomes of the latter process is that demand for electronic mail has increased. In mid-1970s, when commercial electronic mail started, the question was "will E-MAIL succeed?" and now it is "when will E-MAIL compete with other messaging systems?" In fact, in many cases it is a better alternative to traditional mail systems.

E-MAIL is not really a new facility, it has been around since Telex. In the Baha'i world as well as in business, Telex is a common way of sending messages and receiving them from many parts of the world. In comparison to electronic mail system (EMS), Telex is slow, expensive, and seems unable to accommodate new benefits of computer and communications technologies. Currently, there are many international businesses that rely on EMS for transfer of information from one point to another. Also, many commercial enterprises are offering similar services to the public as well as to organizations.

What is making EMS grow so fast? There are two main reasons for such growth. First, communications are going through a phenomenal progress. Earlier in this century, it was a luxury to speak to someone overseas using a telephone. Usually an operator was required to do the dialing, and after several hours of waiting to make the connection, a caller found that the lines were often full of static and noise. Now it is routine to dial a number across the ocean and expect the voice you hear to be as clear as if you were talking to your neighbor. The telephone services have expanded and the quality has improved through technological innovations as well as uses of satellite and fiber optics. In many cases, the same voice line or satellite facilities are used to transfer computer data. Second, computers are becoming more powerful and less expensive. When communications are combined with a computer having huge storage capacity, distribution of mail happens at a very high speed. E-MAIL is available commercially through many communications companies as well as through traditional mail organizations. Their subscribers are growing constantly as they expand their services to more and more countries. In some cases, one company can connect up to 50 countries.

FUNCTIONS AND SERVICES

To derive the most benefit from electronic mail systems, it is essential to have some basic knowledge about its delivery methods, services, and functions. In the way of mail delivery in an EMS, there are two general categories: direct delivery and centralized delivery. In the first method, when a sender mails a letter the recipient gets it through the network system. The delivery is almost instantaneous. Centralized delivery can be compared to a post office where all the mail is stored till it's picked up. E-MAIL with a centralized method has a central computer with a huge storage capacity through which mail is sent and received. As a user you would check your in basket (or in box), and if there is mail, you can open it. This is also called a "store and forward electronic mail system."

There are numerous commercial enterprises providing E-MAIL services to the public and to organizations.

COMPANY	COUNTRY	TELEPHONE
Source	USA	1-800-336-3366
MCI Mail	USA	1-800-424-6677
Western Union	USA	N/A
Delphi	USA	1-800-544-4005
Compuserve	USA	1-800-848-8990
Porta/COM	Sweden	N/A
Envoy 100	Canada	N/A
Canada Post(E-MAIL)	Canada	1-800-267-0320

Table 8.1 List of EMS Services

Just as the post office and the courier companies offer different kinds of services such as ordinary mail, overnight delivery, and registered mail, similar varieties exist with EMS. For the purposes of our discussion, we have chosen MCI as an example and discuss its four services. They represent a broad range of options available in the industry.

INSTANT LETTER: This is the most popular, cheapest, and fastest service of MCI Mail. For 45 cents, you can send a message of up to 500 characters, or $1.00 for 500 to 7,500 characters. If the recipient is a subscriber it happens instantaneously. However, if the addressee is a nonsubscriber, you have an option of providing the street or TELEX address and sending it as an MCI letter or a Telex for an extra charge.

MCI LETTER: This is for a nonsubscriber recipient. After preparing your message and sending it electronically, it transfers the letter to the MCI postal center nearest the destination. At point, it is printed, placed in a bright orange envelope and given to the postal service for delivery. Usually, it takes one or two days, and the cost is $2.00.

OVERNIGHT LETTER: For overnight service, your message has to reach the MCI office by 11 p.m. E.S.T. on any business day and it will be delivered by noon the following day. This service costs $8.00 and is available across the U.S. continent and many other countries. The message is created and sent just like an MCI Letter.

FOUR-HOUR LETTER: A Four-Hour-Letter costs $30.00, and is the most expensive service. Currently, MCI Mail only delivers such letters to specific metropolitan areas. An up-to-date list is available from MCI offices.

Similar services are also provided by other E-MAIL companies. Other services besides those described may be available, some for no extra charge. For instance, you can include letterhead and a signature in any message you send. To do so, you must first register both of them with MCI Mail; then, by giving a command, you can order laser printer to put the letterhead at the top and signature anywhere you want.

If you use the EMS frequently and the list of recipients is long and varied, it becomes possible to store it. When sending a message, just attach it to your mailing list and every one on that list will receive the electronic parcel. Like a telephone call, it is possible to reverse the charges as a recipient or sender. If you are interested in knowing when the mail reaches its destination, you can request a receipt of all outgoing mail that is recorded, as soon as the recipient reads your message. Or you can ask to call the subscribers and inform them that the message is waiting in their mail box. Finally, you can use your EMS to shop for supplies and services.

Now let's look at some of the functions of EMS. Again, they vary from one product to another. Therefore, we picked DIALMAIL as an example to show the functions it provides once you are connected. The choices are as follows.

```
SCAN      to list your messages,
READ      to see your messages,
CREATE    to prepare a message,
PROFILE   to change user profile,
HELP      for assistance at any time,
MENU      to return to the main menu at any
          time,
EXIT      to leave DIALMAIL.
```

All these choices are given to allow the user to manage the mail easily. Some of the operations include creating cover letters, and attachments, browsing incoming or outgoing mail, scanning the inbasket and outbasket, and providing help in all areas. However, the choices are numerous enough to overwhelm a beginner. Each of the first choices of the above menu presents the user with another screen full of selections; for example, choosing the READ option gives you the following.

```
INBOX     To read messages in your Inbox,
DESK      To read messages on your Desk,
FOLDER xx To read messages in Folder xx,
CONF   xx To read messages in Conference xx,
BBOARD xx To read messages in Bboard xx.
```

Note, some EMS also provide services other than mail services, such as bulletin boards and conferencing.

USING EMS

When using EMS in the Faith or for personal reasons, it may be worthwhile to compare it with the existing services such as the post office, Telex, and courier services. The attractive characteristics of EMS are: that it transfers information instantly, it is available for use day or night, and it is capable of storing any message if needed. But we have to remember that these services and advantages apply only to information transferable electronically, not to parcels, books, or other material.

Now, let's compare the cost of EMS with other mail systems. From Figure 8.5 we note that the cost of ordinary mail in an envelope with a stamp is still cheaper than the lowest MCI Mail charge. However, if your mail has to reach its destination quickly then EMS is a viable alternative. While using the services it is always wise to pay attention to the connect time, otherwise the bill can become surprisingly high. To use the EMS services, you need a subscription to an EMS company.

MCI Mail Services			Competitive Services		
Carrier	Delivery Time	Price	Carrier	Delivery Time	Price
MCI Mail Instant Letter	Within seconds, read at addressee's convenience 500 characters	$1.00 $0.45	(no comparative service)		
MCI Mail Four-Hour Letter	Hand delivered to major cities within four hours	$30.00	Air Courier	Same Day	$70 to $115
MCI Mail Overnight	Hand delivered by noon of following business day	$8.00	Air Courier	Overnight	up to $20
MCI Letter	Usually next day U.S. Mail delivery	$2.00	U.S Postal Service/ Express Mail	Overnight (no pickup)	$9.35

Figure 8.5. Cost Comparison

The fact that the Baha'i Faith is widespread throughout the world, with a network of local and National Spiritual Assemblies, it can use a system with the services and functions of EMS. It is particularly true as the Faith grows and the institutions become time sensitive. We have already seen EMS being used among National and World Centers. One can predict that the use of this service will become cheaper, therefore making it economical for other levels of Baha'i administration to use. Some of the uses of EMS for the Faith are sending orders to distribution services, distributing mailing lists to local and regional areas, and disseminating information from the National Centers to the rest of the country.

Microcomputers have played an important role in making EMS a popular and inexpensive tool. An E-MAIL user concerned about cutting cost must look at some of the benefits of using a microcomputer instead of going on-line with a terminal. To use the EMS, you have to pay for the connect time as well as for the size of your message. During the connect time, the user normally creates, edits, and browses the mail, but these tasks are easily accomplished on a microcomputer. For creating and editing, you can use your favorite word processor, then connect communications software to the EMS. A few of these programs are:

PROGRAM	COMPUTER	VENDOR
Cross-Talk	IBM-PC and compatibles.	
PC-TALK	IBM-PC and compatibles.	Public Domain
KERMIT	IBM-PC and compatibles.	Public Domain

Figure 8.6 List of Communication Programs for Microcomputers

Some of the capabilities are dialing telephone numbers, reading mail box entries, and sending messages. Also, you can prepare your messages and mailing lists at your leisure, and set a timer so that all the transactions are done when the rates are the lowest. This is a good way to cut costs.

The electronic mail system has already gone through the initial stages of development and is being accepted with great enthusiasm. In many ways, it is seen not as a replacement of the traditional post office, but a new way of receiving and sending mail. It is slowly becoming a necessity when dealing with information that has to be moved in a hurry.

8.4 COMPUTER-BASED CONFERENCING

A messaging network such as the electronic mail system is also suitable for group discussions, decision making, and exchange of information among participants that are scattered all over the world. Another attraction is that contributions can be made at a convenient time and place. A system with such facilities is called computer-based conferencing (CBC). It has many of the functions of the EMS. In addition, it provides an environment for consultation, for exploring new areas, for coordination of projects, among other things. While EMS offers mail services, however, computer conferencing is mainly for discussions and exchange of views, and eliminates the limitations of traditional meetings.

Now let's look at some of the ways CBC offers many advantages over face-to-face meetings. It eliminates long-distance travel for members, reducing the cost of a project considerably. It resolves the problem of having conflicting personal schedules, and allows better participation by each individual in discussions and general promotion of an issue. Also, it does not allow individuals, by virtue of personality or position, to control exchange of opinion. Furthermore, the user has time to collect and compose his/her thoughts before logging in to contribute personal views on a subject.

Although the advantages of CBC are numerous, it should not replace face-to-face meetings entirely. In the Baha'i Faith, traditional meetings are essential, can be used to show love and fellowship, and they give a personal touch to working together. However, CBC is useful after an important gathering has taken place, to keep each participant informed of all developments on a given topic. For example, in large countries such as Canada, the Unites States, or Australia, it is important to include members from different regions when forming national committees. Often the traveling cost and conflicting personal schedules make regular meetings impossible, or difficult at best under such conditions. CBC can reduce the number of personal meetings required, yet many aspects of the committee work, such as consultation, making decisions, and exchange of information, can continue regularly.

FUNCTIONS

Often, companies provide electronic mail and conferencing, and likely some of the user interfaces for both are similar. For instance, the choice menu, shown below, includes conferencing as well as electronic mail.

```
MESSAGE        Create a message for mailing,
FOLDER         Create a personal file folder,
FOLDER XXX     Create Folder; it bypasses title prompt,
CONF           Create a Conference,
CONF  XXX      Create Conf; it bypasses title prompt,
LIST           Create a mailing list.
```

Computer conferencing is a conference set up when a group of people have a common goal in discussing a subject. This group can be as small as two or as large as several hundred, depending on the capacity of a service. Once set up, all participants can use it from wherever they are and whenever they like through a network that has access to the services. In such a conference, when the user adds a comment, question, or idea it is called an ITEM. The items are immediately available to any group member. A reaction to such an item is a RESPONSE. Both items and responses are stored in the system, and a printed copy is available at any time. Also, in some facilities it is possible to send messages, notes, or communicate on-line with other members, regardless of the distance separating them.

Within a conference, you can set up topics (subconferences). Members can join any of these topics at any time. Figure 8.7 shows a hierarchy of conferences and topics. At the top level there are two conferences (National Teaching and International Pioneering).

```
CONFERENCE        National Teaching          International Pioneering

                  -----------------          -----------------
                  |    |          |          |    |          |
SUBCONFERENCES    *    |          |          *    |          |
            Ethnic     *          |    Africa     *          |
                  Mass Teaching   *            Needs of      |
                             Deepening         pioneers      *
                                                     Home coming
```

Figure 8.7 Hierarchy of Conferences

Each is divided into many subconferences (Ethnic, Mass teaching, and so on). At both levels, subjects are added or deleted, depending on the needs and goals of the discussion.

Among new users of CBC, a common concern is the security of private information in conferences. Vendors of computer conferencing offer a variety of security levels. For example, COM/Porta/COM (a Swedish conferencing service) provides the following types of conferences, each providing different levels of security. These measures are typical features in many other conferencing products.

OPEN: Anyone able to participate in an open conference.

CLOSED: The organizer(s) of the conference can add new members only to closed conferences.

RESTRICTED: Open to one set of users yet closed to another set.

PROTECTED: The existence of a protected conference is known only to members. It is impossible for nonmembers to find out if such a conference exists. It is like an unlisted telephone number.

WRITE PROTECTED: This kind allows only a selected member to communicate with the conference. However, it is possible for other members to read the contents.

Users of closed conferences are very particular about who is allowed to see their information. Therefore, this puts a lot of pressure on suppliers of such services to exercise great confidentiality and security of data. In some cases, even the vendors' support and service staff is not capable of accessing protected conferences. Enhancements of security measures continue to ensure that absolutely no unwanted eyes can see confidential material.

To make a conferencing session a successful one with lively discussion, prompt responses, and universal participation, it requires that all forums have a moderator. This person's main job is to start a forum, add or delete participants, and facilitate flow of messages among members. Also, it would enhance the conferencing, if the moderator had some technical knowledge about messaging systems to help any members in difficulty but this is not absolutely necessary. Like the chairperson of a Baha'i meeting, the moderator can facilitate the consultation as well as help promote the goals of a particular forum.

Most CBC systems have plenty of help information to get you around the system, if you are just starting. The commands can vary in complexity from one system to the next. In addition to on-line help, you can get tutorial lectures and manuals. Initially you may want to use the menu to get around. Once you are familiar with the system menus and they become boring, you may then move on to the command level. This gets you anywhere by just typing a command line instead of making several menu selections.

Some more uses of computer conferencing are:

1. on-line balloting,
2. survey,
3. search for a key word/phrase/time/person,
4. a printout of conference activities.

To access a CBC system, you need a terminal or personal computer with communications capabilities, a MODEM, and a phone. To get on-line, you will also need a data network provided either by the vendor or a public service. As we have seen in EMS, it would be less costly to use your personal computer to compose your text rather than using the on-line editor.

SERVICES

There are many public conferencing systems. To use their facilities you need a subscription.

NAME	COMPANY	TELEPHONE
PARTIPATE	Participation System Inc.	617-729-1976
EIES	New Jersey Institute of Technology	201-420-5111
Porta/COM	Stockholm University Computing Center	46 8 679280
eFORUM	Network Technologies International	313-994-4030
CoSy	Institute of Computer Science University of Guelph	519-824-4120 ext. 3712

Figure 8.8. List of CBC Vendors

Figure 8.8 shows a list of CBC vendors and their phone numbers. Each has different capacities and is intended to serve the needs of specific communities such as academic, business, or private organizations. Porta/COM is very well-known worldwide, especially in Europe. It was developed in Sweden and is very popular in Europe. You can access to any E-MAIL or conference in the world by using it. It provides gateways to other networks and messaging systems throughout the world, including those in the United States and Canada. eFORUM and CoSy are newer entities in the CBC world.

GLOBAL FEELING

To appreciate the advantages of computer conferencing, we'll look at a realistic situation where it can be applied. Earlier, we briefly mentioned the promotion of an economic and social project (initiated by Baha'is), using a computer messaging system. We'll expand this example to show the importance of rapid efficient flow of information among participants, especially if they reside in many different parts of the world. The main issue here is that flow of information should implement discussion and consultation, and should eventually help get the job done. It can be applied to many projects in the Baha'i Faith, both at national and international levels as in the case of teaching, pioneering, audiovisual projects, education, and so on.

The social and economic development project that we will use as an example is in a fictitious country called Ubamba. It is a national undertaking, involving several levels of Baha'i administration as well as some government organizations. As it is a fairly new experience for the Baha'is of Ubamba, they want to benefit from successful projects elsewhere in the world by including experts from countries where such a project has taken place. A team is formed to include Ubambans and Baha'is from India, China, Australia, United States, South America and Europe.

To begin with, everyone is invited to a meeting to discuss the issues and formulate a plan of action. At the end of the meeting, the group saw a need for improvement in the following areas:

1. Education of family,
2. Vocational Training,
3. Agriculture,
4. Culture and technology,
5. Spiritual needs.

In addition, it is critical to finish this project within a relatively short time. To achieve this, the group lists a few operational guidelines for every member to consider during the lifetime of this project. They are:

1. continuous and prompt flow of information from one member to another,
2. minimal duplication,
3. keeping the cost low,
4. maximizing efficiency,
5. resolving problems through timely consultation.

Obviously, these suggestions are important in making the project a success.

Other discussions include many social and economic goals, and means by which thay could be implemented. When the meeting is over, the participants living in Ubamba got to work and the rest went to their respective countries.

Fortunately, there is a worldwide communications network and a computer conferencing that can connect all the members together. After choosing a moderator and subconferences (topics), everyone is able to go on-line at one's own convenience. While the project progresses, every member of the group joins in on discussions of any or all topics, making comments, giving fresh ideas or just simply browsing through the information in the data base. Occasionally, there are personal notes and messages flowing among members.

One can really appreciate the benefits of CBC in times of emergency. In such situations, every member is informed immediately about a concern. Any message from Ubamba can be broadcasted over the CBC within minutes. Also, crucial telephone conversations can be initiated through this method too.

CBC is most cost effective when the group working together is spread far apart throughout a country or the world. Before using it, of course, the need has to be justified. In many cases, old traditional methods work just fine, but there are cases, such as in our example, where the quick flow of information is necessary to a project. In the Baha'i Faith, there is a great need for face-to-face meetings, and our suggestions of using computer conferencing is not meant to replace them, but rather to save them only for instances where they will benefit. Currently, it is rather costly, but as the subscribers of this service increase, it will likely become cheaper and in many cases worthwhile to use on a regular basis instead of phone, Telex, or telegram.

8.5 ON-LINE DATA BASE

So far we have described what is known as on-line services such as bulletin board, E-MAIL, and computer conferencing. Also, there is another product called on-line data base which is a combination of communications and computer data bases. Such a data base is stored in a remote computer for subscribers to use. There are many companies that sell access to such information. They are called data base vendors. Those who compile and organize it are known as data base producers. Data bases provide from one subject to hundreds, ranging from airline information to scientific reports. In fact, the number of subjects currently available in data bases is too long to mention here, and there are strong indications that the list will grow greatly.

In the Baha'i Faith, we feel there are several possible uses for such data banks. The Official Airline Guide (OAG) is related to traveling. It's a huge bank of information about schedules and fares for about 700 airlines around the world. While looking for the best schedules and fares, you can also book the flight. Soon similar facilities will be added for hotels, motels, and car rentals. Using OAG will likely save up to 30% in air fare.

The other area of interest is data bases with enormous amounts of information on subjects such as medicine, psychology, agriculture, education, and so on. In the Baha'i Faith, if individuals or administrative bodies have to research any subject, these pools of data can be invaluable. They contain facts, statistics, research papers, newsletters, and so on. The user interface and search capabilities are well refined in these services. By giving a word, phrase, or sentence, you can retrieve data with context and relations. Third area of possible use for the Baha'i Faith is in investments and finances. This program is called Dow Jones/Retrieval.

Accessing to any of these data bases is similar to using E-MAIL or computer conferencing. In the United States or Canada you can access them through Tymnet, Telenet, or Datapac. There are many companies such as Compuserve and Source that provide both utility services (E-MAIL, conferencing, etc.) as well as data bases.

NAME	USES	TELEPHONE
NEWNET	National & International news	1-800-345-1301
DIALOG	General information data base	1-800-227-5510
Dow/Jones Retrieval system	Financial, stock and other data	1-800-257-5114
Official Airline Guides (OAG)	Airline schedules and reservations.	1-800-323-4000

Figure 8.9. List of Data Base On-line Services

CHAPTER NINE

EDUCATIONAL HELP

Although we have seen a burst of new interest in computer-aided learning only during the last few years, this technology was first used to promote education in the early 1960s. In those days, only the researchers at academic institutions with costly mainframes had experience with different ways of using computers for educational purposes. In the 1970s, the minicomputers, because of their lower costs, made computers available to more schools and teachers. But it was only in the 1980s, after the influx of inexpensive microcomputers, that the uses of computers moved from the academic environment to real application in the classrooms.

In the early 1980s, when government offices and businesses decided to put microcomputers such as Atari, Apple, Radio Shack, and IBM-PC, to work in developing educational software, the microcomputer generated new excitement in schools and showed a lot of promise. Individualized teaching, self-testing software, tracking and reporting a student's progress, and motivation through graphics were just a few capabilities that excited users. Computers had the potential to manage the total learning process that much was obvious. Within a short time, many schools bought classrooms full of computers to teach subjects such as mathematics, physics, chemistry, and so on, through simulation of physical phenomena and sequential instruction programs. Also, accompanying these tools were management programs that tested the degree of success with which students acquired their learning.

Soon, however, the promises began turning sour. Many teachers, software developers, and researchers now believe this industry has not completely held its promises. The main stumbling block has been the premature release of instructional or management programs. When they reached the classroom, these programs were not robust enough to work flawlessly, and in some cases they did not perform as advertised. The results were disastrous as they hampered the learning process while leaving many teaching staff confused about the great promises of computers. There is also another aspect that does not help produce quality software. It is the lack of exchange among the teachers, learning experts and programmers while developing software for the classroom. In many cases, it is the software developers who are responsible for designing, implementing, and testing these learning tools. The result is usually a product with mediocre quality and with inadequate instructions. Furthermore, there is a tendency, for economic reasons, to try to replace a teacher with a computer. Considering the social and spiritual nature of a student, it is doubtful whether a computer can replace a teacher in a classroom.

Considering the early stage of computer-aided learning (CAL) and the need to reevaluate the effective use of computers, it is important that Baha'i institutions, educators, and parents who contemplate using it, take cautious steps. There is no doubt that the computer is beneficial as a general learning tool, and it can be applied to many aspects of the Baha'i Faith. Since youngters, between the ages of 9 to 12, are fascinated by computer simulations, it can be used to teach subjects such as history, and the lives of the central figures and the principles of the Baha'i Faith. For adults, going through a sequence of screens full of information, one can learn about administration, pioneering, teaching, and so on.

We also know the computer is an excellent tool for communication, and this can be applied in education. It can be used to establish forums where educators, parents, and other interested individuals can have dialogues among one another to explore many different ideas about education as seen in the Baha'i Faith. Similarly, it can promote Baha'i scholarship. Given the clear emphasis on both these areas, education and scholarship, in the writings of the central figures, the Guardian, and the Universal House of Justice, computer-based conferencing can definitely help in a deeper exploration of these topics, and can also provide a way of getting a better understanding of both.

As word processing and printing become cheaper the computer can help to provide literature in a radically different way than our present methods have, and promises to be a great force in eradicating illiteracy. In many remote villages of many countries the greatest hurdle in deepening the Baha'i is a limited ability to read and write. It has been found that one way to promote literacy as well as teach Baha'i principles is to transcribe prayers and stories into dialects of the local villages. When combining a word processor and printer, this process becomes simple and quick. Additionally, texts for reading can be produced at a cheaper rate.

In this chapter, we will discuss all these ideas of promoting education through computers, and show how the technology can apply to the Baha'i Faith. We should warn you that these discussions are not about theories or analyses of computer-aided learning. Rather, the emphasis is on how education can be enhanced using computer-aided instruction and management. Also, we will provide an example of instruction for the "Three Onenesses." In addition, we will show how computer conferencing provides a forum to share ideas and promotes discussion about education and scholarship. Finally, a brief explanation will show the benefits of this modern technology in a basic literacy program.

9.1 EDUCATION AND SOFTWARE

Before we can use this technology for the purpose of teaching the Baha'i Faith, it is essential to gain some understanding of educational software and why it is attractive to students as well as teachers. First, technological improvements are producing fast, powerful computers, with storage capacities that exceed many millions of characters, and the recent sudden explosion of computer applications is bringing down prices as well as sizes. But above all, it is a very patient machine, endlessly taking commands from its users and doing countless operations. With a TV-like high resolution monitor it can produce amazing pictures, texts, graphics, and animation. Furthermore, the user can interact with the computer through a keyboard, which combines sound and the visual image, making the computer both a useful and fascinating tool. All these features are good but it is the possibility to program a computer to suit many different learning aims that is the most attractive feature to educators.

Among youngsters, especially between 9 and 16 years of age, interaction with the computer makes learning more interesting. Compared to other learning tools, such as pen, paper, and chalk board, it is the most fascinating in modern times. Also, it is a fact that young students are easily distracted, but the flashing text, popping objects, questions, and quick responses do keep their attention on their lessons.

In Baha'i schools, all these features of the computer can be used to teach many subjects such as the history of the Faith, and lives of the central figures. Learning can happen at a pace with which the student feels most comfortable. It is very effective in improving progress among high-achieving and low-achieving students alike. Similarly, adults can use computer-aided instruction (CAI) to learn about many aspects of the Baha'i Faith. In these two categories, adults and youths, the subject matter may be the same, but the objectives of learning may differ considerably. Therefore, the learning needs do dictate the kind of CIA that is developed to satisfy each group. In the rest of this section, we will discuss the three most important areas of computer in education. They are:

1. Computer-aided learning,
2. Computer-managed instruction,
3. Computer-aided instruction.

It is impossible to exhaust the discussion of these areas, but we hope it will arouse some interest among teachers and Baha'i institutions and encourage greater use of them.

9.2 COMPUTER-AIDED LEARNING

Historically, people have always been able to use a new technology as a tool for learning. When the first computer was built, it was used to learn simple arithmetic as well as to give better understanding of the technology itself, namely, the transmission of electronic impulses. Designers, learning through the first computers and those subsequent to them, improved this technology so as to produce more capable computers. Currently, it is used in many different ways to acquire various skills. As an example, students rely on it to learn various subjects in classrooms, psychologists use it to understand behavior, and secretaries do word processing. Also, it is used as a learning tool in almost all fields, including engineering, nursing, and aerospace. Regardless of the subject, it is the intellectual nature of the user that is stimulated to gain a better understanding of a subject through the help of software.

In recent years, learning centers, such as public schools and universities, have invested unprecedented resources into CAL in order to improve cognitive learning of students. For many popular computers, such as Atari, Apple, and IBM-PC, there is already a variety of programs to create the environments for learning how to think. The focus of the software developers and educators is on the problem-solving processes of the user. One example of such a program is LOGO, which is very popular among young students. They use it happily, for it gives them control over their own learning process. LOGO is based on the Piagetian idea that the child is an active participant in the construction of intelligence. In LOGO turtle graphics, the student not only experiments and discovers knowledge, but also puts intuitive knowledge to use to create other objects. Many students face similar challenges when using programming languages such as BASIC to program games or simulation. While doing so, they learn logic, programming skills, and subjects such as physics or mathematics. Or, it could be composition and editing learned through word processing. The computer industry is constantly producing new and improved software to enhance learning. Recently, the software has been connected to interactive video systems to improve the multisensory effects. Also, through data communication it is possible to conduct a class where the trainer and students are scattered throughout a country or area. However sophisticated this technology may get, to a teacher or trainer, CAL is a tool to be used only in addition to books, libraries, field trips, and laboratories.

Before we list some of the ways CAL can be used in the Baha'i Faith, it is important to ponder some philosophical issues surrounding CAL. It is proven that individualized learning, where one tutor teaches one pupil, is very effective in developing competence. In past centuries, affluent families had private tutors for their children, and the successful results came from the following facts:

1. The students get immediate results, instead of sharing the teacher and the teacher's reinforcement,

2. The lessons are administered according to learner's needs,

3. There are immediate rewards or punishments,

4. The student learns from a tutor with expert knowledge of a subject.

Today, there is a tendency to replace the teacher with a computer for all the above reasons as well as for its ability to analyze the learning process through tracking the responses of the students. These ideas, proposed by educational theorists, may be valuable in some cases, but if they are pushed to extremes where learning is happening only through a computer, then they raise some serious questions. There is no doubt that CAL has many virtues, but, it is important to realize a computer is a machine and a student is a human being. As Baha'is, we also understand each human being has a physical as well as spiritual nature, and great intellectual capacities.

Furthermore, artificial intelligence is being developed using computers, and the industry is marketing great promises of applying it to software. As a result, computers can talk, listen, and even act in a flexible manner, in imitation of the human being. With all these sophistications, it is still unreasonable for CAL to take over all the teaching activities at schools.

When we see humankind as spiritual, it is very clear that the appropriate environment for a human being to learn in is a human one rather a mechanical one. Learning is best achieved not only by absorbing facts but also through interaction with other spiritual and social beings such as teachers and peers. Collectively and individually, it is better to have spiritual qualities, such as kindness, courtesy, compassion, and so on (as well as to acquire knowledge) than to be an unscrupulous product of high technology sadly lacking in spiritual and social qualities. In a situation where one has to deal with peers and teachers, opportunities to communicate as well as to test one's own personality arise. This is a fertile ground in which to evaluate and develop one's own spiritual growth. But if the student spends most of the learning time with a computer, this opportunity for interaction, this chance for social and spiritual development, is completely missed. It is, therefore, a challenge to combine all the benefits of CAL and keep all the interaction among peers and teachers.

One approach to combine both worlds is to have computer-aided cooperative learning. In this situation, a task is given to the students such that interdependence is necessary to complete it. One arrangement is to assign two or more students to one computer and see that each contributes one part to finish the whole task. Some of the advantages of computer-aided cooperative learning are as follows:

1. Positive interdependence,

2. Social skills and spiritual qualities are developed,

3. Teacher observes and intervenes,

4. Individual is accountable,

5. Working in groups is encouraged.

Given the important cautions, we will now look at how CAL can be used in teaching the Baha'i Faith. As the computer is becoming more popular in schools and work places, we can assume many Baha'is are gaining some degree of skill in using the basic components, the disk, keyboard, screen, printer, and so on. Therefore, while designing a courseware, training in handling the different components is not always essential. Here, our focus is to develop software that promotes the learning among Bahai's, whether within a formal class situation or at home. Also, we should bear in mind that in many cases the students are of different ages: children, youths and adults.

It is the multisensory medium of the computer, where touch is engaged through the keyboard and sight through the screen, that fascinates many of the users. It is especially true for children as young as five years old. We know software can simulate real life situations. Also, there are numerous children's books relating stories about central figures, heroines, and heroes. These two tools, the book and the computer, when used together, can heighten the learning process. The element of interaction as well as having one child to one computer, gives the child control of the learning pace. This environment is also conducive to gaining certain independence that helps build self-esteem.

The software can be designed in such a way as to assess the learning at the end of a session. To do this the software saves all the responses while the session lasts. Extracted from the child's responses, it produces a report about the progress of each child. In using this feature, the creativity of an experienced teacher can be channeled to ensure that children are achieving the educational objectives, and to guide them whenever help is needed.

Similarly, there are many areas in the Faith that may interest the youths and adults equally. However, in each case the content of instruction and objectives of learning as well as the software design may be different. The following are some suggestions of subjects for consideration:

1. Learning about the history of religions,

2. Basic facts about the administration,

3. Lives of the central figures of the Baha'i Faith,

4. Nature of the soul/spirit/body,

5. Pioneering.

9.3 COMPUTER-MANAGED INSTRUCTION

In choosing a method to promote learning, it is necessary to devise a plan to evaluate its effectiveness, so that we can decide whether such a program should continue. Computer-managed instruction (CMI) is often used to collect students' input while using the computer as a learning tool. From the detailed records of students' responses to questions, the software analyzes and generates report information about the learning process of a particular educational program.

Over many decades, CMI has existed in mini and mainframe computers, but the recent proliferation of microcomputers has brought this tool into the hands of many teachers in public schools. Today, there are CMI programs sold for Commodore, Apple, IBM-PC, and PC compatibles. In any educational program attempting to computerize learning in the Baha'i Faith, some kind of CMI is a must. Mentioned below are some of its major functions.

DATA BASE: The choice of information collected through a CMI system is crucial in processing and reporting the performance. It includes the following three types:

1. Student information, such as name, identification number, and demographic characteristics,
2. Class identification, such as subject and period,
3. Curriculum information, such as tests, answer keys, objectives, and prescriptions.

PROCESSING: The processing of performance data should include:

1. Entering and storing data into the CMI system,
2. Summarizing the information.

REPORT: The benefits of a CMI system depend on the quality of the reports. They are generally grouped into the following four categories:

1. Performance of individual students,
2. Average performance of a class,
3. Parent reports,
4. Analysis of curriculum.

9.4 COMPUTER AIDED INSTRUCTION

To use the computer for any kind of learning, it is programmed to impart instructions to students. In this section, we will discuss many aspects of computer-aided instruction to show the necessary steps in developing it as teaching tool, with special interest for the Baha'i Faith. CAI has been around for many years, and much research has been done on how to best use this versatile tool. However, the users have been disappointed for lack of good quality software. The main reason for this shortage is a lack of principles guiding designers during development of courseware.

To produce good quality CAI, it is not enough to have just an instructional expert, teacher, or programmer. An ideal team will consist of all three. The expert guides the team with the knowledge of the content as well as the characteristics of the student. The teacher or designer contributes to the quality of the product by applying principles and theories about learning as well as her or his experience in teaching. Finally, the programmer, with the understanding of computer technology, translates the instructional design into a well-developed CAI. In the industry it has been shown that it is a well-balanced team that produces a well-balanced product, and to overlook this will likely result in poor quality software.

Many psychologists and educators, through numerous years of research and refinements, have produced strategies to develop CAI. While doing so, many other disciplines from cognitive and educational psychology to computer science and artificial intelligence have been used. The subject of design, implementation, and assessment of CAI is so broad, combining many theories about instruction, learning, and teaching, that it is beyond the scope of this book. For an in-depth discussion, there are numerous books and articles written on this subject (see Appendix A). However, we will list some commonly used strategies.

1. Drill and practice,
2. Tutorial,
3. Exploratory,
4. Simulation,
5. Games.

In designing the instructions, these software strategies are used to produce events such as:

1. Gaining attention,
2. Informing the student of the objective,
3. Stimulating recall of prerequisite skills,

4. Presenting the stimulus material,
5. Providing learning guidance,
6. Eliciting performance,
7. Providing feedback,
8. Assessing performance,
9. Enhancing retention and transfer.

To implement any of these events, graphics menus, animation menus, text, and other menus are used.

9.5 AUTHORING SOFTWARE

There are many different ways to develop CAI. For many years, teachers or programmers have used computer language such as BASIC, FORTRAN, or PASCAL to develop instructions to teach physics, mathematics, history, and so on. The main drawback is that a teacher, while interested in developing CAL, is forced to become a proficient programmer. Given the work load of teachers, many do not have the time to invest in the programming of CAI using computer languages.

In recent years, tools to create CAI without using programming skills have emerged for the microcomputer. They are called authoring software. In recent years, this software has attracted the attention of teachers as well as CAI developers. The main reason for this new interest is that it requires little time to learn how to use it. Once a certain degree of skill is attained, a set of instructions is easily translated into CAI for students to use.

Now, let's look at some of the characteristics of authoring software that make it valuable in building CAI. First, let's look at the differences between teaching and using the computer. Teachers, through many years of teaching a subject, are accustomed to an instructional logic that makes learning possible. This logic is the interaction, with meaningful dialogue, that teachers use to respond to a student's queries. The teachers, after many sessions, learn certain truths about teaching individuals and groups. On the other hand, computers operate with a logic that differs from the instructors. One is based on human interaction and intelligence which can perform several processes simultaneously, while the computer logic is controlled by electronic circuitry in sequential steps. Authoring software is the instrument that translates an already proven set of instructions into a computer program. Since teachers, with few exceptions, are not familiar with the information processing and reasoning skills required by computer logic, this tool relieves them of the task of learning computer programming. It allows teachers to concentrate on directly translating their valuable experience into CAI.

The other attraction of the authoring system is the simplicity with which it operates. There are some, like Super Pilot, that require simple syntax to produce instructions. One such command is equivalent to a dozen lines of BASIC commands, one of the easiest computer languages to learn. There are also other authoring software that are fully interactive, therefore there is no need to learn a single syntax. Such software guides you through the different steps, and by making choices from instructions it provides, you can easily produce sequential instructions. Without being aware of the computer logic, the author (teacher) plans and develops the CAI according to his or her instructional point of view and experience. Some of them are so versatile that, with some imagination in planning and implementation, they provide the opportunities of using computers as an interactive and adaptive program for students.

Although authoring software uses features such as text, simulation, gaming, sound, questions, and help menus to develop instruction, they are not its primary strength. To add the adaptive and interactive qualities, it uses some unique techniques. To show you some examples of these techniques, let's look at an authoring product called Teaching Turned Author (TTA). It will be used later in this section to develop instructions to teach the "Three Onenesses." The features discussed are common to many authoring software available for microcomputers.

In a computer system, the viewing device is the screen, therefore each screen can be considered a page, just like in a book. In TTA, a page may contain text, graphics, and questions. This software provides the author with word processing functions to edit the text on any page. After creating or editing a page, you can immediately play it back. Any of these functions are performed interactively within minutes. The software saves the instructions according to pages.

With the text, you can combine any graphics, and TTA has the ability to draw circles, rectangles, lines or fill a box with color with a few key strokes. In addition, if you have a color monitor, you can choose from 16 different colors. While using the graphics, any pictures can be saved, and called up later for another page. With these functions, the author includes sketches, pictures, or illustrations in instructional pages.

Another capability of authoring software is testing and branching. In a design, this can be used to check the degree of learning taking place, so that proper steps can be taken based on the responses. For example, if the response is not correct, then it branches to remedial pages; otherwise it continues toward the end of the instruction. In TTA, the students provide four types of responses to questions. They are:

1. Fill-in the blank responses,

2. Multiple-choice responses,

3. True/false response,
4. Press any key to continue.

As the training environment is being used, TTA keeps a record of each student's responses. This is fully integrated with the rest of the software. You can print timely reports on student progress and check the effectiveness of a course. The record keeping features are:

1. Complete question record keeping,
2. Separate instructor's disk to access student records,
3. The instructor may view the question numbers that each student missed,
4. Student log-on/log-off course software (or courseware) restarts on the page of previous departure.
5. Prints copies of student and class records,
6. Student cannot access or modify records.

This software is used to design any courseware regardless of subject matter, but there are many other programs that are specific to certain subjects. For example, there is TEACHER'S QUIZ DESIGNER to set up multiple-choice and true or false questions. Also, there is ELECTRIC POET for simple graphics, animation, and music. Another software package with more functions is PIRATE TUTOR, for developing an interactive learning program.

9.6 AN EXAMPLE: THE THREE ONENESSES

After our discussion on CAI and CMI, we are ready to apply this technology in the Baha'i Faith. As mentioned earlier, it is useful for all categories of students from children capable merely of touching keys to adults. Of course, the objectives of learning are different in each case, and the differences dictate the instructional designs.

Designing CAI is as involved as preparing a book, especially if it is to impart knowledge. Given the interactive aspects of the computer, which is used to control the learning process, it is important for the courseware developer to reflect on educational objectives and theories so as to provide the best learning tool. For many years, educators and psychologists have had many theories that apparently helped in designing a successful CAI. It should be noted that this area of computerized education is still at its early stage of development, therefore there is plenty of room for improvement. Here, we will mention some of the effective ideas in good CAI design. They are:

1. In CAI, feedback messages are easy to produce after a student's response. However, if used effectively, it promotes learning, otherwise it can be counterproductive,

2. It is important for the student to be aware of the objectives of instructions,

3. The student is tested to see if these objectives are met,

4. The design of screen should arouse the curiosity and interest in the student using graphics, simulation, sound, and so on.

In designing a CAI, the objective is to achieve certain educational goals. To do this, the developer chooses a strategy, such as drill-and-practice, tutorial, or simulation, to evaluate the effectiveness of the software. There are many educational theories that can be applied. Some of them are

1. B. F. Skinner's technology of teaching,

2. Information-processing theories,

3. Robert Gagne's conditions of learning,

4. Jean Piaget's cognitive development theory,

5. Albert Bandura's observational learning theory.

In the Baha'i Faith, a CAI product can be used for many different reasons; the size in terms of instructional pages can also vary, from a few pages to hundreds of pages. To illustrate a design of CAI, we have chosen a simple example. It is instruction for youngsters, from 9 to 14 years of age, called "Three Onenesses."

First, we will show a flow chart, a sequence of pages, and the logic in which they are presented to the student.

As shown in Figure 9.1, this set of instructions consists of 9 pages, the first 5 of which are instructions. The next two (pages 5 and 6) give questions to test how much information the learner has absorbed. If an answer is not correct, the program branches to a remedial page; otherwise it continues to the next question. For example, if the answer to the question on page 5 is correct, the program moves on to page 6. If the answer given is incorrect, it refreshes the mind of the student with previously shown information. When both questions are answered correctly, it ends. After determining the logic of the instructions, we then build each page of instructions, using authoring software TTA (see Appendix B for a list of authoring software).

```
                    THREE ONENESSES


......................................
:  INTRODUCTION  (Page 1 )           :
:....................................:
                  :
                  :
                 \:/
......................................
:  ONENESS OF GOD  (Page 2 )         :
:....................................:
                  :
                  :
                 \:/
......................................
:  ONENESS OF RELIGION  (Page 3 )    :
:....................................:
                  :
                  :
                 \:/
......................................
:  ONENESS OF MAN  (Page 4)          :
:....................................:
            :
            :
           \:/
..................... NO   .......................
:   QUESTION (Page 5) : ---->:REMEDIAL PAGE (Page 8):
:.....................:     :......................:
          :                       :
          :<-----------------------
          :         YES
         \:/
..................... NO   .......................
:   QUESTION (Page 6) : ---->:REMEDIAL PAGE (Page 9):
:.....................:     :......................:
          :                       :
          :<-----------------------
          :         YES
         \:/
......................................
:      END  (Page 7)                 :
:....................................:
```

Figure 9.1 Instructional Logic

One of the first things we want to do is to show the student the objective of this session, as shown in Figure 9.2.

THREE ONENESSES

WELCOME

In this session you will learn the THREE ONENESSES

They are :

1. ONENESS OF GOD.

2. ONENESS OF RELIGION.

3. ONENESS OF MAN.

At the end of this lesson you will be given two questions to answer, therefore please pay attention.

Figure 9.2 Page 1

The next three pages are about the three onenesses.

ONENESS OF GOD

ONENESS OF GOD means there is one Supreme Being who made every thing. He made my mother, my father, myself, everybody around me. Also, He created the mountains, trees, stars, and the sun.

He is very kind, loving, generous, and has many other divine qualities.

Figure 9.3 Page 2

ONENESS OF RELIGION

God send His Prophets to everybody to learn about God.

Some of these prophets are Christ, Mohammad, Krishna, Moses, the Bab, and Baha'u'llah. The Prophets start a religion to teach about God.

Some of these religions are:

Christianity	started by Christ.
Islam	started by Mohammad.
Hinduism	started by Krishna.
Judaism	started by Moses.
Babi	started by the Bab.
Baha'i	started by Baha'u'llah.

Each religion teaches us how to become a better person by developing divine qualities so that we can get along with other people.

Figure 9.4 Page 3

ONENESS OF MAN

Everybody is created by GOD. My mother, father, sister, brother, and I are all created by GOD. My neighbor, friend, and teacher are created by GOD. Everybody who lives in this country and other countries created by GOD.

Some are tall. Some are small. Some are black. Some are white. But each belongs to ONE family. It is called the family of man.

Figure 9.5 Page 4

To build these pages using TTA, you just answer the appropriate questions and enter the text. We have only shown text, but you can add illustrations. Note, that these pages are arranged in a sequential order; after reading one page, the student presses a key to move to the next one. The next page, as shown in figure 9.6, provides a multiple-choice question. If the answer is "1," then page 6 is shown; otherwise it moves to remedial page 8, as in Figure 9.9.

```
                         QUESTION ONE

                   WHICH ONE IS A RELIGION ?


                  1.  Hinduism

                  2.  Toyota

                  3.  Europe


                      Select : ...
```

Figure 9.6 Page 5

```
Some of the religions are :

     Christianity   started by Christ.

     Islam          started by Mohammad.

     Judaism        started by Moses.

     Hinduism       started by Krishna.

     Babi           started by the Bab.

     Baha'i         started by Baha'u'llah.

Each religion teaches us how to become a better person so that we can get along with
other people.
```

Figure 9.7 Page 8

Then it goes back to page 5, to answer the question. The following, Figure 9.8 is a question of the type "fill-in the blank." The remedial page is on Figure 9.9.

```
QUESTION TWO, FILL IN THE BLANK


        All people come from ---.
```

Figure 9.8 Page 6

```
        All people come from GOD.
```

Figure 9.9 Page 9

Finally, this session ends, as shown in Figure 9.10.

```
    This is the END of this lesson.


    Hope you enjoyed it.


    Thank you for your participation.
```

Figure 9.10 Page 7

9.7 FORUM

In the Baha'i Faith, while examining any form of teaching task, whether it is at summer school or at home, often we have to ponder whether or not every step we take is in harmony with the principles of our belief. This requires educators, parents, and other interested individuals to reevaluate constantly some of the current theories, teaching materials, and learning environments, to see if they satisfy the needs of educational standards in the Baha'i Faith. To enhance this process of evaluation we need an environment where individuals as well as institutions can freely exchange ideas and conduct consultation on any aspect of education.

In previous chapters, we saw how data communication is used to establish conferences and electronic mail. We saw how the forum, set according to a subject, becomes an electronic meeting place to get a better understanding of that subject. In similar ways, a computer with the capacity for distant data communication can be used for discussion and exchange of ideas in any imaginable area of education. In this section, we will show a few benefits of forums (discussions) when used in education. There are many advantages, but the most important one is that it can provide opportunities to exchange ideas among participants about promoting educational standards in the Baha'i community.

In teaching children, through Sunday classes, summer schools or a formal institution such as in India and Haiti, many educational issues such as discipline, curriculum, teaching material, and so on, have to be looked at with a fresh approach at every instance they are used. In the Baha'i World, there are no hard rules applying to education, except that the fundamental principles be used. Although every educator is free to develop programs in the best interests of learning, it is also important to avoid duplication of work every time a new class or school begins. In other words, if there is a network and a pool of information regarding previous research work, the duplication is less likely to happen. When starting a learning center, one cannot merely draw upon this resource, but must also contribute fresh ideas and comments. As education grows, so will this pool of information.

To implement this in a conferencing system, a subject starts whenever the need arises. As the forum develops, more subjects are added. A user can connect to one of these forums, at one's own leisure, and browse, or contribute if necessary. Contributions and exchanges are not only in terms of ideas but also materials. Some of these subjects are:

1. curriculum,
2. disciplines,
3. preparation of children's books,
4. spiritual and moral education of children.

At a different level, a computer-based conferencing system can also help promote scholarly studies and procedures. One obvious forum would be to encourage discussion on the fundamental issues of Baha'i scholarship. Here the objective would be to understand the definition of scholarship and how it can be promoted in the pursuit of knowledge. If the users and the forum network expanded across a country or throughout the world, the quality of the results would be better, as it would bring the input of people with different cultural experiences. Furthermore, in such a place where exchange of ideas occurs, new truth's would arise, giving scholarship a new meaning.

Second, a conferencing system can provide easy, prompt access to information. One such type of information is the papers submitted by many participants at conferences organized by the Association of Baha'i Studies. Each paper requires numerous hours of research and careful thought to prepare, and, without doubt, each has some value, although the Association may decide not to publish it. To allow access to them, a computer conference system can be used to provide a directory of all the papers. Any paper could be transferred on request within a short period of time. Again, with this technology, the text is easily moved from one place to another. From a practical point of view, once such a system is set up, the authors can submit their material on storage media such as a floppy disk, relieving the Association of the task of putting them on disk.

9.8 LITERACY

In recent years, the Baha'i Faith has entered many remote places of the world. Many of these new believers experience a spiritual understanding of the Faith through listening to their teachers rather than through reading because they have little ability to read and write. To gain any further understanding, such new Baha'is have to depend on someone else to teach them prayers, or to read newsletters and books to them. Additionally, many aspects of Baha'i administration require basic literacy. Unfortunately, in many places, no local schooling facilities are available, and it is urgent that they develop the learning skills to participate in Baha'i activities to a greater extent.

There are two principles that motivate Baha'i institutions to promote literacy. First, it is a wish of Baha'u'llah that there be education throughout the world, and that citizens of all nations have a chance to develop learning skills. As Baha'is, it is our privilege to help in this goal any way possible. Second, the growth of the Baha'i Faith is taking place where many adults have had no chance to get a formal education. In such areas, to provide a healthy and sound foundation for the Baha'i community, it is essential to have some kind of schooling. A teacher, with the purpose of deepening the knowledge of new believers, may find it necessary to teach basic reading and writing skills while teaching Baha'i principles, to ensure that students retain their lessons.

Here, we are suggesting how the computer technology can help in a program providing basic literacy. In these situations where material has to be produced in a short time and there are no rigid requirements for things such as binding and illustrations, a word processor with a printer is a very useful tool.

As seen earlier, the word processor is very versatile in managing text. Its capabilities, such as editing, formatting, and indexing are real time savers. You can easily prepare any kind of text from memos to books and pamphlets. When buying a word processor, it is important to remember that they are not all alike, and they differ in price as well as in the functions they can perform. Therefore, it is your responsibility to investigate what is available and decide which one meets your publishing needs.

Similarly, printers differ in size, price and capability. In addition to producing basic print characters, some come with many fonts, languages, and graphics. You must ensure that the word processor is compatible with the printer, and that you can use all the functions of both tools.

The great challenge to a Baha'i teacher is how to improve the learning skills effectively in a short time. In many places, the people know only a local language that remotely resembles a national or universal language. Sometimes, it is easier to improve the literacy in the local language than to teach a new one, that is popular nationally. Research has shown that students learn faster when the language is familiar to them. One way to teach using dialects is to tape Baha'i or other stories in the local language and transcribe it using a word processor. When the master copy is completed, you can make many more copies through a printing shop or photocopying machine.

In a Baha'i community in a village, or in any other place, the age group may vary from children to adults, and there is always a need to provide some form of learning for all of them. Obviously, different curricula are needed for each group. Again, a word processor is a useful tool for its flexibility in arranging a text while it is being prepared. It is likely that material will keep changing to adapt to new situations, and not only can the word processor keep a copy of text in its storage device, but it can also recall an old one for further changes or additions.

In conclusion, there seems to be a certain degree of urgency for the Baha'i Faith to educate those who live in remote areas of the world. This education should happen at two levels: acquiring basic learning skills, and a deepening in understanding of the Faith. It must be remembered that many of these new adherents had little or no formal education in their lives. If the planning of an educational program is done carefully, both levels can be intertwined together. The computer technology has the potential of helping prepare any size or any kind of material. There are many different brands of word processors and publishing software, and their numbers are increasing while the costs of purchasing and using them are decreasing.

CHAPTER TEN

TEXT RETRIEVAL SYSTEM

In the last chapter, we saw mammoth data bases located far from the user, and constantly baffling him with huge amounts of information. Here, we'll look at a different kind of data base, made for microcomputers either to benefit one individual or to benefit the administration of the Baha'i Faith. This is a text storage and retrieval method that accomplishes two main objectives: access and organization of documents. There are many programs on the market designed to manage and retrieve segments of documents. Such software can be used in keeping of minutes, organizing notes, letters or other texts that have certain relations between words or phrases. Such a tool is only beneficial if the information base is too big to access adequately and to organize with a manual system. For the Baha'i Faith, some of the direct applications of text retrieval software are in the areas of research, managing minutes, or maintaining catalogs.

Here, we will discuss the capabilities of text retrieval software. To demonstrate these facilities, we will build a data base using text from *The* `Hidden Words`. Then, with a commercial software, called SIRE, we'll build a retrieval system as well as show some of its uses. Other applications, such as keeping up a library and keeping minutes will also be briefly described.

10.1 WHAT IS TEXT RETRIEVAL SOFTWARE?

As a personal computer user, you know how files easily grow, especially if you create new ones daily. In a short time, the floppy or hard disk is full of files about minutes, reports, letters, and so on. It is realistic to have hundreds of these files with text on diverse subjects. Unfortunately, most of us are not capable of keeping track of many of them, and knowing what each file precisely contains. If you want to know about a subject, teaching in the Rama Reserve, for example, in all the minutes, reports, or notes, you will have to pull all the related text files and leaf through them, looking for references to teaching in the Rama Reserve. The task is not only time consuming, but becomes more complicated if the mention of the subject you are looking for is scattered throughout many files.

Word processors, used to prepare the documents, do have commands to search for words or phrases. However, these commands, though useful, are not sufficient to do searches when contexts and relations between words and phrases are needed. In addition, with most word processors if you have to look at many files, you have to load each file and then do the search. If the files are too big, say over 50,000 words, searching through them may take a long time.

There is a problem with the name of the microcomputer file; it is too short. For instance, PC-DOS allows up to 11 characters. Such limitations make file names cryptic and difficult to remember, especially after not using one for a long time.

In these situations, where word processors are in-adequate, a text retrieval program locates words and phrases within a given context and relates documents found in many files. To do a fast search, this software first produces an index of every word of every file in a directory. However, common words such as "is," "to," "this," and so on are ignored. Indexing is like a "hook" to "catch" the spot where each word is found. For instance, if you are searching for "children's school" among minutes, the program will quickly locate these words in every file.

Next to indexing, the way of doing a search is the most important function of any text retrieval software. Unlike word processors, it uses Boolean operators. These operators are used to locate occurrences of text, and also provide the context and relations among them. Let's say you are looking for all the decisions made about the "Rama Reserve Teaching Project." The command to do this would be: *"Decided AND Rama Reserve AND Teaching" WITHIN 100 WORDS*; when the search is over the program shows you the text with all these words within 100 words of all the minutes files. Another example is locating all instances of "Teaching" OR "Deepening" among committee reports. This will show any segment that has either of these two words. These words AND, WITHIN, and OR are called Boolean operators.

Many programs allow use of wild-card characters (* and ?), a standard used in PC-DOS. When using it, searching for "soft*" would locate "software," "softly," and "softness," and "h?t" would find "hat," "hot" and "hut."

Most data retrieval programs are designed that setting up requires no programming, and they are usually user friendly. In fact, one program, called ZyIndex, allows search soon after a file, prepared by a word processor, is indexed. Generally the process of indexing is straightforward and doesn't take much time. With ZyIndex a page of text takes about 30 seconds to index. One thing to remember about indexing is that to get the best results this process has to be done often enough to include all new and updated files.

One drawback about text files with no structures (such as letters, reports, and memos) and using a program like ZyIndex is that context is lost during search. For more precise search, there are programs that require some form or structure. This is useful when all the documents have the same format. A few such examples are catalog data of books, minutes, and personal information of members. A program that needs a structured document to be input is INMAGIC. It requires some start-up procedures to define the structure before indexing files and using it for text retrieval. But this extra step is only worthwhile if the search requires precision and correct context.

Many of these data retrieval programs also have other benefits. Of course, these benefits vary from one product to the next. Some of the most common facilities are printing a located text, sorting the text, and producing a thesaurus of all the indexed text.

The cost of these programs ranges from 150 to 800 U.S dollars. The price seems to depend on the program's capacity to handle documents. At the low end, one program indexes a maximum of 500 files, while the most costly one accepts up to 15,000 files. Another cost-dependent feature is the number of unique words allowed per index list, which varies from 125,000 to 500,000. However, every real text retrieval software supports Boolean operators and some form of indexing.

NAME	VENDOR
ZyIndex	Zylab 233 East Erie Street Chicago, Illinois 60611 312-642-2201
Inmagic	Inmagic Inc. 238 Broad Way Cambridge, MA 02139 617-661-8124
SIRE	Cucumber Information 5611 Kraft Drive Rockville, MD 20852 301-984-3539

Figure 10.1. List of Text Retrieval Software

10.2 APPLICATIONS

Among the many uses of a text retrieval system, a common one for Baha'is is research and study of the Faith. Many of us are familiar with the card system, a collection of references and extracts from different literature put together according to subjects. This is very useful while preparing talks, or simply while increasing one's own understanding of the Faith. Of course, other ways to reference are to look up the index, table of contents, or concordances. These methods work well for most of us, as long as the volume is not too great, and the desire to locate text is not too frequent. To achieve speed as well as search through a volume of documents, we need a computer text retrieval system.

What can text retrieval software offer? A lot of literature on the Faith, such as *The Hidden Words*, compilations, and letters, have no index. This tool can index many thousands of pages within a short time, as well as produce a thesaurus if needed. Using the Boolean operators, within seconds you can find your favorite passages, sometimes difficult to do even with a book index. Therefore, it would be preferable to include all the text (with or without an index) in this kind of system. Pulling different segments of letters, compilations, and books, and seeing them on the screen, has two main advantages:

1. Seeing the context in which a phrase or word is used,

2. Seeing same word or phrase used in different contexts.

Because of the numerous sources of Baha'i Writings, from the central figures, Guardian, Universal House of Justice, and Assemblies, it is important to see relationships and contexts while doing any kind of research. No doubt, it will bring better understanding to the student of the Faith. In addition to indexing, this software can find relevant documents out of thousands or millions of them. And it is much faster than any manual method.

Like the card method, it takes time to build a computer text retrieval system. In this case, most of the work is in entering the text into the computer files. We hope that in the near future all the publications about the Faith will be available on disk. This would make building your own text data base and retrieval system easier.

As an illustration, we will describe all the steps taken to build a small retrieval system. The text is the *Arabic Hidden Words* and the program is SIRE. Let's start this exercise by first describing what SIRE can do. The following list shows all the functions of SIRE. Some of them have been mentioned earlier, and others are extra features provided by this product.

1. Accepts files made by a word processor (Converted to ASCII file),

2. Index of all source files,

3. Automatic installation,

4. Each document should have at least one field. Example, -fieldname- at the beginning of each document, report, or text, and a corresponding end for that document using the label -end-. Each

document can be divided into smaller portions or fields (maximum of 256 allowed),

5. It supports Boolean operators (AND, OR, NOT),
6. It's command resembles natural language requests,
7. It produces an automatic full-text indexing and manual indexing,
8. It produces an automatic statistical small thesaurus,
9. Its output is printed or shown on the screen,
10. It matches words or characters using wild cards (*, ?),
11. It also uses adjacent operator (ADJ) to look for words next to each other.

The next step is to enter the text of `Hidden Words` into the file using a word processor. It would take a few hours of typing. This book is divided into parts that are numbered from 1 to 71. The structure consists of two parts, combined to make one document (record). Each part is a field that starts with label FIELD1 or FIELD2. Thus all the 71 parts are grouped in this manner. For example:

```
-FIELD1-
1. O SON OF SPIRIT!

      .
      .
      .

-FIELD2-
2. O SON OF SPIRIT!

      .
      .
      .
-END-

-FIELD1-
3. O SON OF MAN!

      .
      .
      .

-FIELD2-
4. O SON OF MAN!
      .
```

```
      .
      .
-END-
      .
      .
      .


-FIELD1-
70. O SON OF HIM THAT STOOD BY HIS OWN
    ENTITY IN THE KINGDOM OF HIS SELF!

      .
      .
      .

-FIELD3-
71. O SON OF MAN!

      .
      .
      .

-END-
```

The reason for grouping two `Hidden Words` into one document is that the SIRE program we are using is a demo version. Therefore it only allows a maximum of 38 documents to be part of a data base. Such grouping is necessary to include all the 71 parts. When such restriction does not exist, you can structure your documents in any way that satisfies your particular needs.

With an IBM-XT and a hard disk, it takes a little over 3 minutes to index this text and build the dictionary. Now, we are ready for a "test drive."

First, let's start with a few searches. To find the instances of the word **love**, the command is

```
get love
```

or simply

```
love
```

As a result, SIRE shows every document where **love, loved**, or **loving** are found, and there are 19 occurrences (any of these records can be sent to a file, a way to separate this portion from the main text).

SIRE has an EXPAND command to list words that are closely related to the words of the query. The result of the command.

EXPAND love

is this:

```
love      seekest
essence   servant
perish    enter
pleasure  therein
Beauty    Mayest
lovest    creation
Dominion  find
lover     trial
know      Son
```

This is also suppose to be a thesaurus list. However, it is difficult to imagine **love** is synonymous with many of these words. So we did this query

love AND Dominion AND enter

The result is this passage

6. O SON OF BEING

Thy Paradise is My love; thy heavenly home, reunion with Me. Enter therein and tarry not. This is that which hath been destined for thee in Our kingdom above and Our exalted dominion.

Here **love** is equated to **dominion** and **enter** is related as a verb. You can see the usefulness of this command, but it does not produce a true thesaurus.

This program accepts English language-like commands. Therefore, the following is acceptable.

I want love and essence

It searches for love and essence, and shows these two passages.

3. O SON OF MAN!

Veiled in My immemorial being and in the ancient eternity of My essence, I knew My love for thee; therefore I created thee, have engraved on thee Mine image

```
and revealed to thee My beauty.


13. O SON OF SPIRIT!

I created thee rich, why dost thou bring thyself down to poverty? Noble I made
thee, wherewith dost thou abase thyself? Out of the essence of knowledge I gave
thee being, why seekest thou enlightenment from anyone beside Me? Out of the
clay of love I molded thee, how dost thou busy thyself with another? Turn thy
sight unto thyself, that thou mayest find Me standing within thee, mighty,
powerful and self-subsisting.
```

ALPHA is a command to list words alphabetically surrounding a given word in the data base dictionary. For example this command

```
ALPHA love
```

produces this list with a number of occurrences of each word.

```
lead      2
less      1
life      6
lift      1
light     10
limit     1
live      2
long      3
lord      2
love      19
lover     2
lovest    3
made      7
magnify   1
main      1
majesty   2
```

Sometimes, looking for a quote in the Writings can be frustrating, especially when you don't remember where it is, or have forgotten some of the key words of the passage. With a software retrieval system, searching for a particular passage becomes easy. Let's say we are looking for a word in the *The Hidden Words* that sounds like rejoin. The command is

```
get rejoin
```

It gives a message

No document retrieved, meaning there is no occurrence of **rejoin.**

The next step is to look for words alphabetically surrounding **rejoin**. It gives a list of 9 words.

```
recount   1
reflect   1
regard    1
rejoice   4
remember  1
renounce  1
repose    1
rest      2
return    2
```

The word **rejoice** is closer to what we are looking for, and there are four such instances. After looking at each one, we find the following:

```
52. O SON OF MAN!

Should prosperity befall thee, rejoice not, and should abasement come upon
thee, grieve not, for both shall pass away and be no more.
```

Looking for this passage takes only a few minutes.

Another use of this retrieval program is to manage minutes at any administrative level. How many times were you unable to recall decisions made months or years ago? Among hundreds of them made each year by Assemblies or committees, it is impossible to remember them all. Or the staff at a National Center may find it necessary to search through piles of previous minutes to locate important decisions, policies, or references. This problem is easily resolved by using text retrieval software. To use it effectively, the minutes must have some structure. In Chapter Two, we described a structure, with key words planted in each minute, and gave file names to help identify them easily. A program such as SIRE, that recognizes structure yet uses text prepared by a word processor, is appropriate to manage the minutes.

Until recently, managing library information required data base programs such as DBASE III or RBASE:5000. They need programming before using them. Now, with data retrieval packages, it is easy to maintain the entire catalog of a library, and no programming is needed. Since the information (such as name, author, title) of each book has the same format, it is preferable to have software that requires some structure for its inputted data. Both SIRE and INMAGIC are suitable for this application. In fact, INMAGIC comes with another program called BIBLIO, and both are combined to build data bases, produce reports, and handle all the needs of working in libraries.

Some uses of BIBLIO and INMAGIC are that they:

1. Have on-line catalog information of all kinds of material (books, films, clippings, reports). This data base can be used by the staff as well as the users of the library,

2. Manage ordering and acquisition of books and other materials. They also give reports, mailing labels, and acquisition lists,

3. control and manage circulation of all items.

These programs are designed in such a way as to require minimal setup procedures and they come in a ready-to-use format. However, if you want to design your own catalog management system, SIRE will do the job well. Information about each book can be grouped as a record. This record is divided into different parts or fields. Figure 10.2 shows an example of a record and some fields. A similar structure can be designed for any other material.

```
Title
Author
Date Borrowed
Date Due
Name of Borrower
Access Number
Publisher
Subject Matter
```

Figure 10.2. Record and Fields to Contain Book Information

Finally, note that the programs mentioned in this chapter are merely suggestions of possible applications. It should not be taken generally to satisfy all the needs in any of these areas. Our purpose of using SIRE is to show only the usefulness of this kind of software. To get the most from a document retrieval system, one of the most important steps is to decide your own particular needs. Then, you can effectively search for a program that does all of the critical tasks. By taking these two steps, any rewards of document retrieval system using a computer will come your way.

APPENDIX A

Bibliography

Alabi, G. A. Design of a Microcomputer-Based Circulation System for Nigerian Academic Libraries. *Microcomputers for Information Management* (Mar. 1985) pp. 43-52.

Arca, Julie Anne. Practical WordStar Uses. Berkeley, CA: Sybex Inc., 1983.

Baha'u'Allah. The Hidden Words, Wilmette. Il: Baha'i Publishing Trust, 1971.

Bell, F. Why is Computer-Related Learning so Successful. *Educational Technology* (June, 1974) pp. 15-18.

Bell, M. E. The Role of Instructional Theories in the Evaluation of Microcomputer Courseware. Educational Technology (Mar. 1985) pp. 36-40.

Bork, A. Learning with Computers. Bedford, MA: Digital Press, Digital Equipment Corporation, 1981.

Burke, Robert L. CAI Source book. Englewood Cliffs, NJ: Prentice-Hall, 1982.

Cain, Thomas and Cain Woodard, Nancy. 1-2-3 At Work. Reston, Virginia: Reston Publishing Company, 1984.

Cambron, Jim. The First Primer of Microcomputer Telecommunications. Blue Ridge Summit, PA: Tab Books Inc., 1984.

Ciarca, Steve. Turnkey Bulletin-Board System. *Byte* (Dec. 1985) pp. 93-98.

Cohen, V. B. A Reexamination of Feedback in Computer-Based Instruction: Implications for Instructional Design. *Educational Technology* (Jan. 1985) pp. 33.

Davies, Denise M. The Organizations of a Computer Software Collection Using an Information Storage and Retrieval Software Package. *Microcomputers for Information Management* (Sep. 1985) pp. 201-210.

Desson, Jim. The Computer in Education: Fundamental Principles and Future Prospects (June 1984.)

Dwyer, Thomas A. and Critchfield, M. CP/M and the Personal Computer. New York: Addison-Wesley Publishing Company, 1984.

Emerson, Sandra L. and Darnovsky, Marcy. Database for the IBM PC. Reading, MA: Addison-Wesley Publishing Company, 1984.

Falk, Howard. Handbook of Computer Applications for the Small or Medium-Sized Business. Radnor, PA: Chilton Book Company, 1983.

Fox, E. A. Automatic Document and Passage Retrieval Methods: Aids to Searching the Baha'i Writings.

Gagne, M. Developments in Learning Psychology. *Educational Technology* (June, 1982) pp. 11-15.

Gallini, J. K. Instructional Conditions for Computer-Based Problem-Solving Environments. *Educational Technology* (Feb. 1985) pp. 7-11.

Glossbrenner, Alfred. Personal Computer Communications. New York, NY: St. Martin's Press, 1983.

Gorth, W. P. and Nassif P. M. A Comparison of Microcomputer-Based, Computer-Managed Instruction (CMI) Software Programs. *Educational Technology* (Jan. 1984) pp. 28-32.

Hancock, Chris. Common Ground (Microcomputer Based Conferencing System). *Byte* (Dec. 1985) pp. 239-246.

Hass, Lou. Going ON-LINE with Your Micro. Blue Ridge Summit, PA: Tab Books Inc., 1984.

Johnson, D. W. and Johnson, R. T. Computer-Assisted Cooperative Learning. *Educational Technology* (Jan 1986) pp. 12-18.

Jonassen, D. H. The REAL Case for Using Authoring Systems to Develop Courseware. *Educational Technology* (Feb. 1985) pp. 39-41.

Lambert, Steve. On Line, A Guide to America's Leading Information Services. Bellevue, WA: Microsoft Press, 1985.

Lewis, Ted. 32 VisiCalc Worksheets. Blue Ridge Summit, PA: Tab Books Inc., 1983.

Lewis, Sasha. Plugging In, The Microcomputerist's Guide to Telecommunications. Radnor, PA: Chilton Book Company, 1984.

Los Nietos School District. Computer Assisted Instruction, How it Raises Children's Achievement Scores. Edited by N. D. Crandall, CA, 1977.

Lundeen, G. and Tenopir, C. Microcomputer Based Library Catalog Software. *Microcomputers for Information Management* (Sept. 1984) pp.215-228.

Meeks, Brock N. An Overview of Conferencing Systems, *Byte* (Dec. 1985) pp. 169-184.

Myers, Roy E. Microcomputer Graphics. Reading MA: Addison-Wesley Publishing Company, 1982.

Myers, Roy E. Educational Software Directory. Tallahassee, Fl: Electronic Communications, Inc., 1985.

Norton, Peter. Inside the IBM PC. Bowie, MD: Brady Communications Company, Inc., 1983.

Palme, Jacob. Database Structure in PortaCom. *Byte* (Dec. 1985) pp. 195-200.

Penniman, W. David. Microcomputers in Libraries: If they are the answers, what are the questions? *Microcomputers for Information Management* (Mar. 1984) pp. 31-38.

Puotinen, C. J. Using the IBM Personal Computer: WordStar. New York, NY: Holt, Rinehart and Winston, 1983.

Rosenbaum, D. J. WordPerfect, Advanced Techniques. Carmel, Indiana: Que Corporation, 1987.

Salton, G. The Smart Retrieval System. Englewood Cliffs, NJ: Prentice-Hall, 1971.

Simpson, Alan. Advanced Techniques in dBase III. Berkeley, CA: Sybex Inc., 1985.

Smith, P. L. and Boyce B. A. Instructional Design Considerations in the Development of Computer-Assisted Instruction. *Educational Technology* (July 1984) pp. 5-11.

Trudell, Libby. Options for Electronic Mail. White Plains, NY: Knowledge Industry Publications, 1984.

Waite, Mitchell and Arca, Julie. Word Processing Primer. Peterborough, NH: Byte/McGraw-Hill, 1982.

Willis, J. Desktop Publishing, With Your IBM PC & Compatible. Tucson, AZ: Knight-Ridder Press, 1987.

Zager, Masha and Chase, Claire. Using Microsoft Word. Carmel, Indiana: Que Corporation, 1987.

APPENDIX B

SOFTWARE DIRECTORY

WORD PROCESSING

TEXT INDEXER
Publisher: Publisher's Software Network
Hardware : IBM-PC and compatibles
Price : $ 239.00
Features : It contructs an index from a text file. Also, a creates word list, formats the indexed file, which can be further edited.

THINKTANK
Publisher: Living Videotext
Hardware : IBM-PC, compatibles and Apple Macintosh
Price : $ 135.00
Features : It is an idea processor and works like a text processor. It is useful to organize ideas and concepts into an outline format.

VOLKSWRITER 3
Publisher: Lifetree
Hardware : IBM-PC and compatibles
Price : $ 285.00
Features : A powerful and user-friendly word processor. It includes spellchecker, mailmerge, and online tutorial.

WORDPERFECT 4.2
Publisher: WordPerfect
Hardware : IBM-PC and compatibles
Price : $ 205.00
Features : A flexible and powerful business word processor. It includes thesaurus, spellchecker, column format, math functions, split screen, etc.

WORDSTART PROFESSIONAL 4.0
Publisher: MicroPro
Hardware : IBM-PC and compatibles
Price : $ 239.00
Features : In addition to basic word processor functions, it has spellchecker, thesarus, mailmerge. It also features macros, block and columnar functions, pop-up help menus. Available in French.

WORDWRITER
Publisher: Timeworks
Hardware : Atari ST
Price : $ 79.95
Features : A word processing system with spellchecker and thesaurus.

MACWRITE
Publisher: Apple
Hardware : Macintosh
Price : $ 70.00
Features : A word processor using mouse and menues. Merges graphics. Available in French.

MICROSOFT WORD 4.0
Publisher: Microsoft
Hardware : Macintosh and IBM-PC
Price : $ 285.00
Features : A high-power word processor with many desirable features.

DATA BASE

DATAMANAGER
Publisher: Timeworks
Hardware : IBM-PC and compatibles
Price : $ 59.95
Features : Useful for filing and record keeping. It generates reports and labels, including graphics with pie, line, or bar charts.

DBASE III PLUS
Publisher: Ashton-Tate
Hardware : IBM-PC, compatibles and MacIntosh
Price : $ 355.00 (IBM-PC and compatibles)
Features : One of the most popular data base systems, featuring menu operation, Advanced Query System, Application Generation encryption, etc. Also available in French.

DBXL
Publisher: WordTech Systems
Hardware : IBM-PC and compatibles
Price : $ 169.00
Features : A great immitator of dBase III Plus, using Dbase data and program files.

PC-FILE III
Publisher: ButtonWare
Hardware : IBM-PC and compatibles
Price : $ 123.00
Features : This is an easy-to-use data base program, completely operated using menus. Other features include browse mode, full screen editing, reports, macros, etc.

R:BASE 5000
Publisher: Microrim
Hardware : IBM-PC and compatibles
Price : $ 399.00
Features : In addition to basic functions, it includes forms, report generator, and immediate feedback on validity of input.

TRIMBASE
Publisher: Michtron
Hardware : Atari ST
Price : $ 99.95
Features : A relational data management system with ability to exchange data with other application programs.

MICROSOFT FILE
Publisher: MicroSoft
Hardware : MacIntosh
Price : $ 199.00
Features : A data-management system for forms. Interfaces with Microsoft Word.

DB MASTER
Publisher: Stoneware
Hardware : Macintosh
Price : $ 189.00
Features : A basic database manager, using all the MAC and GEM features.

COMMUNICATION

I*S TALK
Publisher: Batteries Included
Hardware : Atari ST
Price : $ 69.95
Features : Communication system based on GEM, including full-screen editing, spellchecker, and macros.

SMARTCOM II
Publisher: Hayes
Hardware : Macintosh
Price : $ 79.00
Features : A communication program using menus.

CROSS TALK
Publisher: Microstuf
Hardware : IBM-PC and compatibles
Price : $ 95.00
Features : Allows creation of a "script" file to establish communication. Operates on dual screen, one for operation and the other for status.

MAILBOX/PC
Publisher: I.P Sharp Associates
Hardware : IBM-PC and compatibles
Price : $ 85.00
Features : Offers electronic conferencing. Files and retrieves messages. On-line help for beginners. Allows communication between PC's.

SPREADSHEET

LOTUS 1-2-3
Publisher: Lotus
Hardware : IBM-PC and compatibles
Price : $ 325.00
Features : A very popular spreadsheet program, also including a mini-data base, graphics, formatting, and advanced programming capabilities.

REPORT WRITER
Publisher: Lotus
Hardware : IBM-PC
Price : $99.00
Features : A report writer using Lotus 1-2-3 worksheet files. It allows creation of custom reports and forms.

SWIFTCALC
Publisher: Timeworks
Hardware : IBM-PC, compatibles and Atari ST
Price : $ 59.95
Features : Allows up to 250 rows, 250 columns, 62,5000 cells. Also includes graphics with bar, line, and pie charts.

INTEGRATED SOFTWARE

FRAMEWORK II
Publisher: Ashton-Tate
Hardware : IBM-PC and compatibles
Price : $389.00
Features : Idea processing, word processing, spreadsheet, data base, and graphics.

GET ORGANIZED!
Publisher: Electronic Arts
Hardware : IBM-PC and compatibles
Price : $ 99.95
Features : Word processing, correspondence manager, index-card file, notepad, calculator, and communications.

SMART SOFTWARE SYSTEM
Publisher: Innovative Software
Hardware : IBM-PC and compatibles
Price : $ 895.00
Features : Word processing, data base manager, spreadsheet, and communication.

SYMPHONY
Publisher: Lotus
Hardware : IBM-PC and compatibles
Price : $ 429.00
Features : Spreadsheet, data base manager, and text editing.

JAZZ
Publisher: Lotus
Hardware : Macintosh
Price : $ 399.00
Features : Spreadsheet, word processor, data base, communications, graphics, and form design.

COMPUTER-AIDED LEARNING

TEACHER TURNED AUTHOR (Starter Series)
Publisher: Raster Technology Inc.
Hardware : IBM_PC and Compatibles
Price : $ 119
Features : Basic authoring functions, mix text, graphics, and questions, some editing, student record keeping.

WRITING TO READ
Publisher: IBM
Hardware : IBM-PC
Price : N/A
Features : To teach five-and six-year-old children to write what they say. Also, it teaches them read what they write.

DATA RETRIEVAL SOFTWARE

BOOKENDS
Publisher: Sensible Software
Hardware : IBM-PC and compatibles
Price : $ 213.00
Features : Mainly for storage of bibliographic references and abstracts. It allows editing, search by key words and authors.

THOR
Publisher: Revolution Software, Inc.
Hardware : IBM-PC and compatibles
Price : $ 79.95
Features : Includes basic data retrieval functions.

ZYINDEX
Publisher: Zylab
Hardware : IBM-PC and compatibles
Price : $ 201.00
Features : Full-text retrieval system. Indexes up to 15,000 files and 500,000 unique words.

INMAGIC
Publisher: Inmagic Inc.
Hardware : IBM-PC and compatibles
Price : $ 650.00
Features : Full-text retrieval system. Also includes password security, report writer, calculator, and editor.

SIRE
Publisher: Cucumber Information
Hardware : IBM-PC and compatibles
Price : $ 550.00
Features : Uses natural language to locate words or phrases. It is flexible and fast with automatic thesaurus.